The Lonely Mirror

Contributing to a lively dialogue with Anglo-American and French theorists, *The Lonely Mirror* sets out to contextualize Italian feminist theory within the international debate. The essays vividly illuminate the specific character of Italian feminism as a political and intellectual movement and expose the differences between the more institutionalized nature of women's studies in the United States and Britain. It will be of vital interest both to general and academic readers who want to explore some of the most vibrant trends in European feminism today.

Sandra Kemp is Senior Lecturer in English at the University of Glasgow. She is the author of *Kipling's Hidden Narratives*, and has edited an edition of Virginia Woolf's *To the Lighthouse* for the Routledge English Texts series.

Paola Bono teaches English literature at the University of Rome. She is associate editor of *Donnawomanfemme* and writes regularly for *Il manifesto*.

The Lonely Mirror

Italian perspectives on
feminist theory

Edited by Sandra Kemp
and Paola Bono

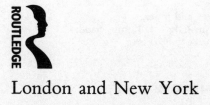

London and New York

First published 1993
by Routledge
11 New Fetter Lane, London EC4P 4EE

Simultaneously published in the USA and Canada
by Routledge
29 West 35th Street, New York, NY 10001

Phototypeset in 10 on 12 point Bembo by
Intype Ltd, London
Printed in Great Britain by
Clays Ltd. St. Ives plc

British Library Cataloguing in Publication Data
Lonely Mirror: Italian Perspectives on Feminist Theory
  I. Kemp, Sandra II. Bono, Paola
  305.42

Library of Congress Cataloging in Publication Data
The Lonely mirror: Italian perspectives on feminist theory/edited by
Sandra Kemp and Paola Bono.
  p.   cm.
  Includes bibliographical references and index.
  1. Feminist theory. 2. Feminism-Italy. I. Kemp, Sandra.
  II. Bono, Paola.
  HQ1190.L66   1992
  305.42'01–dc20

ISBN 0–415–03777–8   ISBN 0–415–03778–6 (pbk)

To Karina Williamson and M. Vittoria Tessitore

Contents

Contributors

Patrizia Magli works in the *Dipartimento di Scienza della Comunicazione* at the University of Bologna. She is the author of *Corpo e linguaggio* (1980), and editor of *La donne e i segni* (1985).

Nadia Fusini is Professor of English Literature at the University of Rome 'La Sapienza', and one of the founders of the *Centro Culturale Virginia Woolf*. Her publications include *Nomi* (1986), *La luminosa. Genealogia di Fedra* (1990) and a new Italian translation of Woolf's *To the Lighthouse* (1992).

Viola Papetti is Professor of English Literature at the University of Rome 'La Sapienza'. Her publications include *Arlecchio a Londra* (1976), and, as editor, *Le forme del teatro* (1990).

Marina Mizzau is Professor of Psychology at the University of Bologna, and is active in the *Centro di documentazione, ricerca e iniziativa delle donne* there. She is the author of *Prospettive della comunicazione interpersonale* (1974), *Eco e Narciso. Parole e silenzi nel conflitto uomo-donna* (1979), *L'ironia* (1984), and of two collections of short stories, *Come i delfini* (1988) and *I bambini non volano* (1992).

Marina Camboni currently holds the Chair of Anglo–American Literature at the University of Macerata. Her publications include *Come la tela del ragno. Poesie e saggi di Adrienne Rich* (1985), an edition of Anne Sexton's selected poems, *La doppia imagine e altre poesie* (1989), and *Il corpo dell'America: Leaves of Grass 1855. Introduzione al'opera di Walt Whitman* (1990).

Silvia Montefoschi is a follower of Jung. Her publications include *L'uno e l'altro* (1977), *Oltre il confine della persona* (1979),

Al di là del tabù dell'incesto (1982), *Il sistema uomo. Catastrofe e rinnovamento* (1985), and *C. G. Jung: un pensiero in divenire* (1985).

Maria Grazia Minetti is a Freudian psychoanalyst, based in Rome, and was one of the founders of the *Centro Culturale Virginia Woolf.* Her essays have been published in *Reti* and *Quaderni di Agape.*

Silvia Vegetti Finzi is Professor of Dynamic Psychology at the University of Pavia. Her publications include *Storia della psicoanalisi* (1986), *Il bambino della notte* (1990), and essays in *I figli della scienza, Bioetica* and *Aborto perché.*

Gianna Pomata teaches the Theory and History of Historiography at the University of Bologna, and Modern European History at the University of Minnesota. Her publications include *In scienza e coscienza: donne e potere nella società borghese* (1979), two chapters of which are included here.

Annarita Buttafuoco works in the *Dipartimento di Studi Storico-Sociali e Filosofici* at the University of Siena. Her publications include *Le Mariuccine. Storia di un'istituzione laica: l'asilo Mariuccia* (1985) and *Cronache femminili. Temi e momenti della stampa emancipaziionista in Italia dall'unità al fascismo* (1988). She was a founder of the *Centro Studi donnawomanfemme* in Rome, and is the editor of the feminist theoretical journal *Donnawomanfemme.*

Adriana Cavarero works in the *Istituto di Filosofia* at the University of Verona, and is part of the feminist philosophical community, Diotima. Her publications include *Dialettica e politica in Platone* (1976), *L'interpretazione hegeliana di Parmenide* (1984) and *Nonostante Platone* (1990).

Angela Putino works in the *Istituto di Filosofia* at the University of Salerno. She is the author of *Trompe l'oeil. Il mito di Narciso in Herman Hesse* (1977), has contributed to *Nuova rivista storica* and *DWF*, and is a founding editor of *Madrigale.*

Gabriella Bonacchi works in the *Fondazione Internazionale Basso*, where she is in charge of the history section. She has contributed to *Les Cahiers du Grif, Reti,* and *Telos,* and is on the editorial board of *Memoria.*

Acknowledgements

The excerpt from Sylvia Plath's 'Last Words', from *Crossing the Water*, is used by kind permission of Faber and Faber Ltd. Every reasonable attempt has been made to obtain permission to reproduce copyright material. If any proper acknowledgement has not been made, we would invite copyright holders to inform us of the oversight.

Introduction
Without a leg to stand on

Sandra Kemp and Paola Bono

The project that became *The Lonely Mirror* had been to edit an international collection of essays on feminist theory which included all those feminisms that got left out of the political debate between the Anglo-American and the French (the Italian, the German, the Spanish, the Canadian and the South American). I [Sandra Kemp] met Paola Bono at a British Council conference in 1986, and we began working together on the Italian material. This was scarcely known outside Italy because it had rarely been translated. There was so much of this material, and it was so fascinating, that I set the other project aside, and for the last five years Paola and I have been working on the Italian feminist debate.

Now, in 1992, the project has divided again – into two books. The first, *Italian Feminist Thought: A Reader* (published by Blackwell in 1991), uses extracts from books, articles, journals and newspapers to chart twenty years of feminist theory (1966–89) in Italy, although it does contain a number of full-length articles as well. It looks at the different women's centres and groups all over the country, their manifestos and publications. The Blackwell reader also contains sections on the debate on social and political issues, including the laws on abortion and contraception, terrorism, military service for women and political representation. The book has a detailed chronology, and a complete bibliography of Italian feminist books and journals published during these years.

This second project, *The Lonely Mirror*, is less historical/political in nature, offering complete scholarly articles, rather than journalistic or documentary extracts. The material is drawn from different subject areas (language, literature, semiotics, psychoanalysis, history and philosophy). The essays span a decade (1979–89).

In the Blackwell reader Paola and I tried in short space to give as full an intellectual and political history of Italian feminism as possible. Rather than repeat ourselves here, we have tried to reconstruct our early discussions of the particularity, or the difference, of Italian feminist theory. The historical and theoretical material we touch on is presented in more detail in the Blackwell book. But we thought it would be useful, and would provide a slightly different gloss, to personalize and contextualize the issues in this way. Obviously, the division into question and response is an artificial one. The argument presented here is a summary of a number of years of our talking and writing together on Italian feminism, and represents our shared view of the area and of the material. In the later sections of the introduction, we locate the essays we have selected within the frameworks of the contemporary international feminist debate.

I

When Paola and I began talking about Italian feminist theory, there seemed to be four areas that were particularly distinctive or characteristic. First, in Italy, women's studies, or gender studies, is not institutionalized. But women's groups, often attached to bookshops and publishers, are more than consciousness-raising groups. The regional nature of the groups is significant, as is the fact that they are constantly engaged in debate and conflict. Second, there is the strongly political character of Italian feminism. In a sense it has never left the streets, and hasn't been divided into 'first– ' and 'second-wave' feminist theory, as British and American feminism has. Third, following from these two, Italian feminist theory offers a very different sense of what it means to have a collective identity as well as an individual identity. Finally, there is the whole question of the relationship of Italian feminist theory to other cultural institutions; for example, to the Church or to communism.

SK *Regarding the first point, the non-institutionalized nature of the debate. What is surprising to us is that it doesn't take place within the universities.*

PB In a sense the debate has moved off the streets in Italy as well, because there haven't been any mass demonstrations in the last few years. But it depends on what you mean by on or off the streets. If you mean 'grass-roots feminism', as opposed to the theoretical or the academic, then that distinction has never been as strong in Italy as it has become in Britain and the US. Particularly in the US, there is a definite gap between the two. This is something de Lauretis mentions in 'The essence of the triangle', when she tries to characterize Italian feminist theory by contrast with the Anglo-American and the French.

> Another way to say this is that the essential difference of feminism lies in its historical specificity – the particular condition of its emergence and development, which have shaped its object and field of analysis, its assumptions and forms of address; the constraints that have attended its conceptual and methodological struggles; the erotic component of its political self-awareness; the absolute novelty of its radical challenge to social life itself. This is what is being addressed in the recent writings of some Italian feminist theorists, while their Anglo-American counterparts seem for the most part engaged in typologising, defining, and branding various 'feminisms' along an ascending scale of theoretico-political sophistication where 'essentialism' weighs heavy at the lower end.[1]

De Lauretis also talks about the fact that feminism in the US is becoming entrenched in the academy in spite of the fact that much of the theory is about being able to talk to the 'woman on the streets' as well. This has resulted in division and lack of communication. In this respect, the feminist community in Italy has always remained very closely knit, though of course it is still an élite. There are still thousands of women who don't know much about it, or if they do they are not interested, and so on. But in terms of the social composition of a feminist meeting, let me give you an example. The last time Luisa Muraro came to Rome, to a workshop at the Virginia Woolf Centre to talk about authority and female authority and what that could mean, of the one hundred and fifty people who were there at least half were not academic. I don't think this would be common in Britain or the US.[2]

SK *Supposing someone asked you why it is that in Italy there aren't* *organized departments of women's studies or gender studies as there are now in Britain and America. How would you account for that? In a sense it is really surprising that, being so highly theorized, Italian feminist theory doesn't take place within the academy.*

PB   In Italy, in the last few years, feminist theory has begun to find a place within the universities. But not in an organized or high-profile manner. For example, the Diotima group is composed of women who mostly work in the universities, although not all of them do.[3] But Diotima is connected with the university in the sense that because some of these women are in the university they are able to apply for a research grant through institutional channels. Thus in their own subject disciplines they are 'teaching' feminism. But still only in an individual and low-key way. It is also the case that there is still a resistance towards having women's studies departments as such because most Italian feminists see these as an Indian reservation where you are allowed to run free – without affecting or changing the system. Finally, it is also the case that most of the women within the academy became feminists independently of their being academics. This is particularly true of the older generation who became feminists out of their own unease as women. They worked in and through the *autocoscienza*[4] groups, where the emphasis was so much on personal experience, and the experience of personal relationships.[5]

SK   *Could you briefly recount the history of the growth of what we're calling Italian feminist theory?*

PB   I would locate the beginning of the kind of feminism we're talking about in the late 1960s. There is of course the older history (the history of the movement for suffrage, or of women's organizations at the end of the 1880s and the beginning of our century, not to mention the women in the wartime resistance movement and so on).[6] From our perspective now we can look back at this and see threads of continuity and difference. But history is always created *post factum*. As it actually happened, there were real breaks and earlier achievements were forgotten. The Italian feminist movement is like a river which disappears underground and then comes up again. While it is underground, in a sense nothing is lost. At the same time, everything is lost because when it appears again it has to recover the memory of its previous existence each time. That is why history has been such an important discipline for feminist theory, particularly at certain stages. So you could say that Italian feminism started with women's movements after the Second World War. For example, one could cite the Unione Donne Italiane (Union of Italian Women) (UDI), the great women's movement which was created immediately after the war by left-wing women.[7] But I would locate the beginning of the feminism we are talking about at the end of the 1960s when, paradoxically, the emancipatory struggle had been largely achieved: in a sense women had become significantly more equal than ever before. What is interesting is that this new-wave feminism (at the end of the 1960s and at the beginning of the 1970s) came at a moment when women were a lot less 'oppressed' in their daily and in their professional lives. At this point, the real discovery was that emancipation had not got rid of oppression – that it was part of it. Getting equality didn't change things at root. In *Historical Capitalism*, writing about colonialism, Wallerstein argues that the gifts of civilization and equality are a kind of poisoned chalice:

> The gift itself harboured racism, for it gave the recipient two choices: accept the gift, thereby acknowledging that one was low on the hierarchy of achieved wisdom; refuse the gift, thereby denying weapons that could reverse the unequal real power situation.[8]

By analogy then, the Italian feminists argued that emancipation actually revealed the contradiction of being emancipated but *still being* oppressed: you were less oppressed on a material level but more oppressed on a subjective and 'symbolic' level. Thus Carla Lonzi talking about the problems of equality as early as 1970:

> Equality is a juridical principle. . . . Difference is an existential principle which concerns the modes of being human, the peculiarity of one's own experiences, goals, possibilities, and one's sense of existence in a given situation and in the situations one wants to create for oneself. The difference between woman and man is the basic difference of humankind. . . . Equality is what is offered as legal rights to colonised people. And what is imposed on them as culture.[9]

SK *So could you trace the stages of this new feminist theory.*

PB The beginning is usually identified with the 1966 Demau manifesto. This was the first document of Italian feminism. The Demau manifesto (acronym for Demistificazione dell'autorità patriarcale [Demystification of Patriarchal Authoritarianism]) contained the suggestion 'that no solution could be found to the problem women pose to society as long as women themselves do not address the problem; that is to say, as long as the terms of the question were not reversed, and women were the subject, rather than the object of "the woman question" '.[10]

Then there was 1968. And that was another experience which marked many women who were university students at that time, and who participated in the student movement, but who also realized that they were equal but not equal. At around this time as well women's groups started being formed.[11] The Italians adopted but transformed the American consciousness-raising model. The name given to this practice in Italy, *autocoscienza*, indicates its distinctively Italian character. Women meeting to talk about their own affairs is something which has always existed, perhaps especially so in Mediterranean street cultures like the Italian. It is usually called gossip! But Carla Lonzi first used the term to denote a philosophical and a political practice. This involved transforming an age-old debased practice (gossip) into the self-determined and self-directed process of achieving a new consciousness or awareness. The discussion takes place in the context of theoretical speculation which has already moved away from the mere analysis of oppression to envisage the autonomous production of interpretative categories of reality. *Autocoscienza* is the process of the discovery and reconstruction of the self, both the self of the individual woman and a collective sense of self: the search for the subject-woman.

For some women, these groups, the being with other women and building things with other women, became their only political practice. Others still felt that they wanted to be in the public domain – the political institutions (in parties and in political groups as well).[12] At the same time, these other women were conscious, and couldn't but be, that there was a strong contradiction there: that they were invited to forget, or repress, the new sense of self that they were developing in the groups, in order to fall into the categories of conventional political thought and behaviour. As a result, some left the political parties. Thus, for example, in the early 1970s, Lotta Continua, one of the groups of the extreme left, was shaken by feminist critique and almost disappeared. In the Communist Party as well the presence of women who were also undergoing another political experience and an alternative political practice in the feminist groups, and who wanted to commute between them, resulted in change. One could cite here the instance of the abortion law where the position of the Communist Party changed significantly because of the women in it.[13]

Finally, a massive feminist movement in the streets was also particularly characteristic of the 1970s.

SK *What about feminist publications at this time? The constant exchange of feminist documents and manifestos that we recorded in the Blackwell book seems particularly characteristic of Italy.*[14]

PB This was slow to start, and has remained low-key. Manifestos and other documents were usually circulated in more amateur, impromptu and even personal ways. But, for example, Rivolta Femminile founded their own publishing house at the beginning of the 1970s, and published Carla Lonzi's influential *Let's Spit on Hegel*. The Edizioni delle Donne was founded in the mid-1970s, as were a number of magazines and journals, for example, *Effe* and *Sottosopra*. At about this time as well, a number of left-wing publishing houses started printing feminist material.

SK *Returning to the history. What happened in the late 1970s, and after?*

PB From the mid-1970s onwards, what characterizes Italian feminism is not so much the growth of feminist publishing houses, but the creation of women's cultural centres. These do seem to me one of the hallmarks of Italian feminism. Some women who had been involved in the UDI and/or in the feminist movement in the 1960s, but who were also active in the universities, the media, or the arts, felt that there was a split between their interest in traditional culture, and the emphasis in the feminist movement on experience, and on drawing upon one's own experience as the real and only source of knowledge. They founded the centres as a result of their desire to be accepted in the feminist movement even though they were academics, and, at the same time, to be actively feminist in the places where they were working as well. In this sense their situation was analogous to that of the women in the political parties.[15]

SK *Italian feminism is separatist, isn't it. I do think that that is another difference.*

PB Yes, particularly in the 1970s it was strongly separatist. It still is, but it was even more so at that time. The Italian feminists have always felt that first and foremost they want to relate to *other women*. As I have said, they prioritize their place in the groups, and in the wider feminist movement, over their role as academics, in teaching and in research. For example, Luisa Muraro and Nadia Fusini. Luisa Muraro is probably the most influential Italian feminist theorist. But she's influential not because she's an academic, but because she's a good thinker, and because she has been in the feminist movement right from the beginning. And because she's still involved in it. Nadia Fusini is less involved in the women's movement now, but she was one of the founder members of the Virginia Woolf Centre, and she was very active in the feminist movement earlier on. By contrast, Viola Papetti, who teaches at Rome University, is often invited to give papers at seminars for women's groups. But she gets invited as an academic who is a woman, not as an influential figure in the movement.[16]

SK *Can we move on to the 1980s and the 1990s?*

PB The late 1970s saw the end of the last massive demonstrations (except for Chernobyl in 1986). The 1980s saw a turning inwards, a *riflusso*, or going back to private concerns. But although women were no longer in the streets in their thousands, there was a lot of work going on in the centres and new journals, like *Memoria* (1981), *Orsa Minore* (1981) and *Via Dogana* (1983), were established. There was a strong sense that things were still happening, although not in the public domain.

If Italian feminism had been initially marked by the Demau document, the movement into the 1980s was heralded by a special issue of *Sottosopra* entitled 'More Women than Men'. This represented a turning-point in that it argued that what it called static separatism had done its time, and although having separate women's spheres would always be important, it advocated the creation of dynamic separatism: a separatism that existed in the world outside the groups. The term they coined for this was *affidamento* (entrustment).[17]

Many feminists argue that entrustment doesn't work, that it

merely emphasizes power differences and relations *between* women. But this document marked a new phase of interest in the position of women in the workplace. The notion of measuring yourself against another woman's work rather than by the standards of the world, and of having another woman, or women, as the measure of your worth, was liberating. It had established new forms of organization within the organizations.

The mid–1980s also saw a kind of watershed in the first national conference of women's centres.[18] And in 1986 Chernobyl saw the strongest moment of interrelationship between the feminist movement and the Communist Party.[19]

SK *We've talked about the growth of Italian feminism since the 1960s. I mentioned distinctive features earlier. What would you say these were?*

PB Whatever Italian feminist theory has taken from other feminisms (and there are resemblances), has been rethought and restructured in the context of Italian politics and practice. One thing which is different is the greater emphasis on the relationships between women. For the Italians, the source of knowledge, and the source of politics, is located precisely in the relationships between or among women. Italian feminist political practice consists in the recognition and the struggle for the symbolization of a link between women, and in having women as your primary reference. (I'm not saying that this thereby excludes differences or conflicts between women, or that it is to suggest that all women are the same. These conflicts and differences should be increasingly recognized and prioritized. Women should be able to fight and to hate one another, but without losing sight of the fact that they are women, and that being a woman is a value *per se*.) In general, for Italian feminism, a historical concern with the 'real' world cannot be separated from an investigation of the symbolic structures which both express and shape reality: 'Sexual difference . . . is neither a biological nor a sociological category, but is located at the intersection of these two levels with the symbolic dimension.'[20]

SK *The other differences?*

PB As I mentioned above, the strongly political character of Italian feminism, its close and continuing links with whatever is going on in mainstream politics. The way I would put the question of the relationship, would not be how feminist theory has related to communism, but how feminist practice and theory have related to the existence of the Communist Party, to its politics, to the existence of the trade unions and their politics, in the specific situation that we have had in Italy from the 1960s until now.

II

The essays in this collection cover a decade, and are drawn from literature, linguistics, semiotics, history, psychoanalysis and philosophy. Each essay examines some aspect of 'The Lonely Mirror'.[21] We chose this title for the anthology because it submits to positive and negative definition. Women have traditionally been regarded as mirrors for men, and as dependent on men's gaze for their sense of themselves. But, as the essays here suggest, women have started being mirrors for one another, and these positive reflections have become the basis of new models of individual identity, and community.[22]

We begin with the negative (before moving on, in the second part of this Introduction, to suggest more positive aspects of the mirror).

Mizzau's analysis of Dostoyevsky's story 'A meek young girl' in 'A double-voiced silence' (1987), which is chapter 4 in this volume, is typical of the revisionary textual readings of the 1970s and 1980s which reveal hitherto unread female plots. Narrated retrospectively by the husband in an attempt to make sense of what happened, the story tells of a poverty-stricken young girl who marries a pawnbroker, discovers unhappiness, and commits suicide. And because it brings together a number of the issues central to Italian feminist theory, it is worth looking in some detail at Mizzau's analysis of Dostoyevsky's story in order to frame the larger debate.

'A meek young girl' is predicated on the notion that the woman lacks a self. She is entirely sublimated to the man's image of her in a deforming and gratifying mirror. At the same time, the man's identity is confirmed through his power over the woman whom he perceives as an object. In his eyes, she is incapable of autonomous thought, or of desiring subjectivity. Each resists the other's subjectivity, and silence becomes the story's catastrophic means of communication. Thus in Mizzau's analysis of 'A meek young girl', silence, or the figuration of silence, disconfirms the other, and nullifies his or her discourse, or renders it enigmatic.

But the dynamic of silence and enigma is problematic. In her definitive silence, the meek young girl constitutes herself for ever (untouchably and as an enigma). She can be seen as acting critically on her everyday situation in order to transform her position within it. The story offers images of subjectivity, not as the source of meanings, or as the object of a quest, but as an elusive starting-point.

Mizzau sees the woman's situation in the story as paradigmatic of that of all women: she is the absent interlocutor operating (in Bakhtin's terms) through 'the loophole word'. Anne Freadman, writing in an analogous context on George Sand, notes that what is at issue here is the woman's need 'to transform discursive material that in its untransformed state leaves a woman no place from which to speak, or nothing to say'.[23] The meek young girl's need is not met. She fails to transform the discursive material she is landed with. She displays all the symptoms of classical hysteria:

> Unease and rebellion show themselves in the only way which is socially codified, if not accepted, through analogical and iconic modes. . . . Hysteria is a form of indirect communication which asks the question while sheltering from the frustration of not receiving a reply, and at the same time permits the formulation of a request (for affection, confirmation, existential recognition).
>
> (pp. 71–2)

The story plays on the conjunctions of the body and of identity, and on the impossibility of separating outside and inside, sexuality and self.[24]

In the end, Dostoyevsky's meek young girl fails to establish communication within the given social and cultural conventions. Nor can she find a voice that would change the rules of the game. She is in the classical double-bind. Whatever she does, she loses, and the contradictory messages she is constantly receiving from the man (and he from her) cannot be resolved because they are part of the very condition of their communication. The consequence is a reaction of absolute impotence and total mistrust in her own psychic capacities. In this context suicide becomes the only possible response, a radical response of withdrawal.

Silence – or, in Cavarero's words, 'the figuration of silence' – is a central concern of a number of the pieces in the literature and philosophy sections of this book. In 'Towards a theory of sexual difference' (1982), chapter 11 in this volume, Cavarero is concerned with how to think sexual difference through a system of thought founded on not thinking it: the problem of the woman who speaks and thinks, but not beginning from herself.[25] The difficulty then becomes finding a structure that would contemplate the woman as subject without believing in an original femininity which history has defeated and concealed: 'in the representation of a lost essence we can mourn ourselves, but not find ourselves.' For Cavarero, the female subject is not a mythical essence to be reclaimed, but exists in the here and now. It is the same and different in every woman. It is 'the true, the originary differing in sex which everyone carries in their flesh like living and dying'.[26]

For Cavarero, then, being lost is not the locus from which the movement of finding ourselves proceeds. As she argues elsewhere, Ulysses, the archetypal male wanderer, was in fact never lost. He always had a place to go back to. But for the woman who stayed at home, it was not her home. She had nowhere to return to:

> But woman did not have a house from which to distance herself. Her being, for ever distant in language, cannot remember or regret. . . . So for man distance is holiday, while for woman it is drudgery: a finding herself distant which does not involve leaving home or arriving in a foreign place. Because language, as the word of the other, already estranges her.[27]

We are lost as long as we accept the disorientating discourse of the other. If we discard it, we find ourselves. Paradoxically, then, this movement consists in finding oneself without ever having lost oneself. Cavarero is concerned with thinking about sexual difference without giving priority to the notion of difference, emphasizing instead the notion of self. In this way, she completely alters, or displaces, the terms of the debate.

'The discourse of passion' (1984), 'Woman-graphy' (1986), 'The erotic woman writer' (1990), and 'Language in the crucible of the mind' (1986) (chapters 1, 2, 3 and 5 in this volume), address the same issues as Cavarero. But rather than taking silence as their starting-point, these authors begin with the premiss that bodily experience is at the base of psychic structure, and that male language is inadequate to the expression of female sexuality. As Fusini puts it: 'it is impossible to appropriate the sexual body in the word.' These pieces centre on the relationships between women, bodies and writing.[28]

Fusini begins with Lawrence's 1929 essay 'Pornography and obscenity' in which Lawrence reconstructs the etymology of the word pornography. From *pórnē* (harlot, prostitute) and from *gráphō* (to write), we get pornography. 'Woman-graphy' explores how the word takes away the body, substituting for it the body of the word. Using Lawrence's novels and *My Secret Life*, Fusini explores how 'the something which language cannot arrive at a complete knowledge of is the body traversed by this sexual drive'. *My Secret Life* is a meticulous record of the sexual adventures of its Victorian (male) author. And yet, as Fusini points out:

> the more we read on the more we cannot help but understand that in all this description what eludes the writer is precisely that which obsesses him, his failure to capture the act of sex. It seems to the gentleman that without being captured in the *word*, the *act* is not in itself enough. . . . The repetitiveness which lies at the heart of sex, its mechanical nature, seems to strike a deep wound into the gentleman's identity, a wound which is healed by the act of writing; by registering, calculating, taking notes, the gentleman turns into a work of art the sexual work which he performs with a mechanical rhythm akin to some extent to the rhythms of the factory production line.
>
> (p. 40)

By contrast, in Lawrence's novels language is summoned only to dissolve in the violence of the body. And for Lawrence there is an unreclaimable gap between sexuality and word, word and body. For this reason, Fusini argues, 'Lawrence rightly defends himself from the charge of pornography'.

We may take issue with this, but Fusini's perception that pornography makes us realize there is a limit to representation is central to Papetti's argument in 'The erotic woman writer' as well. Drawing her examples from 'perverse, fragmented examples of erotica – texts which have slipped under others', slipped from notice (by Behn, Montagu, Colette, Woolf, Wharton), Papetti suggests that women writers of erotica are rare precisely because they fear the kind of narcissistic loss of self/falsification of experience in writing which happened to the author of *My Secret Life*: Fusini argues that 'in this sense when the object is enclosed in the representational order, it is precisely the object which slips away, in other words what succeeds in evading pornography, the writing of the body in the sexual act' (p. 43). Fusini and Papetti both argue that there is no figurative model of the female body's pleasure embedded in tradition. 'The discourse of passion' looks at how language's expressive system may be represented by the body and constructs a semiotics of gesture:

> If we consider the body as the theatre of the passions, the possibility emerges of a semiotics originating in a score of vital impulses, of which the gesture, the gaze and the facial expression would simply be the end-point of a line running from the interior to the exterior. The body is the superficial structure where the deep structure of the passions emerges and becomes visible. In this dynamic of emergence and visible expression, in this becoming language and communication of the deep structure of human emotions, the entire historical and cultural destiny of the passions is played out. Culture projects a selective grid on to the inchoate mass of emotions, drives, intermittences, reveries, like a net whose shadow cuts and segments an undivided surface into separate portions. We know from phonology how each language selects only a limited number of sounds from the continuum of sounds which the human voice is capable of producing. Similarly, culture creates a language from human emotions and a legible text from the body by circumscribing, isolating, codifying and attributing pertinence to just a limited number of expressive and semantic units.
>
> (p. 34)

Like Magli, Camboni is interested in the interaction of physical and mental experience. Looking at texts by Woolf, Stein, Sexton and Fraser, she characterizes 'the mental crucible in which experience is transformed into writing', and argues that, paradoxically, it is the 'uselessness' of words that makes them 'ethical':

> The truth of a word lies in the cohabitation of meanings within it. The coexistence of tensions within a human being is what this truth reveals.
>
> (p. 93)

Her project involves detaching language from a referred world in order 'to cultivate the very silence out of which a woman's life might surface'.

III

In different ways, Fusini, Papetti, Magli and Camboni are all concerned with the combinations of bodies, passions and writing. Camboni calls this 'projective criticism': 'in which there is an interaction of physical and mental experience'. 'Maternal role and personal identity' (1978), 'In search of the mirror' (1988) and 'The female animal' (1984) (chapters 6, 7 and 8 in this volume) examine the relationship between the body and the economy of subjectivity in specifically psychoanalytical terms. In the latter pieces Minetti and Vegetti Finzi are particularly interested in shared collective projects: the 'body' of the group.[29]

'Maternal role and personal identity' draws upon Jungian analytical psychology to explore the character of what Montefoschi calls, in a part of the paper not published in this translation, 'the social reality of women which motivated the psychic dynamics that theories of the maternal present as being natural facts'. Montefoschi examines both the negative and the positive in the cult of the mother, and the use of psychoanalysis in feminist theory and practice, potentially either liberating or repressive. The danger is that psychoanalytical practice can end up by merely 'confirming already institutionalized subject roles'. On the other hand, according to Montefoschi in the original paper:

> Jungian analytical psychology could be a theoretical base (on a psychological level) for the feminist movement, and the practice of the psychoanalytical process could serve as an instrument of individual awareness and transformation, and could be used along with a collective political practice.

Subtitled 'Fusion and differentiation in women's groups', 'In search of the mirror' also asks if it is possible to see the women's group 'as an effective maternal mirroring function'. Minetti argues that women's needs are answered by the group as the child's are by the mother. Her article examines group experiences to see what narcissistic needs feminism has, or has not, fulfilled.

'The female animal', meanwhile, seeks to identify the missing female subject through institutional modes of working together. Vegetti Finzi unravels the genealogy of the modern subject from ancient Greece to Foucault. 'The female animal' examines the representation and the regulation of the female body, of images of women, and of the roles allocated to them. Vegetti Finzi describes the now familiar double-move: man needs woman to mirror to him his own aggrandized self-image, the woman meanwhile is resistant to the image given to her by man, but has not expressed an autonomous and alternative version of herself. By exploring the nature/nurture debate at selective historical moments (she is particularly interesting on female mystics), Vegetti Finzi discovers an oblique method of 'constructing a memory of the future', and thereby 'making the silence speak'.

Relationships between past, present and future also figure in 'Premiss: a figure of power and an invitation to history' (1970) and in 'On "mothers" and "sisters" ' (1980) (chapters 9 and 10 in this volume). Pomata and Buttafuoco side-step from psychoanalysis to history. These pieces share with the previous essays their concerns with the body and with the maternal metaphor. But the emphasis is now on the history of such formulations.[30]

Pomata's 'Premiss', for example, begins with the issue of women's control of their bodies. Citing the text of Italy's 1977 abortion bill, Pomata analyses the anonymous subjectivity of scientific knowledge and its powerful bureaucracy:

> The relationship between doctor and woman is defined as an interaction between a minor to be protected and a competent person in charge. . . . The power of protection is based on the ability to ensure for the minor the right to a 'good' which is determined and defined by the guardian himself: in our case 'the physical and mental health' related to 'the social value of motherhood'. So the doctor's power is that of defining the area of realities and values within which the woman's rights can be considered, even before they can be exercised.
>
> (pp. 155–6)

For Pomata the power which the law delegates as the 'guardian of human life' is inseparable from the development of what she calls 'the bourgeois state':

> We have been so fascinated by the bourgeoisie beheading their king that we have not noticed the figures with which bourgeois order has surrounded us, the doctor and the teacher, the scientist and the judge. . . . Perhaps we have been too busy . . . to notice the multiform and elusive nature of bourgeois power.
>
> (p. 158)

Pomata's 'Premiss' then is that the bourgeoisie has, as it were, created 'a crowd of beings marked by a new specificity' (woman and criminal, child and madman), and that these beings are characterized by medical, biological, moral and social norms, created from and by a scientific definition which imprisons them. 'Perhaps woman has become a "question" only when, under the spotlight of practical reality, women were focalized as a distinct object, and therefore as a new and specific object,' Pomata says.

Pomata's concern with 'the poverty and frailty' of individual women's lives (as opposed to the collective woman's body as defined by the bourgeois state) is again the subject in the Epilogue in chapter 9, which takes its title – 'To room nineteen' – from Doris Lessing's story of that name. Here the moral and social 'norm' at stake is the institution of motherhood. In 'Maternal role and personal identity' (see p. 15), Montefoschi had argued that 'the woman must sacrifice the mother she carries within herself'. The happily married woman in room nineteen is only hazily aware that to want a room of her own is to want to escape the constraining cult of motherhood. 'To have a room all to oneself is to ensure the possibility of movement, of metamorphosis.' But, as Pomata points out, the power that has defined and built 'woman', and has assigned a specific space for her,[31] is insidious and hard to place:

It is difficult to understand from what form of oppression the woman in room nineteen is seeking relief. Never has authority been so invisible or, if it has shown its face, never has that face been so ordinary and innocuous, so capable of fitting perfectly, like a mask, to our own face, of blending with our own identity. An attempt to distance ourself from authority, to express our difference as compared to its definitions, can begin . . . with the search for a place where we can let it fall, where we can be another person, or, simply, be ourselves.

(p. 165)

Buttafuoco's 'On "mothers" and "sisters" ' is another non-victimist historiography. She acknowledges that the theoretical reference points have been drawn up by male historians. But, like Cavarero, she is uninterested in the absent place. Instead, she asks what kind of collective planning ahead persuades us to 'make history' today. Like Cavarero, Buttafuoco is interested in the here and now: 'the actual society in which we live':

The present/past dynamics, in fact, interests me rather for the third dimension which opens up and which is rarely considered when one ponders the meaning of history: that is, the choice of which features of the past to illuminate through historical observation is determined by a present which already poses a hypothesis of the future.

(p. 173)

Buttafuoco is alert to the problem that 'women are not woman', that our lives are shaped by different political, social and economic structures, and that when we recover the women of the past from their limbo, we are effectively describing them only in terms of their affinity with, or difference from, our own lives. At the same time, she sees the strength of a collective or communal feminist historiography

to combine ideas and techniques for a knowledge which is concerned neither with an analysis of the individual self (as it is in the case of psychoanalytical therapy), nor with the study of 'broadened' selves, groups of individuals who feel bound to a vast and consistent range of common features (as in the case of the 'practice of the unconscious' and of the little groups of *autocoscienza*): a knowledge which needs to overcome the barrier of the death of women who have gone before us and of their movements. This is a knowledge which tries to retie the thread of memory that Ariadne lost or that Theseus broke after having made use of it to get out of the labyrinth. . . . [It is on this that] we build our identity for today and propose it for tomorrow.

(p. 174)

IV

The various articles we have examined so far reflect the difficulties, the pitfalls and the risks inherent in seeking to recover the female subject who cannot identify herself in the mirrors of history and of philosophical thought. But the papers in this book also reveal positive projects, and the contributions to knowledge, made by feminist speculative and theoretical thought. The very existence of these essays – their shared interests and their differences, their potential dialogue or exchange with other now recognizable 'communities' of women – is evidence of both a continuing challenge, and a real achievement.

For example, we have already seen the ambitious quality of Cavarero's project (see p. 12). Rethinking the whole western philosophical tradition[32] without, as it were, a leg to stand on is also the intention behind Putino's piece. 'Jumping' (1983) (chapter 12) involves assuming responsibility for a new female self in a different context of desire which is placed outside all known philosophical and verbal paradigms:

> 'Run away, run away, don't let them catch you, if you're there you won't be here any more.' Not wanting to be tamed, this is thinking for oneself. A flickering, a revolt which combines the joy of being in the world and the desire to be strangers. An adolescent game which invents not another street, but another space. The intensity of the untamed in my thinking makes me turn to another woman, a concrete other, with a name or to other women with names. Maybe here, without ever pronouncing we, I say we. We is a challenge, it is not familiar territory. It is . . . a map of connections, glances, remedies, writings.
>
> (p. 224)

Putino's 'we' carries the notion of the strength of relationships between women, who operate as mutually mirroring selves, each reflecting an image on and of the other. This is a positive recurrent feature in many of the essays in this anthology. Minetti's 'In search of the mirror' (see p. 15) frames the 'we' explicitly in the context of the emotions and the relationships generated within the women's groups. Bonacchi's 'On the female word and its "spirit" ' (1980) (chapter 13) argues a similar genesis:

> This founding act was the loving, 'thoughtful' addressing of a word, for the first time destined by woman to woman. . . . Reciprocal address has transformed being female from a fact into an *event* which established relationships among women. This relationship is the originary event of our movement's history and politics. . . .
>
> In the groups of the 1970s, each woman was first of all a mirror where the other woman could recognize her own 'body'. This recognition has created culture, weaving the web of interpersonal relationships. . . . Sometimes, the groups have succeeded in the delicate cognitive process of constructing a bodily image as object (whole), at the same time as considering

this image as subject, that is as an active source of self-representation.

(pp. 231–2)

This shared concept of the foundation of women's thought and
action, their reciprocal acknowledgement and validation, is seen
as the source of their inner power and self-knowledge: 'being-
woman' in 'being-together'. Thus the attempt to create the female
subject becomes a reality. At the same time, as Putino points out,
each 'we' contains many individual selves:

> Without being tamed by the landscape, here I move and another
> woman moves. If I am able to look at her in this space she is
> clearly visible, not far from me but separate. If I have this
> space I know her difference and mine, my fear and hers, but
> also her courage and my fear. . . . But without imitating her,
> without identification, because in this space, which is imposs-
> ible to manipulate according to external limits and signs, we
> are at the same time a tribe and individuals, and each woman
> fights her own war.

(p. 224)

In this context, it is worth noting that Bonacchi's piece was
written for a seminar called 'Individue: Nascita del Soggetto Morale
Femminile' [Female Individuals. Birth of the Female Moral Sub-
ject], held in Rome (11 March 1989), which was organized by the
Centro di Studi e Ricerche delle Donne of the Istituto Gramsci. As
Francesca Izzo, also a speaker in the seminar, explains the term
individue is a neologism which genders the neutral (but grammati-
cally masculine) individuo (individuum):

> There is no doubt that the term 'female individual' points to
> the current trend of dismantling women's social and cultural
> tradition founded on a relative homogeneity in their reflected
> consciousness, a growing trend that is aimed at achieving real
> (not just formal) subjective freedom. Yet to speak of the 'moral
> female subject', however one wants to understand it, is to
> indicate the birth of a trans-individual identity. The conjunction
> of 'female individual' with 'moral subjectivity' provokes an
> issue completely ignored in the modern idea of the subject. By
> linking the two terms we attempt to bring together women's
> thought and action on a plane quite different from the tendency

to particularize, emphasizing all the various differences, the multiple subjects and figures that operate in today's post-industrial societies.[33]

Both Bonacchi and Izzo frame their very different discussions of female ethics within the context of postmodernism. But like so many contemporary feminist theorists, they are suspicious of the place and uses of feminism within the postmodern debate. Bonacchi, for example, (unlike Cavarero) sees the need for a 'rootedness' in feminism which would undermine the 'experience of a presence without a foundation' which is so crucial to postmodernism:[34]

Women's political presence is a hybrid. It testifies on the one hand to this movement of history towards the 'unmentionable community' [Blanchot], a community without foundation; on the other hand to the anxiety about the lack of foundation – or lack of symmetry, which amounts to the same thing – and to the search for a new, solid foundation which can fill the void left by the traditional one.

(p. 234)

But the revision of established categories along the lines advocated by Izzo and Bonacchi (the rethinking of Kant and Hegel in the case of the former), also means venturing away – as Cavarero says – from places where we have never been, and recovering a language we have never lost. Marina Sbisà locates this 'Between interpretation and initiative' in a piece from 1985, not published in this collection. She brings together the problems and successes of the creation of the subject as agent and enunciator, and offers a linguistic reworking of the reconciliation or the reconnection between self and body. Sbisà's project is to prevent the short-circuiting that so often happens between theory and practice, and which leads women to minimalize their own linguistic acts:

It is a matter of seeing if there can be semiotic and linguistic mediations that will be able to confirm and verify a solidarity between presentations of the self that are not subordinated to the traditional feminine stereotype and the support that offers its energies and particular form to such presentations, the (or rather, a) female body.[35]

V

The female body (individual or collective, silent or speaking) is at the centre of all the essays in this collection. We started with Mizzau's analysis of Dostoyevsky's silent girl. The three silent women in Marleen Gorris's 1984 Dutch film *A Question of Silence* replay the social and cultural conventions of the story a century later. The film, as Linda Williams describes in 'A jury of their peers',

> is about the spontaneous and unmotivated murder-mutilation of a male boutique owner by three women shoppers. They commit the crime after one of them – a near-catatonic house-wife – is caught shoplifting a dress. Instead of meekly returning the garment as the smug male shop owner seems to expect, Christine stubbornly shoves it back in her bag. Two other women . . . come to her defence and then, slowly, deliberately, join in her offence, taking garments themselves. . . .
>
> During the courtroom investigation, the psychiatrist earn-estly attempts to find psycho-social explanations for their acts. But each woman resists the imposition of a clinico-juridical discourse that would explain her crime by judging her mad. . . . The psychiatrist must finally agree that they are three 'very ordinary women'. . . .
>
> The film ends when the psychiatrist leaves the courtroom, and once again encounters the chorus of silent women. She turns to look at them, and on this look the frame freezes. The spatial, experiential and metaphysical realms of female differ-ence are recognized in her look, though they have still not been spoken.[36]

The point is that the women in the film have perceived a common identity, but they cannot articulate it. They can only share it in silence, or, at best, in the raucous, disruptive laughter that expresses their solidarity in the courtroom. As we have seen, Dostoyevsky's meek young girl was not aware of her condition or situation, let alone able to express it (verbally, or by some other means). The violence in her story – the revolver scene – is merely potential. Framed between the story and the film, the theoretical writings of a decade of Italian feminism are, in some sense, equally resistant to speech. As Cavarero points out:

> There is no mother tongue, since there is no language of

woman. Our language is a foreign language which we have not learned by translation from our own tongue. And yet, it is not ours, it is foreign, suspended in a faraway place that rests upon the missing language. That which we perceive in this foreign tongue, which yet we are and cannot be, is thus the distance which separates us from it; the tongue in which we speak ourselves but do not recognize ourselves. In this distance is preserved, as a possibility, the missing language, a need for translation which lies in the foreign tongue like a desire to return to the language which has been translated, and is nevertheless missing, present only in the translation like an original which is not lost, but rather has never been granted.

(p. 197)

At the same time, the essays also show that the silence has been broken, and that we can now discern the contours of a recognizable self in the mirror. In putting together these pieces in 1990, and in discussing them in this Introduction, we were aware of two problems. First, that we have selected pieces as arbitrarily different from each other as we could find; second, and paradoxically, that we may have made the 'contours' clearer and more unified than they actually are. We have taken this risk, however, because we believe that the issues framed within the last decade are still crucial, and framing them in this (necessarily subjective) way will at least outline some of the parameters of the debate. Obviously the emphases could fall differently, and we could ourselves make different patterns out of the material. We would ask our readers to remember, in Putino's words, that 'Jumping' is always the name of the game.

NOTES

1 Teresa de Lauretis, 'The essence of the triangle or, taking the risk of essentialism seriously: feminist theory in Italy, the U.S., and Britain', *Differences*, 1989, vol. 1, no. 2, p. 4.

2 The second half of the 1970s marked the birth of a new type of feminist association, which became known as the *Centri* or women's centres. These constituted themselves as separate and autonomous sites of sexually controlled research, in order to preserve, transmit, produce culture as/for women. In 1986, when their first nation-wide conference took place in Siena, there were over a hundred of them spread all over Italy. More than a third had assumed a formalized legal structure. See the 'Table of Women's Centres' in Paola Bono

and Sandra Kemp (eds), *Italian Feminist Thought: A Reader*, Oxford, Blackwell, 1991, pp. 368–70.

The 'Virginia Woolf', also known as 'the Women's University', is one of the most important feminist cultural associations in Italy. Founded in Rome in 1979, it has annually organized courses, seminars and conferences on a wide range of subjects. More than three hundred women a year have attended the centre, women from very different walks of life, many of them not otherwise involved in the politics of feminism.

Luisa Muraro, a leading figure in Italian feminism, belongs to the Milan Women's Bookshop collective, and is also a member of the Diotima group. (See n. 3 below.) *Sexual Difference. A Theory of Social Symbolic Practice* by the Milan Women's Bookstore Collective, has recently been translated with an introductory essay by Teresa de Lauretis, Bloomington, Ind., Indiana University Press, 1991.

3 Diotima is a women-only philosophical research group, or, as its members would prefer, a philosophical 'community' of women. It was formed in Verona at the end of 1983 by women already engaged in the field of philosophy. They have since published a number of papers, *Il pensiero della differenza sessuale*, Milan, La Tartaruga, 1987, and *Mettere al mondo il mondo. Oggetto e oggettività alla luce della differenza sessuale*, Milan, La Tartaruga, 1990.

4 Self-consciousness or consciousness of the self – 'the term coined by Carla Lonzi for the practice of consciousness-raising groups which Italian women adapted from North American feminism to suit their own socio-cultural situation' (de Lauretis, from her introduction to *Sexual Difference*, op. cit.).

5 For the practice of consciousness-raising groups, or *autocoscienza*, see p. 6 and pp. 121–3.

6 There is no space here to illustrate this historical background and its sociopolitical and cultural aspects in any detail, either in general or with respect to women. In their studies on Italian feminism, both J. A. Hellman, *Journeys Among Women. Feminism in Five Italian Cities*, Oxford, Polity, 1987, and L. Chiavola Birnbaum, *La liberazione della donna: Feminism in Italy*, Middletown, Conn., Wesleyan University Press, 1986, deal with this aspect at some length. S. Bassnett, *Feminist Experiences. The Women's Movement in Four Cultures*, London, Allen & Unwin, 1986, is also interesting in this respect. More recently, see de Lauretis, Introduction to *Sexual Difference*, op. cit., and Maurizia Boscagli, 'Unaccompanied ladies: feminist, Italian, and in the academy', *Differences*, 1990, vol. 2, no. 3. On women in postwar Italy, see L. Balbo and M. P. May, 'Women's condition: the case of postwar Italy', *International Journal of Sociology*, 1975/6, vol. 5, pp. 79–102. On women, Marxism, the PCI (Italian Communist Party) and the extra-parliamentary groups, see A. Buttafuoco, 'Italy: the feminist challenge', in C. Boggs and D. Plotke (eds), *The Politics of Eurocommunism: Socialism in Transition*, Montreal, Black Rose Press, 1980, pp. 197–219; D. Dobbs, 'Extra-parliamentary feminism and social change in Italy, 1971–1980', *International Journal of Women's Studies*,

1982, vol. 5, no. 2, pp. 148–60; Y. Ergas, '1968–79 – Feminism and the Italian party system: women's politics in a decade of turmoil', *Comparative Politics*, 1982, vol. 14, no. 3, pp. 253–79; S. Hellman 'The "New Left" in Italy', in M. Kolinsky and W. E. Paterson (eds), *Social and Political Movements in Western Europe*, London, Croom Helm, 1976, pp. 243–72; R. Lumely, 'Social movements in Italy, 1968–78', unpublished PhD dissertation, University of Birmingham, 1983; A. Melucci, 'New movements, terrorism and the political system: reflections on the Italian case', *Socialist Review*, 1981, vol. 56, pp. 97–136; T. Pitch, 'Notes from within the Italian Women's Movement: how we talk of Marxism and feminism', *Contemporary Crises*, 1979, vol. 3, pp. 1–16; V. Spini, 'The New Left in Italy', *Journal of Contemporary History*, 1972, vol. 7, pp. 51–71; and K. C. von Henneberg, 'The Italian Communist Party and the feminist movement', unpublished honours thesis, Harvard University, 1983. On the Unione Donne Italiane (UDI), see K. Beckwith, 'Feminism and leftist politics in Italy: the case of the UDI–PCI relations', *Western European Politics*, 1985, vol. 8, no. 4, pp. 20–37. Some general studies on Italy and Italian politics include P. A. Allum, *Italy – Republic without Government?*, New York, Norton, 1973; J. A. Hellman, op. cit.; and P. Lange and S. Tarrow (eds), *Italy in Transition: Conflict and Consensus*, London, Frank Cass, 1980. Obviously, many more works are available in Italian.

7 The UDI was founded immediately after the Second World War to fight for better conditions for women. It is an original and interesting development of women in the anti-fascist struggle. It came into being within the framework of the political left, gradually building up its own political and organizational autonomy.

8 Immanuel Wallerstein, *Historical Capitalism*, London, Verso, 1983, p. 85.

9 Carla Lonzi, *Sputiamo su Hegel*, Milan, Rivolta Femminile, 1971; translated into English as *Let's Spit on Hegel*, in Bono and Kemp, op. cit., pp. 40–59 (this quote from p. 41).

10 Manifesto, Demau, 1966. Translated and quoted in Bono and Kemp, op. cit., pp. 34–5. De Lauretis, Introduction to *Sexual Difference*, op. cit., p. 5.

11 A characteristic feature of Italian feminism is its diffusion through a number of diverse groups, which operate in many cities. For the work of a number of important Italian feminist groups (including Rivolta Femminile, Movimento Femminista Romano, Libreria delle Donne di Milano, Il Centro Culturale Virginia Woolf di Roma and Diotima), see Bono and Kemp, op. cit., pp. 1–207.

12 Throughout the 1970s, the issue of 'double militancy' – of the simultaneous participation/involvement in the feminist movement and in the activities of an organized party or political group – was a crucial one. For 'double militancy', see Laura Lilli and Chiara Valentini, *Care compagne. Il femminismo nel PCI e nelle organizzazioni di massa*, Rome, Editori Riuniti, 1979; Maria Luisa Boccia, 'Dentro e fuori le istitu-

zioni. Le intellettuali tra professionalità e politica', *Memoria*, 1989, no. 9.

13 In Italy, as elsewhere, the issues of abortion and sexual violence, and their links with a sexuality imprisoned in the norms of patriarchy, have been central to the feminist movement, and have involved women from remarkably different social, intellectual and political backgrounds. For documentation on the law, see Bono and Kemp, op. cit., pp. 211–31.

14 For the exchange of documents and manifestos between the groups, see, for example, Rivolta Femminile, Manifesto; Movimento Femminista Romano, broadsheets; *Donnawomanfemme (DWF)*, editorials. Translated in Bono and Kemp, op. cit., pp. 34, 64–8, 187–207.

15 See n. 12 on 'double militancy' above.

16 See articles by Fusini and Papetti, chapters 2 and 3 in this volume.

17 The practice of 'entrustment' advocated by the Milan Libreria delle Donne insists on the need to acknowledge not simply differences but actual disparities between women in order to overcome a 'static separatism' – the idea of a separate woman's world as a haven of peace – in favour of a 'dynamic separatism', at play in the social arena. See the chapters on 'Pratica dell'Inconscio' and 'Libreria delle Donne di Milano' in Bono and Kemp, op. cit., pp. 82–138. See also an unpublished paper by Luisa Muraro, 'Love as a political practice: the example of the love for the mother', given at the conference 'Feminist Theory. An International Debate', held in Glasgow, 12–15 July 1991.

18 The first National Conference of Women's Centres was held in Siena in 1986. Collaboration and teamwork are the practice of many Italian feminists, and quite a few of the publications have collective authors.

19 For the Italian feminist movement and Chernobyl, see Bono and Kemp, op. cit., pp. 23, 317–38.

20 Rosi Braidotti, 'Feminist epistemology: critical theories and a woman-defined philosophy of sexual difference', unpublished paper given at the international seminar on 'Equality and Difference: Gender Dimensions in Political Thought, Justice and Morality', held in Florence, December 1988. Quoted in Bono and Kemp, op. cit., p. 23.

21 Title quotation from W. H. Auden, 'My dear one is mine as mirrors are lonely', from *The Sea and the Mirror*.

22 See Jenijoy La Belle, *Herself Beheld. The Literature of the Looking Glass*, Ithaca, NY, and London, Cornell University Press, 1988.

23 Anne Freadman, 'Sandpaper', *Southern Review*, 1983, vol. 16, no. 1, pp. 162, 171.

24 See Mary Kelly, *Interim*, Cambridge, Mass., Harvard University Press, 1986. See also Mary Kelly, '*Interim* part 1: *Corpus*, 1984–5' and 'Re-presenting the body: on *Interim* part 1', in James Donald (ed.), *Psychoanalysis and Cultural Theory*, London, Routledge, 1991, pp. 51–67.

25 Teresa de Lauretis, *Alice Doesn't: Feminism, Semiotics, Cinema*, Bloomington, Ind., Indiana University Press, 1986, pp. 7, 165. See also Patrizia Violi, 'Language and the female subject', in Giuliana Bruno

and Maria Nadotti (eds), *Off Screen. Women and Film in Italy*, New York and London, Routledge, 1988, pp. 139–50.

26 For the ways in which the whole question of essentialism is perceived differently in the Italian context, see de Lauretis, 'The essence of the triangle', op. cit. Much Italian feminist theory is running the risk of essentialism as it has hitherto been perceived. Taking that risk 'seriously', de Lauretis argues, may seem to speak essentialism, but it enacts a new kind of empiricism.

Irigaray works closely with the Milan group. She has written explicitly about Italian feminism and Italian politics. When the whole issue of representation became crucial, and collaboration seemed possible with women in the Communist Party, Irigaray was a speaker in the party's summer festivals, and debated the political significance of sexual difference in the party's newspaper *L'Unità*. She gave papers on various occasions between 1986 and 1989 in Italy at meetings of communist women. See her introduction to the published collection of these papers, *Il tempo della differenza. Diritti e doveri civili per i due sessi. Per una rivoluzione pacifica*, Rome, Editori Riuniti, 1989.

27 Adriana Cavarero, 'Essere presso di sé. Noi che non fummo ad Itaca' [Being with oneself. We who never were in Ithaca], *DWF*, 1986, no. 4, p. 12.

28 See Mary Jacobus, Evelyn Fox Keller and Sally Shuttleworth (eds), *Body Politics: Women and the Discourses of Science*, London, Routledge, 1990; Mary O'Brien, *Reproducing the World. Essays in Feminist Theory*, Bloomington, Ind., Indiana University Press, 1989; Teresa Brennan (ed.), *Between Feminism and Psychoanalysis*, London, Routledge, 1989; Richard Feldstein and Judith Roof (eds), *Feminism and Psychoanalysis*, Cambridge, Mass., Harvard University Press, 1989.

29 See n. 11 above.

30 See Sandra Harding (ed.), *Feminism and Methodology*, Open University Press, 1987; Cheryl Wall, *Changing Our Own Words. Essays on Criticism, Theory and Writing by Black Women*, New Brunswick, NJ, Rutgers University Press, 1989; Chandra Talpade Mohanty, Ann Russo and Lourdes Torres (eds), *Third World Women and the Politics of Feminism*, Bloomington, Ind., Indiana University Press, 1991.

31 In addition to the obvious Virginia Woolf, *A Room of One's Own*, London, Hogarth Press, 1929, for the maternal metaphor see the work of Kristeva and Jacobus.

32 For feminism and philosophy, see C. C. Gould and W. Wartofsky (eds), *Women and Philosophy: Towards a Theory of Liberation*, New York, Capricorn, 1976; Jean Grimshaw, *Feminist Philosophers. Women's Perspectives on Philosophical Traditions*, Brighton, Sx, Wheatsheaf, 1986; M. Whitford and M. Griffiths (eds), *Feminist Perspectives on Philosophy*, London, Macmillan, 1989; Rosi Braidotti, *Patterns of Dissonance: A Study of Women and Contemporary Philosophy*, Oxford, Polity Press, 1991; Moira Gatens, *Feminism and Philosophy: Perspectives on Difference and Equality*, Oxford, Polity Press, 1991.

33 Francesca Izzo, 'Immagini del soggetto moderno. Etica e soggettività'

[Images of the modern subject. Ethics and subjectivity], *Reti*, 1989, nos 3–4, p. 123.

34 For feminism and postmodernism, see Jane Flax, *Thinking Fragments: Psychoanalysis, Feminism and Postmodernism in the Contemporary West*, Berkeley, Calif., University of California Press, 1990; Susan J. Hekman, *Gender and Knowledge. Elements of a Postmodern Feminism*, Boston, Mass., North-Eastern University Press, 1990; Linda Hutcheon, *A Poetics of Postmodernism. History, Theory, Fiction*, London, Routledge, 1988; Linda J. Nicholson (ed.), *Feminism and Postmodernism*, London, Routledge, 1990; Meaghan Morris, *The Pirate's Financée: Feminism, Reading, Postmodernism*, London, Verso, 1988.

35 Marina Sbisà, 'Fra interpretazione e iniziativa', in Patrizia Magli (ed.), *Le donne e i segni*, Ancona, Il Lavoro Editoriale, 1985, p. 48. For feminism and linguistics, see Deborah Cameron (ed.), *The Feminist Critique of Language*, London, Routledge, 1990.

36 Linda Williams, 'A jury of their peers: Marleen Gorris's "A Question of Silence" ', in E. Ann Kaplan (ed.), *Postmodernism and Its Discontents*, London, Verso, 1988, p. 108.

Part I

Language, Literature, Semiotics

Chapter 1

The discourse of passion*

Patrizia Magli

Psychoanalysis has maintained a long silence on the subject of passion. This, at least, is the claim made by some contributors to the issue of *Nouvelle revue de psychanalyse* entitled 'Passion'. One of the reasons for this silence is presumed to be the futility of defining terms such as love, fear, or nostalgia in any greater detail, as these words are of such common usage that there already exists a consensus of opinion as to their meaning. And so the passions would seem to be no more than fragments of day-to-day semantics, words that have been impoverished by the wear and tear of a common vocabulary. But psychoanalysis has built itself a home with and within this very vocabulary. For the analyst there is no reality beyond the bounds of discourse: it is through the word that the subject becomes immersed in her/his own representation, describes, seeks and liberates her/himself. The word is the place where one encounters the other and makes oneself known to the other.

But language is not only a place where people meet. It is also a battlefield, a place where negotiations and manipulations take place continuously. Agents of force of a word which not only informs but also attempts to seduce, to provoke and to intimidate: these are the passions.

The science of meaning has begun to consider the passions with growing interest, studying them as sense-effects caused by both pragmatic and interpretative action. Besides, it is well known that since earliest times certain forms of passion have been closely connected to certain topics. These relationships have been codified in classical rhetorics, in genre theory and in the theory of comedy;

* First published as 'Il discorso', in *Memoria*, 1981, no. 1. Translated by Maureen Lister.

it is well known, for example, that *terror*, *pity* and *laughter* were considered to be stimulated by certain discursive structures. And what are tragedy and rhetoric themselves but complex agents of passionate transformations?

To answer Michel Deguy's curious question, 'If the heart is structured like a language . . . what is to stop us from seducing a heart with rhetoric?', we should look back to Aristotle who, in his *Rhetorics*, speaks of the passions as *effects* that an orator must produce in his listeners. However, these passions are not just a collection of essences but rather what everyone believes the passions to be. In other words, a collection of opinions: 'the general opinion', declares Aristotle in a surprisingly modern tone, 'is the measure of being.' Thus the passions are *doxa* and as such have the power of real social forces, dictating the models and modes of human behaviour.

And it is Aristotle, again, to whom we owe the notion of passion as 'a modification of the soul caused by an action undergone'. This notion has pervaded the entire history of philosophical thought, loaded sometimes with negative connotations, as in the opinion of the Stoics that 'the passions are the disease of the soul', and sometimes with positive ones, as in Hegel's opinion that 'there is nothing great in the world without passion!' What seems to be of particular interest in the Aristotelian notion is the fact that the profoundly relational nature of the passions is taken into consideration. This nature was pointed out by Descartes, who said that 'what is passion in relationship to a subject is always action from another point of view'. Passion appears to be the effect of a process of manipulation in which at least two subjects are always involved: 'passion regarding the subject who undergoes it', declares Descartes, 'or action regarding the person who causes it'.

But passion in this dual relationship is above all a sense-effect arising from a reading of the other, of her/his pragmatic action. And the symbolic order – knowledge, power – intervenes in this interpretative process.

The symbolic is thus connected to the existence of the subject, constituting her/his reason for living and passion for being. In 1828, Broussais himself admitted that 'this culture of the intellect may spawn a multitude of artificial passions', although he is talking about the physiological roots of the passions. The passions, therefore, are ruled by cultural models and thence subject to profound metamorphoses related to the vicissitudes of the great symbolic systems. Think, for example, of the evolution that the idea of love has undergone. The archetypes of social mythology play a vital role in the illusions of the 'passionate' man. 'If I address you so coldly it is to make you understand that I am not carried away by passion,' says a character in Urfé's *Astrée* (*c.* 1610–27) who is trying to persuade his interlocutor of the absolutely rational nature of his own behaviour. But just a century later there is such an epidemic of convulsively passionate outbursts in the same social milieu that they are institutionalized exactly as if they were theatrical performances.

The destinies of social mythologies and of the metamorphoses of passions are thus closely interrelated in the history of the symbolic. Being cultural units, the passions are grouped in different semantic constellations in different cultures. But the semantic system of a culture coincides with this culture's world-view. So that, while the lexical repertory and syntactic structure of a language condition the speaker's world-view, the various systems of passions determine how they are experienced. The passions, more than any other psychic event, seem to be rooted in the body and to draw on the reality of an absolutely unique experience; but in fact they too belong to the formal domain of signs, to the content they signify and to the relationships which they establish with things. Everything must pass through the immense labyrinth of language: this is the law of western culture. Madness is incomprehensible because it is aphasic or cryptic. But in the great theatre of the passions, the urgency of communicability takes priority.

The language of the passions is based on the correlation of two mutually referential systems: an expressive system, frequently represented by the body, and the semantic system of the passions. Deguy writes, for example, that 'everything that moves the heart is written in the face'. The body is indeed the great stage of the passions. This is what Damish means when he speaks of 'masks' in connection with the range of emotional expression in the work of the seventeenth-century painter Le Brun. These expressions form the visual alphabet by means of which passion is articulated.

They are inscribed in a syntactic system of co-ordinates, constructed on a basic figure, tranquillity. The translations from one passage to the next are illustrated along the parallel lines of the drawing, as in a musical composition. This game of tranformation is governed by a process of *deviation*: in the condition of tranquillity the lines of the mouth and eyebrows follow the horizontal, each deviation from this initial stage indicating the movements of the different passions.

Similarly, on the level of content, the great philosophical systems have based the semantic universe of the passions on a system of differences. The passions are in fact organized in opposing pairs in relation to a positive or negative characteristic of the object: thus love is in opposition to hate, desire to repulsion, joy to sadness. Indifference, the *apateia* of the ancient Stoics, represents the zero degree of this system. Barthes actually speaks of indifference in this dual sense: as absence of passion and as absence of difference. It is no coincidence that *wonder*, the first of the Cartesian passions, is considered as pure and simple perception of the difference of an object, thus opposing itself to indifference. According to Giorgio Agambem, the entire semantic system of the passions is based on the original exclusion of *indifference*. The passions, therefore, take form as language on the basis of a system that relies on a process of deviation, of 'difference', both at the level of expression and at the level of content.

If we consider the body as the theatre of the passions, the possibility emerges of a semiotics originating in a score of vital impulses, of which the gesture, the gaze and the facial expression would simply be the end-point of a line running from the interior to the exterior. The body is the superficial structure where the deep structure of the passions emerges and becomes visible. In this dynamic of emergence and visible expression, in this becoming language and communication of the deep structure of human emotions, the entire historical and cultural destiny of the passions is played out. Culture projects a selective grid on to the inchoate mass of emotions, drives, intermittences, reveries, like a net whose shadow cuts and segments an undivided surface into separate portions. We know from phonology how each language selects only a limited number of sounds from the continuum of sounds which the human voice is capable of producing. Similarly, culture creates a language from human emotions and a legible text from the body by circumscribing, isolating, codifying and attributing pertinence to just a limited number of expressive and semantic units.

Common words and passions thus seem to be subject to a perverse paradox: 'You wouldn't look for me if you hadn't already found me' the logic of language seems to reply, according to the well-known principle of Pascal, to a person who is struggling to find the words to express what to her/him seems unique, 'unspeakable', confused. For the logic of language, what can be spoken has already been spoken again and again: the word has gone before it, understands it, defines it and forgets it. But the discourse of the passions is a complex and intricate web made up not only of the spoken but also of the unspeakable, the unspoken and the not yet spoken.

A reflection upon the word tells us how speaking constitutes a deviation from the unspeakable. The unspeakable is the very horizon of speaking. One of Bergson's most famous theses claims that the life of consciousness, which is essentially continuous, becomes so deformed when one tries to describe it by means of language that it appears to be a discontinuous juxtaposition of distinctly separate elements. A colour consists of an infinity of shades, but language obliges me to use only the denominations that it is able to provide me with. And so the word 'blue' leads me to believe in outlines and divisions where there is really only a continuity of gradations. With the passing of time, for example, my impressions are continually modified by a series of slidings and imperceptible changes. But words prevent me from expressing the continuity of these passages, and so I am led to believe that my impressions remain the same for the whole period of time that depends on the same word, and I see it change abruptly when language forces me to describe it differently. Language is indifferent to shades of meaning and dissects reality with words. These are the abstractions that divide the continuity of experience and make it seem like a juxtaposition of masses each of which is internally homogeneous, but clearly separated from the others. Language, being essentially a categorization, a creator of objects and of relations between objects, is the most powerful instrument for shaping the world: forming experience, language forces experience to be seen as it is expressed. We also reconstruct and analyse dreams with a certain linguistic framework. It is a characteristic of language to express only what it is possible to express. The entire nervous system of our knowledge and our emotion is drawn within the perimeter established by words. Thus the individual, as a historical subject, is predetermined in her/his choice by the discourse formation of the culture s/he lives in. At any given moment in her/his unique experience, the subject finds in society's systems a certain number of possible choices and excluded possibilities. In the same way it is possible, in language, to choose from several words, excluding all the others: 'speech is a legislation,' claims Barthes, 'language is its code. We don't see the power that language possesses because we forget that each classification is oppressive: *ordo* can mean either apportionment or intimidation.' Jakobson has shown how language may be defined not so much by what it permits us to say as by what it compels us to say.

But apart from the unspeakable upon whose absence human communication depends, discourse is also interwoven by the unspoken. According to Foucault's well-known theory, the production of discourse in every society is controlled, selected, organized and distributed by means of a certain number of procedures, of codified protocols. In each social group, even those that are apparently the freest, there exists a considerable number of linguistic taboos. There are topics totally forbidden and protected by a sort of law of silence; there are activities and feelings that are not spoken of. The discourse of the passions is affected by many different prohibitions. It would be possible to hypothesize a cultural typology based on the hierarchy of passions which condition its value systems. A society that places *audacity* at the top of this hierarchy will organize the behaviour of its members in order to favour the explicitation of this passion, whereas other passions will be silenced. Thus *fear*, *awe* and *tenderness* will constitute the unspoken of this discourse.

The story of the passions lives on this kind of cancellation, of shadowy areas, of elaborate rituals, of times allotted to the word and times prescribed for silence.

Yet there also exists a *not yet spoken*, sometimes perceptible through the gaps in discourse, which preserves the mute strength of a text which is closed in upon itself. It is perhaps only through eventual rifts and fractures in discourse that one can intuit the becoming-word of this hidden story. It cannot be excluded that an unlimited discourse, continuous and silent, may reign beyond the limits of linguistic grids: a discourse which has been repressed or removed from these categories. Our task, then, would be to allow it to emerge into words.

This new affectivity is perhaps already secretly present, lost in the depths of memory, stuttering and whispering in the murmuring of things. Perhaps it is lying still unexpressed, awaiting a word, or perhaps it has already been spoken, but is still imprisoned by the prohibitions of a symbolic system, of knowledge, of power.

But then the passions would have no reason to exist as discourse, or they would have to begin again by finding a language that is new and still being contended.

Chapter 2

Woman-graphy*

Nadia Fusini

There is a 1929 essay by D. H. Lawrence called 'Pornography and obscenity', in which Lawrence reconstructs the etymology of the word 'pornography'.[1] From *pórnē* (harlot, prostitute) and *gráphō* (to write) we get pornography, which thus combines the idea of writing with the figure of the prostitute. If we follow this etymology then pornography becomes 'the sign of the prostitute': an inscription 'of the prostitute' which maintains in its genitive form its ambiguity, signifying both the mark left by the prostitute and what is predicated about the prostitute.

It is well known that Lawrence frequently and willingly found himself on the side of the prostitute: his art was frequently and willingly called *pornography*. And yet Lawrence did not write about prostitutes at all. He wrote about the body, about sexuality, about woman and about man with regard to sex. In a sort of innocent utopia Lawrence sought the truth about man and woman in sex. But his contemporaries did not understand him, and were not interested in his utopia of liberation of the body. They declared him a pornographer, a pornographer for them evidently being etymologically someone who wrote about sex, about man and woman in terms of their sexual relationship.

But why is the figure of the prostitute (*pórnē*) called upon to speak the interweaving of the body, sexuality, pleasure, enjoyment? As far as this interweaving is concerned the prostitute is only, we might say, a synecdoche, in the sense that she represents only a part, a particular aspect, a specific position of the body and of sexuality: and yet she arrogates to herself the right to allude to the whole. And just as in poetry every metonymy has

* First published as 'Donna-grafia', in *Memoria*, 1982, no. 3. Translated by Sharon Wood.

a slightly metaphorical shade of meaning and vice versa, so in the discourse of sex the prostitute is both metaphor and synecdoche of the body and its performance; in this way she is placed at the centre of a constellation of meanings which are held together in her, or which spread out from her.

That this figurative weight is given to the *prostitute* reveals immediately how access to sexuality is linked to *one sign* in particular, which is given by the harlot; it is the sign of exchange, of equivalence. The word *pórnē* reveals this relation in its root: *por* takes us to the Latin *par* (equal) and to the vulgar Latin *paria*. The figure of the prostitute and the idea of exchange are indissolubly tied together in this movement towards equivalence: both make the *same*, one set of goods equals another, body for money. Both *par* and *pórnē* are close to the verb *pérnēmi*, which means to sell.

The idea of equality which the prostitute evokes is diabolical and sinister, not just because it is tied to the notion of money but, rather, because the relation between the sexes is here restored to its precise content of the sexual act; to that act which every member of the species can perform irrespective of any difference or privilege.[2] Precisely in this *indifference* (because for her all men are equi-val(i)ent, they are all worth the same, i.e. money), precisely for this reason the prostitute is the free body – and it is no accident she was to become a figure akin to the worker in those metaphorical equivalences Marx would institute between the worker and the whore.

So pornography has to do with the body captured in this exchange. But this is not immediately so, because pornography, as we saw at the beginning, also puts into play the idea of writing, *graphia*. We have here the body/discourse split which is the specific characteristic of human sexuality – which takes us back to the specificity of man's desire. So here too man reveals his symbolic vocation, his essence, according to Cassirer's definition, as a 'symbolic animal', a 'symbol-maker': an animal who lives in discourse, who emanates/constructs signs. In this sense human sexuality is always a spectacle, a stage-set, in the simple and essential sense that it is always put into words. There is a constitutive relationship between word, body and money, between pleasure, writing and exchange, which forms the basis of the specificity of man's sexual desire. Sexuality, in other words, is not enacted unless it is also spoken; or unless it is written.

A fine example of this is *My Secret Life*,[3] by a Victorian gentleman who, as we know, spent his life pursuing sexual pleasure and found it perhaps more than anywhere else in the eleven volumes in which he meticulously described all his encounters, all the ways and positions in which he knew the body in its sexual aspect. And yet this diary, which is the obsessive record of a life dedicated to sex, tugs at our heart; the more we read on the more we cannot help but understand that in all this description what eludes the writer is precisely that which obsesses him, his failure to capture the act of sex. It seems to the gentleman that without being captured in the *word*, the *act* is not in itself enough, is reduced to a pleasure of the organ which is lost as it occurs, flows out into the void. And since its aim is not 'and nine months later' there is no evidence that it has ever happened, that it has ever taken place. The repetitiveness which lies at the heart of sex, its mechanical nature, seems to strike a deep wound into the gentleman's identity, a wound which is healed by the act of writing; by registering, calculating, taking notes, the gentleman turns into a work of art the sexual work which he performs with a mechanical rhythm akin to some extent to the rhythms of the factory production line. The very banality which ensues, inevitable given the endless repetition of the act, always the same despite all the different positions: that sad, obsessive, repetitive release which reduces the gentleman to an anonymous machine whose rhythms are a slave to biology, is as if redeemed by the gentleman's devotion to writing, by his will to know sex, testified by his patient recording of it, by the imaginative as well as crudely physical spending which engages him *in* as well as *beyond* the work.

However, the meticulous recording of the gentleman's entrances and exits is only a *diary*. By which I mean that it is not a *novel*. I think this is important; like Lawrence I too think that in the Novel, in the Book, pornography cannot exist.

By Book I mean that fundamentally classic form of representation, that space in language, that mode of expression tied to the modern age, and to the idea which accompanies it that man is Lord of the Earth which he possesses through his speech. When Lawrence began to write, what he measured his own language with and against, was precisely this: the body. And what he found was that language was impotent in its efforts to represent the body. Precisely because it substitutes for the body, language could not represent this outside-of-itself. Lawrence as writer is effectively caught in this double-bind: because he really believes that there is an outside of language – the Open, Nature, the Body – which the western white man wants to close and contain in the word. In this way the word *takes away* the body, putting in its place the body of the word, which is only a pallid substitute for that natural concreteness which Lawrence attributed to man's body-nature. Yet Lawrence wrote, he was a writer; and as a writer all he had were words. And yet the word was his enemy: hence his indifference to form, his inattention to the avant-garde, which many took for traditionalism, a vocation to restore the past, what was gone.

In fact the word for Lawrence, in one way, does not count. For him literature is a place which points to what lies outside it, and his object is not language in is positive aspect but the emptiness revealed in it when it is measured with what is outside it, which is the body. For Lawrence every discursive language is summoned to dissolve itself in the violence of the body. In this respect Lawrence – who seems to keep his distance from the twentieth century with what I described as his 'indifference' to form – aligns himself with radical experiments of this century, such as that of Artaud. He takes a path which Nietzsche had already taken, and like him attacks western metaphysics, beginning with its grammar.

This 'outside' which Lawrence is continually trying to represent in his novels is an instinctual energy which overflows the word, which continually threatens it as something against which language measures the limit of its own capacity of representation. The something which language cannot arrive at a complete knowledge of is the body traversed by this sexual drive, 'reality of what we will never be able to know, a vital, sensual reality, which will never be transformed into an object of the mind, but will remain outside, living body of obscurity and silence, mystical body of reality'.[4]

It is impossible to appropriate the sexual body in the word. Indeed this will to know and have power over the body is the western curse that Lawrence flees from, towards the south, to Mexico. In this too Lawrence repeats or inaugurates a movement carried out by other twentieth-century writers, leaving Europe and moving towards the Arcadias of the twentieth century: Bali, or the country of the Tarahumara, the Indian, the Mexican – all places where the body has not been 'removed' by the word.

The western body is sick, says Lawrence, and the illness which afflicts it lies in the heart of the man–woman relationship, the union which itself gives evidence of the incomplete condition, the difference which makes man the separate being he is. Captured in the abyss of his solitude, of his open being, waiting, man is an incomplete being *par excellence*; the nostalgia which makes him ill is the return of that which could complete him, but which is missing from him more and more. Because it seems to Lawrence that here in the west the subject has only one way of shielding himself from the separation of bodies and things; and that is through linguistic symbolization. But it is exactly this sublimation which Lawrence rejects. For Lawrence one can shield oneself from this exile of the body only by pushing it further: towards another exile, also a geographical one. Going elsewhere, going 'outside'. Since this theatre of the self, which is the representational space destined to western man, is founded upon the word, then Lawrence must search beyond the word.

Beyond the word for Lawrence means in the senses, and as Lawrence is a writer this might seem an untenable paradox. But this is not actually the case, since for Lawrence the word serves only to indicate what is 'outside' it. This movement can be grasped precisely in the particular narrative modalities of Lawrentian language, which tends to make the word a *means* of description. Where the word is channelled towards the construction of the image, where it is no longer the expressive *medium* of the character, it is enslaved to the construction of a visual experience: an experience which touches all the senses, from sight through to the 'heart's emotion'. The image in Lawrence should be understood precisely in its function of alterity with regard to the word – like the objective arranging and composing, via description, of a scene which identifies its own constructive principle in the visualization of an event, rather than in its verbalization.

For Lawrence the words *loss of consciousness* and *death* indicate a threshold which opens out on to a new existence, which by annulling the self and its discursivity can lead to a reappropriation of the body. In the loss of consciousness (ambiguity of the body, but also the way the body names itself) the subject experiences a radical alienation of itself from itself. This is how it comes to experience; the familiar will become unknown, the known will become strange. Before and outside the word, which is mediation, a bridge between me and the Other, me and the other in me, the body is enigma. What happens within it, before and outside the word, is unknowable. The body becomes again an obscure moment, mere matter: the site of resistance to the illumination and clarity of Reason, Thought and Word.

If to name a thing is to take it away, if language is in its totality substitution and metaphor, by moving towards the non-linguistic Lawrence believes he can find *what has been lost*: we could call his work '*à la recherche de la chose perdue*'.

So Lawrence rightly defends himself from the charge of pornography. Rightly, because if pornography is a discourse which believes it can write the body and sexuality, and claims to make them visible in representation and thus to master and know sex – then Lawrence is absolutely on the other side. Between sexuality and word, between word and body, there is for Lawrence an irremediable conflict and a mutual exclusion. Sexuality, the body, pleasure, cannot be written of as such.

However, to state this limit does not mean to take refuge in a reconciled metaphysic of the ineffable, but to recognize what is proper to writing: that is, metaphor – the movement of taking elsewhere, in which something is also taken away. We could say that in this sense when the object is enclosed in the representative order, it is precisely the object which slips away; in other words what succeeds in evading pornography, the writing of the body seized in the sexual act, is exactly what is made most evident in pornography: the body. In this, pornography is stupid, omnipotent and infantile.

It is omnipotent and infantile because representation, *graphia*, does not know the limits within which it operates, and stupidly believes in the illusion of a totally representable body, erect in its visiblity, visible in its erection; in the representation of the body caught in the sexual moment it falsely reconciles the body–word, the body–representation conflict; of what cannot be spoken about, it will not remain silent.

So pornography is false. It is not by chance that the title of the brothel scene in Joyce's *Ulysses* is 'Circe'. Circe who seduces and distracts with false gifts and illusory promises, who reduces men to *pigs* – and indeed Circe is the goddess of pornography. But why are men reduced to *pigs*?

Because with animal and infantile greed these men presumptuously deny that some things are *impossible*, and they, mere men, want to possess the goddess – who will give herself only to the head, Ulysses, who does not want her. The gluttons delude themselves that they will be able to go on eating and eating, taking more and more pleasure, without any limits. Something which is self-evidently not given to mortals to do.

What pornography in its pride and stupidity will not recognize is that there is a limit to representation, that there is something which *cannot be written*. In this, pornography is the extreme point of the western disease – Lawrence would say, that ineradicable faith in representation.

'The fundamental trait of Modern Man', says Heidegger, 'is the conquest of the world resolved into an image . . . but there is an inevitable shadow which spreads over all things when man has become *subjectum* and the world image'; and he goes on: 'Because of this shadow the site of the modern world is a region which escapes representation.'[5] It is in this sense that I said the Book has become at this moment, our moment, of us postmoderns, an uninhabitable space. The Book is possible when man thinks of himself as Lord of the Earth, because he gives it an image. But what writers like Joyce, Lawrence and others point out to us is that contemporary or postmodern man is no longer contained by the Book and by language, because 'the site of the modern world is a region which escapes representation'.

I believe that the most radical experiments of the twentieth century should be seen in this way. Derrida, for example, suggests that this is the way we should read Artaud. Artaud amounts to this experiment in the twentieth century: the rejection of Metaphor. Artaud wants to stop speaking, because metaphor is innate in language, which means that the word is expropriation of the body by the word. In order to signify this expropriation of the body by the word, Artaud reaches the point of 'expressing an existence which refuses to express'.[6] The structure of 'theft' for Artaud is already situated within the relationship between word and language: the word is stolen from Language, and the body from the word. Life cannot be seized by forms, for Artaud as for Lawrence. 'My body has always been stolen from me', says

Artaud. And again: 'all writing is filth. . . . Everybody who is
master of his own language is a filthy pig.'[7]

'All writing is filth': in one way all writing is pornography,
because by *turning it into representation* it destroys the body. It is
here we should seek the truth about pornography: pornography
unveils the truth about the body precisely because it betrays it
the most. It unveils the truth about writing because it is an
absolute lie. In this sense pornography finds itself at the end-
point of the path of emancipation–representation of the body,
which betrays its truth right here: in the sense that here it unveils
the impasse of which it is made.

OF THE BODY AND ITS SEX

My putting together pornography and emancipation will not
sound so strange if we think about the word again in the etymons
which make it up and which, as we have seen, put into play the
idea of selling and exchanging, of money and equivalence. These
are the very movements of the *body* on its path to emancipation.
Movements and ruptures which the body *passes through* like stations of some cross and which, once it has rid itself of the
humanistic-Platonic harmony, will lead it to looking at itself
afresh.[8] The modern look at the body is a look which begins as
the will to know/know about the body; its inaugural moment is
when it approaches the body to reduce its opaqueness, its difference, its otherness – when it wants to penetrate it. When it wants
to perform its *anatomy*.

The word 'anatomy' burst forth in the seventeenth century,
taking the place of another key word-image, which had upheld
until then the imaginary of man's relationship to the world: the
word 'mirror'. The sixteenth century in England had seen a whole
flurry of publications whose titles all included words like mirror,
or glass, or speculum. This was the continuation of the medieval
tradition of moral *exempla* which, presupposing a clearly defined
code of morality which was not open to questions or doubt,
offered men 'a mirror', an objective representation of facts in
which they could recognize themselves and from which they
could draw warning and edification. But from Lyly's *Euphues*
(1579–80) onwards

another metaphor gradually substitutes for that of the mirror. *Euphues* is an *Anatomy of Wit*, and many other anatomies were to follow this one: *The Anatomy of Abuses* (against the corruption of customs), *The Anatomy of Absurdity* (against excessive moralism), and in the seventeenth century *An Anatomie of the World* by Donne himself and *The Anatomy of Melancholy* by Robert Burton (1621). . . . Anatomy: no longer the mirror, the acceptance of models and examples put under the eyes of man, but the precise investigation, the dissection of facts to discover their nature and their conditions.[9]

'Anatomy' then indicates a process of knowing which sees itself as a cut, a dissection. It is not by chance that this process begins in the first instance with the dead body, because the *other* of knowing is precisely reduced to a dead body, a thing, an object. No longer the *mirror* of the universe, man and his body become objects of a knowing which involves the gesture of appropriation by the subject of that which appears as other to it, unfamiliar: that is, not already signified in the chain of correspondences in which medieval knowledge had found room for man, and for his body.

No longer imprisoned in a sense which transcends it: thus the body begins its emancipation. And first it will be the concrete body, the living machine, to be analysed; then it will be the abstract body which precisely in the abstractness and formality of its own operations will find its *free being*. The free body is an active body, which works and produces: knowing it is a more complicated, risky operation. It is clearly not enough to take it literally, or in the actuality of its production. The outside look which names it will not in effect be able to know it, that body finding rather its own sense and value in the process of valorization which the body itself activates. It is this abstractly free and equal body which Marx makes analagous to the prostitute; this body which is simultaneously placed in and removed from the process of valorization and sense of work – a process which gives it liberty, and simultaneously takes liberty away.

The paradoxes of the productive body repeat, in a certain sense, the paradoxes of the love–body of the prostitute. The two bodies are akin in that in both the body is reduced to its generic content of sexual energy, to the act which any member of the species can perform. In this way the value of the body is made measurable, evident, visible. And so the body in itself has no value: it exists in so far as it is expropriated.

This is precisely the truth of pornography, also in the sense of the truth which pornography reveals. That is, the paradox by which the maximum production–representation of the body turns into its maximum expropriation. It is true that work has 'liberated' the body. It is also true that representation of the body as sex has liberated sexuality from the pockets of repression and taboos. But the opposite is also certainly true, if we tell ourselves today (if we are told) that today we find ourselves in the presence not of bodies but of simulacra of bodies. For this reason I don't think we can *believe* in pornography, as if it were a good democratic thing. For this same reason, however, we must believe in it, because nothing else comes closer to the 'truth' than what lies.

Some social forces, however, have opposed the pornographic spectacle: feminists, for example. Feminists have fought for the emancipation of sex, and surely it is not because they are afflicted by ghosts of supposed 'good manners' that they have expressed their indignation at pornography. Yet feminists have invoked censorship and have shown themselves to be decidedly in favour of conserving the *value* of the body, in favour of *valuing* the sexual act. Indeed they have spoken of the reappropriation of the body (*my body is mine* . . .), of the consciousness and the language of the body, of the liberation of the body. In this they have opposed pornography, which is the commerce of the female body and its images.

Besides, women have never been great consumers of pornography. It seems they do not need these images in order to imagine, and to enjoy, sex. This *distance* of women from pornography is the 'mystery' which I would now like to approach, trying to offer some hypotheses. I will try to imagine possible interpretations of the 'mystery', as if solving this enigma really was a complicated business; waving aside easy explanations such as 'because women have been repressed more than men', and so three cheers for the emancipated women who go to see pornographic shows which have the male body as object. I would like to convince you of the distance that I see, that I hope you see, between women and pornography, not in the sense that women are displaced or held back, but in relation to the position of women with regard to sex and sexuality.

It is clearly impossible to speak of the position of Woman with regard to sex and sexuality without turning back to Freud. It is psychoanalysis which has spoken and speaks about sexuality. So I believe we must return to it and to Freud, who inaugurated that particular way of looking at the body. Now, what does psychoanalysis tell us about the body? And especially, what does psychoanalysis tell us about the female body? Or to be even more precise, what does psychoanalysis say about sexual difference?

If you would consent to hear this story (which is well known anyway) I would tell it, very briefly, like this. I would say psychoanalysis tells us that sexual difference hinges around one scene, or one myth: around Oedipus. The story of Oedipus, which is in each and every one of us, fundamentally has two moments, or two acts: omnipotence and castration. The resolution of the Oedipus crisis leaves man with a castrated body, a body which cannot do everything, which cannot deal with all women (or all men), a body which knows the limit. A body is sexed in the face of castration: we could say that sexuality exists only by virtue of this scene in which desire and interdict are knotted together, in which omnipotence and impotence come dangerously close to each other. Pornography, in so far as it has to do with the wretchedness and splendour of the body as sex, has to do with this scene of potency and castration: its truth and its lie, its goodness and its evil, its wretchedness and its splendour, are realized in the moment when it offers itself as an imaginary screen on which a *weak* body projects in the form of fantasies what it cannot sustain in real life. Pornography is an illusion in that it offers the spectacle of a fictitious body which *does not recognize* and which *does not believe in* castration.

If we want to go on with this attempt to analyse pornography I think it is necessary at this point to remind ourselves of one of the meanings which run through the word: the idea of prostitution which, as we saw at the beginning, goes with it. The spectre of prostitution, a spectre which is not so much female as of feminization, forms part of the pornography addict's pleasure. We said that what is interesting about the bodies in pornography is that they are for sale, sold, or saleable. That the representative of the female sex should be, starting with the word itself, a prostitute, is therefore decisive. Tying his pleasure to the exchange-value of the bodies he looks at, the pornography addict ties it to the female being in every body: 'flesh is always feminine in order to be sold'.[10]

The pleasure of the pornography addict seems to concern not simply an organ, but more especially a drive, the scopic drive: to look, to look at a female body offered for sale, this is the desire of the pornography addict. In looking, that look focuses on both his own sexual organ and the sexual organ at which he is looking: in other words, the sexual organ of the other sex, or that which in the scene carries out the opposite and complementary function. The scene which is described here is that of castration, whose decisive moment, in Freudian terms, is the sight of the female sex which precipitates it.

In this sense the real object of pornography is woman and the matter in question is castration. The pleasure of the pornography addict would then be that of avoiding pleasure, since he cannot sustain it, with pleasure taking him close to the edge of that link between pleasure and death – the true area of eroticism according to Bataille – which has to do with the absolute sovereignty and the rupture of representation: where pornography speaks, represents, discourses and, especially, fragments. The pornography addict cannot sustain the body as a whole and so takes it to pieces, so that he can deal with just one fragment at a time; it is with these fragments that he entertains himself and passes his time.

We could say that in the case of eroticism, if we wished to make it speak, we should choose for our discourse a metaphor capable of sustaining the symbolic force of the sexual encounter, the pushing-beyond of that experience; on the contrary, pornography is by its very nature discourse and representation. If any figure is proper to it, it is not metaphor but synecdoche. We know from Jakobson that synecdoche and the metonymic process are the narrative *mode* of prose, while the *mode* of poetry is developed more particularly on the metaphorical axis. So pornography is prosaic, realistic, literal.

Pornography has to do with *pleasure*, with *this* pleasure of *this* or *that* organ. Hence it fragments bodies, and it is in this sense, I think, that the cinema, or at least the photograph, is its most congenial *medium*. Because when we want to use the word pornographically, in some sense it evades us: it is like radio reception which cannot be totally controlled. The word is ambiguous: it does not *show*. And to see is what the pornography addict wants to do. He wants to see the body and its organs. A fragmented body: leg, hand, vagina, anus. He cannot bear an entire body, that is, a body which is not only erect in its organ but erect symbolically. This is why he prefers to see female bodies, flesh which shows so clearly hole, absence, lack: the *pas-tout* which Lacan speaks of in his seminar on love, and which is on the side of the Woman – even if Lacan adds, 'Il y a des hommes qui sont aussi bien des femmes.'[11]

If castration for the little boy has something to do with the loss of the penis, and this in its turn is the pivot which pornography circles round endlessly, woman will have a different relation to it. Women's relationship with castration, and with pleasure, is different. Psychoanalysts tell us that the position of the little girl with regard to Oedipus is different: sexual difference, it seems, is structured around 'a tempo which is slightly quicker for the little girl than for the little boy.[12] This quicker tempo of the little girl is the time it takes her to enunciate the phrase 'I want the phallus'; which also means 'I love the Father'. This is evidently a phrase which rather than releasing her from Oedipus, besieges her more or less definitively within it.

If this is the case, we could explain the indifference of the woman to pornography by this hypothesis: that woman's sexuality hinges on something which we might improperly call an *Ideal*. And if Freud says, 'If led by an intelligent seducer the uneducated adult woman can find every kind of perversion to her taste',[13] and again, 'Prostitutes exploit the same polymorphous, or infantile, predisposition to the ends of their own profession', which is to say, if Freud means to tell us that the woman is on the side of the *Sexual*, we could argue in contrast that if woman has nothing to do with pornography as an enjoying subject it is because she is on the side of the side of the *Ideal*. If we read carefully Lou Salome's essay of 1914 on the feminine type,[14] we find a very interesting analysis of how in the sexual relationship the woman experiences something which is of a different order from simple bodily pleasure, which Salome defines as the Ethical; whereas we know what man is looking for there – he looks for the body, the Sexual.

The theatre Salome constructs is the classical one: the stage which makes Weininger commit suicide, the stage of Wedekind and Kraus. Today this is possibly a little old-fashioned, given the sexual hybridism we have come to, which makes names and positions more unsteady, more difficult to define. And yet, even at the risk of showing a dated photograph, I believe that yes, that theatre is interesting and still describes the difference of woman. I believe that for a woman something else is at play on this stage which isn't simply of the order of a fragmented, metonymic pleasure, the 'organ's pleasure'. 'The feminine has a paradoxical structure', Salome tells us, anchoring herself in the Freudian word. Its first paradox is that through the conversion of the sexual on to herself, woman can allow herself to separate sexuality and the drive of the I, 'in so far as she associates the two'. The feminine is thus 'divided in itself', while the masculine 'remains univocally aggressive'. But the feminine is also 'unitary' where for man uninhibited aggressiveness splits, 'more sexual or more egoistical', in opposed directions. In man sexual aggressiveness is directed towards the passive, towards woman; hence the fact that however much he may idealize sex, his ideal of the self can never be realized in his sexual partner: this ideal will remain with the Father, or the male figure. So 'man passes from the unilateralism of sexual release to the unilateralism of social tension'. For him the *ethical* and *sexual* remain apart.

For the woman on the other hand the *ethical* and the *sexual* coincide. The woman is not satisfied by and finds no pleasure in the pure *pleasure of the organ*. 'There is nothing provisory', says Salome, 'in the case of the erotic for women.' She speaks of the 'female tendency to erect the ideal right there where she abandons herself'. Or there is the consequent paradox for woman, such that she succeeds in 'grasping the sense of the lived in the most spiritual way where, covered bodily, it remains most inexplicable psychically'. In short the feminine succeeds in the profound paradox of 'living the most vital like the most sublime'.

In this, woman unites what man always keeps divided: the *sexual*, which he lives out in turning to woman, and the *ethical*, which remains orientated towards the figure of the Father. The *père(e)version* of the man is in this separation, which will always make him say 'Woman, what have I to do with you?' to the woman, and to the Father, 'Thy will be done'. Female *père(e)version* is of a different kind altogether: in turning to the Father she will ask at the same time 'for her own sexuality and her own sanctity'.

So by following the discourse of psychoanalysis we are brought to the point of the *particularity* of woman in the sexual setting:

as if Woman held herself here in a kind of suspension, which obstructs her, entangles her, hinders her entrance into the symbolic – 'this entrance being made in its turn beyond any interdict, that is without any relationship to the Law'.[15] It is a suspension which, according to the words of Freud, certainly damages her: 'The formation of the superego must suffer from these circumstances.'[16] It is a suspension which keeps her hanging in a kind of double register, both biological and symbolic: exiled from both, 'in a permanent alternation between nature and culture, language and biology'.[17] Caught between a biological constraint – which means that for her the sexual act is a sort of responsibility to the species, a scenario filled with the spectre of children and maternal accomplishments – and a symbolic construction which would have her belong not only to nature but to culture, woman cannot live in her body an experience which is pure sexual release. For her there is always a risk and a debt, there is always something there which has to do with spectres; and she cannot protect herself from them as men do, by turning round and taking pleasure from bodies in pieces and in fragments. Rather, she turns towards the Father, to realize in this *pèr(e)version* her desire for the Law, as that which ensures reproduction and continuity. Woman is brought to guarantee them by the only perverse outlet permitted her, her masochism, which would make her the 'final guarantee of sociability'.

> There is a biological memory of the species which inscribes the female body in a teleology: generations, numbers. . . . On the one hand [the woman] adheres to the symbolic register since she talks, on the other she is chained to biology, to the memory of the cells, since the problem of reproduction poses itself physically every month, and psychically all the time: it is the female counterpart of the male obsession with death.[18]

This, it seems to me, brings me closer to what I wanted to convince you of: that female perversion is not enacted in fragmenting or in multiplying the objects of desire. In other words, woman will never follow the perversion of a Don Juan, nor will she become a devotee of pornography. She will never be able to look on her own body, or the man's body, as 'a machine to fuck, to copulate, to fornicate'.[19] What I have tried to keep in balance here have been two objects which are dear to me: woman and writing, the Book and the female. These past years I have dedicated myself to trying to state the relationships of these two objects, how they interweave and betray each other, their metaphysical conjunctions. It seems to me that here too, speaking about pornography, I have found them united, on the same side. Woman and writing, the Book and the female seem again to maintain an aristocratic distance in the face of the 'graphia of the prostitute'; the literary word and woman's position are both strangers to the writing of sex: indeed they hold their distance. Derrida, via Nietzsche, called the women-effect distance. And now I realize that the beautiful book on Nietzsche's style by Derrida was somewhere in my head all the while I was writing these pages, and from that 'oblivion' perhaps guided my hand, in a sort of involuntary memory-quote.[20] Dis-tanz: dance and distance, pirouette and silhouette, distance invites us to a game of fascination in which woman and style, woman and writing, draw to themselves in elusive effects of seduction the metaphysical fascination of presence according to which the discourse of representation conducts itself.

The making present, the blind faith in the order of representation, the entrapment of sex which seem to constitute the essence of pornography, find in the woman, as in the Book, the space of something irreducible, the subversive gesture of resistance. So it seems to me.

NOTES

1 D. H. Lawrence, 'Pornography and obscenity', in Pornography and So On, London, Faber, 1936.
2 Georg Simmel, 'On prostitution', in Selected Writings, ed. D. N. Levine, Chicago, Chicago University Press, 1907.
3 Anon., My Secret Life (1888–92?), ed. Steven Marcus, New York, Grove Press, 1966.
4 D. H. Lawrence, Women in Love, London, Martin Secker, 1921.
5 Martin Heidegger, 'L'epoca dell'immagine del mondo', in Sentieri interrotti, Florence, La Nuova Italia, 1968.
6 Jacques Derrida, 'Artaud: La parola soufflée', in La scrittura e la differenza, Turin, Einaudi, 1971 (1965); translated into English as Writing and Difference, tr. Alan Bass, London, Routledge & Kegan Paul, 1978.
7 Antonin Artaud, 'Il pesa-nervi', in Al paese dei Tarahumara, Milan, Adelphi, 1966 (1925–7).
8 Massimo Cacciari and M. Ciampa, 'Sapere del corpo e corpo produttivo', Il Piccolo Hans, January–March 1979.
9 Giorgio Melchiori, introduction and notes to John Donne: Selected Poems: Death's Duel, Bari, Adriatica, 1968.

10 C. Calligaris, 'Note sulla pornografia', *Il Piccolo Hans*, January–March 1976.
11 Jacques Lacan, 'L'Amour et le signifiant', *Encore: le Séminaire XX, 1972–3*, Paris, Seuil, 1975.
12 C. Calligaris, 'Sessualità femminile. Che ti dice Freud?', *Il Piccolo Hans*, January–March 1975.
13 Sigmund Freud, 'Three essays on the theory of sexuality' (1905), *The Standard Edition of the Complete Psychological Works of Sigmund Freud*, ed. James Strachey, vol. 7, London, Hogarth Press, 1953.
14 Lou Andreas-Salome, 'Zum Typus Weib', *Imago*, vol. 3, no. 1, February 1914.
15 Calligaris, 'Sessualità femminile', op. cit.
16 Sigmund Freud, 'Femininity', *New Introductory Lectures on Psycho-Analysis*, in *The Standard Edition*, op. cit., vol. 22, 1964 (1932).
17 Julia Kristeva, *L'autre du sexe*, ed. J. Dalanay, Paris, Seuil, 1977.
18 ibid.
19 Antonin Artaud, 'La vecchia scatola d'amore Ka-Ka', 1946.
20 Jacques Derrida, *Eperons. Les Styles de Nietzsche*, Paris, Flammarion, 1978; translated into English as *Spurs: Nietzsche's Styles*, tr. Barbara Harlow, Chicago, University of Chicago Press, 1979.

Chapter 3

The erotic woman writer
A special case of hypokrites*

Viola Papetti

No authoress is more restricted than the writer of erotica. Her fantasies rely on a mask, but the writing which pre-exists them opposes this disconcerting opacity: erotica is perhaps pertinent to the feminine today, as Baudrillard suggests, but as praxis, not as word. Eighteenth-century erotic literature, written almost entirely by libertines, did not attempt to speak the unspeakable and located pleasure more at the textual than at the referential level. It ignored sin, boredom and sentimentality, colouring the sensual world with a cool, intellectual light, benevolent and progressive. Erotic biographical literature (diaries, letters and so on) is, in general, realistic – I am thinking here of *My Secret Life*[1] and *Memoirs of an American Maîtresse*.[2] To the fiery presentation of sexual intercourse and genitalia is added a strong period flavour: corsets, sheets, chamber-pots, skirts, shirts and tantalizing scenarios: stations in the dark, shrubberies, brothels and back rooms. The daily life of people, the cost of their sexual activities, that particular market at the bottom of the general trade which abounds in every *couche* of social life. The insignificant becomes central and distracts us; a respite from the erotic obsession which, however, adds new fuel to the explosion of the forbidden. Nobody surpassed the Victorian English writers in organizing the tale so well for its ultimate revelation: making sex visible.

It is not surprising, therefore, that within this literary genre, which has only lately begun to be studied,[3] so eager to reveal what one cannot and must not see and so astute in its deep strategies, we can count only few woman writers of erotica, while there could have been so many. If we think of the number of

* First published as 'La scrittrice erotica. Un caso speciale di hypokrites', in *I labirinti dell'Eros*, Florence, 1985. Translated by Meriam Soopee.

expert and educated '*maîtresses*' who could have written diaries, letters, notes . . . why did they not do so? Perhaps for fear of a narcissistic loss – a fear that the male writer of erotica simply does not have. John Cleland (just one example is sufficient) earned both money and prestige.

Thus, the authoress of erotica finds she must needs be a hypocrite in the same way as an actress: the representation of the female body that they stage tends to slip and fuse with the body of the individual woman who has enunciated the representation, who has put on, so to speak, the mimesis. This means one must either accept the contamination of fiction and life – the most common choice made by actresses – or repress and deny this identification. The latter course is most common among women writers, who are always authors of essays, poetry and narrative with very varied themes.

Yet if, in some way, one can control and deceive the impudent and indecent glance of the reader who merely wants to see what's 'private', how does one repair the plundering that occurs in the memory, in the narcissistic libido of this singular hypocrite? What recognition can she expect, the authoress of erotica who has dared to trespass the dense symbolic layers of that which is maternal and sacred? Via what truth-games has she made public the status of the desiring woman, how has she revealed it to herself and others? One could respond immediately to the questions: very few and rarely articulated. Women writers of erotic are rare, they are liars and are intermittent. The classical dramaturgy of the soul inherent in erotic life and the practice of 'aphrodisia'[4] have as their protagonist a man. The soul who struggles against itself and against the violence of its own desires, against slavery and moral filth, is a virile soul which exercises an active form of self-mastery. Woman, placed by classical medicine at the other end of the libido, would perform not an act complementary to that of the male, but merely a weak, diminished version dependent on the masculine act. Only the addresser is author; and the equivocation is reflected in the literary system too. If one is supposed to split and double oneself in erotic writing, becoming also the literary protagonist, one can only be male. How can a woman reascend from this twice terminal position – in the coitus and in the text? Classical dramaturgy would have to be overturned. The heroine would have to tread the stage no longer cheated of pleasure and honour, but proud of her active-passive interlacing, of the double enjoyment and of the vigilant boy who is buried inside her. However, sex – writes Pierre Bourdieu, commenting on Foucault – 'is produced by a story during which the body is divided against itself by the perverted self-knowledge which the normalizing argument offers it. Hysteria, onanism, fetishism and coitus inter-ruptus are the four exemplary figures with which the political norm reigns over bodies.'[5]

Thus it is most difficult to find a way out of the place the desiring woman commonly inhabits: either on the edge, or extraneous, or in an unbearable position. The case of Aphra Behn, who saves herself precisely by virtue of her assumption of the hermaphrodite:

. . . we the noblest Passions do extend,
The Love to Hermes, Aphrodite the Friend

is rare; perhaps we ourselves have invented it, prompted by the necessity of the present and the forgetfulness of history. However, her position of fullness and of ease was supported from outside by the exultant wave of an ideological movement. The philo-sophy and the libertine practice of the seventeenth and eighteenth centuries assigned woman a privileged position, recognizing her confused but intriguing authority of addresser-addressee, of erotic and heroic writing and life. The Eros who unifies the universe-matter of Lucretius – predilected philosopher of libertines – is not the pathologized figure of Christ, not the transcendental figure of God the Father. Venus and not the Virgin Mary shines out as the feminine archetype in much literature of the period. Seduction is elevated to a ritual strategy, the female body is resplendent on the altar, adored and fragmented into radiant remains, for its wholeness would be unendurable. (Venus is reborn, though shiel-ded, in neo-classical culture.) Idolatry and perversion focus on specific details: the eyes, the breast, a foot. The passive body of the saint in ecstasy – whether sacred or profane – but also the active body of an Amazon, a sexual and cultural warrior. The heroic action which is the foundation of new cultural practices, of a victorious struggle with the monsters of obscurantism, of a mythopoeic blossoming, could well become the predicate of an aristocratic female subject. The absurd *précieuses*, the *bas-bleus*, the viragos, the libertines, make one think that in a restricted social circle, something has happened, that those women have become at least co-authors with the men of a different dramaturgy. Aphra

Behn can represent them all. Her erotic-heroic writing conceals a phallic tension under the mannerisms of the time. Clearly she has shifted – and incites other women to do the same – into the role of the addresser and is not concerned about protecting the 'private'. The term 'prostitute' dogged her throughout English literature, until Virginia Woolf raised her voice, delivering Behn from obscurity and shame.[6]

Also capable of founding gestures for civilization was Lady Mary Wortley Montagu – our somewhat erratic choice examines only excessive or provocative figures. She showed it when she became the first woman in Europe to have her children vaccinated against smallpox, initiating a hard battle against public opinion and the British medical profession. But the 'Angel in the House' as well as the 'Spirit of the Age', which by the second half of the eighteenth century was no longer very liberal, prevented her from becoming a writer of erotica, even though she lived and thought as a libertine. In her letters from Italy, written when she was over 50, she is determinedly silent about her lovers and professes a dominant maternal passion, reminiscent of Madame de Sévigné. Around this alleged centre, revolve the pleasures of reading, farming, fishing and worldiness – pleasures displayed in order to hide other passions and other events (first her passion for Algarotti, then for the Count Palazzo, both of whom were much younger than she). However, too much energy and sensuality filter through the cracks of her writing to be explained by her daily life and works. She is generally admired for being a strong woman, but strong too were her repressions, cruel the separation of a part of herself and her representation, heavy was the mask of the hypocritical letter. We take her here as an example of one of those women who allowed this split to cut into even their body/writing.

Her opposite could be Colette, who victoriously inhabits the doubling and the negation of herself. Her intelligent eroticism plunders her life to turn it into writing: eroticized writing which protects the loss of narcissim. There is no figurative model of the feminine embedded in the tradition which can mislead her. If female pleasure is, as has been stated, visual, invoking, multivalent, all-pervasive, accumulative, her writing is all this. With a sure hand she turned signifier into signified, in the finale of *Il puro e l'impuro*:

I listened to the word 'pure' which issued from her mouth; the brief quivering, the mournful 'u', the 'r' of limpid ice. She aroused nothing in me save the need to hear again that unique resonance, her echo of a drop that forms, falls and unites with invisible water. The word 'pure' did not reveal its literal sense to me. I must only quench an optical thirst for purity in the transparencies which evoke it, in the bubbles, in the dense water and in the imaginary places, sheltered, unreachable, enclosed in a thick crystal.[7]

The impure and its overflowing heat fuse the life and works of Colette, making of them one magnetic material. Beyond the thick crystal in which the purity of impotence encloses us, today we can look at her with envy. This optic thirst for purity rigidifies instead Virginia Woolf's *Orlando*, a tale of haloes, of transparencies, of narcissistic, not to say autoerotic, eroticism. Hermes and Aphrodite alternate and do not simultaneously inhabit this writing; both abandon it before the end is declared (the last pages fade away, no longer figurative). Whether it be a parodic text or a catalogue of events which happen at the cost of the plot, challenging the logical narrative order, its delicate disconnectedness, its unbalanced tension, make one think that the authoress lacked a libido strong enough to nourish – before her writing – her very life. That sparkling imagination seems merely a fantasy-like compensation for the loss of carefree, childlike sexuality, complete and undifferentiated. Orlando goes '*à rebours*', in pure waste. At the centre of the book, there is a grotesque dual character: the Archduchess-Archduke Harriet-Harry of Finster-Aarhorn and Scand-op-Boom:

> this lady resembled nothing so much as a hare; a hare startled, but obdurate; a hare whose timidity is overcome by an immense and foolish audacity; a hare that sits upright and glowers at its pursuer, with great, bulging eyes; with ears erect but quivering.[8]

The archduchess loves Orlando, but the narrative voice warns that love has two faces, one white, the other black; two bodies, one smooth, the other hairy: the vulture, Lust, and the bird of paradise, Love. Classical (and then Christian) dramaturgy is reconfirmed. Orlando the man flees to Turkey to escape Lust. Orlando the woman humiliates, with an adolescent joke, that grotesque hare-phallus. However, left alone, Orlando looks at herself in the mirror. Both life and lover have abandoned her, she thinks – but her intense narcissism shines and lives like fire, or an enchantment. Looking at herself, she loves herself. The boundary of femininity has been reached and a space, risky yet exciting, has opened.

The erotic fragment by Edith Wharton, probably written around 1919, and printed in Italy as an appendix to her novel *Summer*, there published under the title *Estate*, seems to be of an entirely different genre.[9] In the *Corriere della sera* (24 October 1984), Fernando Pivano describes it as a 'passage of surprisingly pornographic vivacity'. When judging erotic literature, it is impossible to put aside one's own knowledge and personal experiences. To me the fragment seems a precise but rather predictable description of heterosexual intercourse, written by a romantic 'she', who uses love euphemisms very common in certain masculine erotic literature: 'bread of the angels' (the Eucharist), 'the secret jewel/bud', 'the closed petals', 'the secret gates', 'bliss' and so on. The authoress never concluded the story to which this fragment was to be added. Perhaps she was aware of its intimate falsity, its inadequacy of duplicating a description already doubled: one thinks of John Cleland who narrates (is narrated?) through Fanny's enjoyment. This writing, unfaithful through being too faithful to the referent, lacks the dialectic which Anais Nin introduces in the act of writing erotica. To the extent to which she denies and forgets herself as body and desire, she manages to skirt the different eros of the male, of lesbian love, of the perverse. Her distancing strategies are manifold. To begin with, she is paid a dollar per page by an invisible, but authoritarian character, the old collector. Then, upon the suggestion of the 'Angel in the House', she chooses her erotic themes from some manuals on sexual perversion, and is thus able to say: look by all means, but you won't see me. Around this void ('I'm not here, I'm elsewhere') turns an elegant and rich text.[10] Those who have read her diaries will know the pitiful sense of guilt and the gratified fantasies on herself, mother and prostitute.

However, she is able to show sex, as both a radiant wave and as a beat, rhythm, opacity. Her erotic tales offer themselves to the reader like furnished sets from a theatre: the fourth wall is missing and the spectators see everything, even if the pretence is that they are not present. Whether icy or fiery, violent or pleasant, these tales make a show of their combinations of bodies and passions. We witness the eroticization of Nin's writing, usually no more than elegantly sensual, fluid and mythologizing. Here instead she manoeuvres rapid and decisive focalizations, touches objects, descends into the detached regions of the 'Id' and there seizes buttons-jewels. Very different from that extraordinary Rachilde (Marguerite Emery) who always imagines the same thing in her novels: the masculinization of the heroine and the feminization of the hero – 'the most perverse path to reach chastity', comments Ginevra Bompiani in her preface to *Monsieur Venus*.[11]

Thus Anaïs Nin succeeds in transmitting to us – one would say figuratively – the effect of 'having in' pen, penis, passion, or at least a persuasive, seductive substitution of the absence of the latter two terms, thanks to the former.

Let us move to the extreme case of an authoress of erotica who exemplifies not the 'having in' but the 'being in': Paola Masino. Her book, *Nascita e morte della massai* [Birth and Death of the Housewife], written between 1936 and 1939 and published in 1982, is today kept at a distance from its writer; it is a book resplendent of a dark light.[12] The Housewife illustrates marvellously the eroticism of abjection beyond the paths of desire that Kristeva has theorized.[13] The Housewife as a little girl is almost entirely symptom, she lives in a trunk, feeds on mouldy bread and is covered in dust and scurf:

> crumbs and the residue of paper got underneath her nails, moss was growing in between the cracks in her trunk. . . . The trunk exhaled an odour of the forest and of decay in which the little girl developed. . . . From the fire and the flood, experienced who knows where, she had created her ecstasies and her children. By now she lived on that unknown sex which dazed her. From her, a strong odour issued forth which prompted her to sing psalms, almost as if she were enveloped in fire, she sang her own imagination.[14]

She huddles in the archaism of pre-object relation, in the lake of violence that separation from the maternal body has created around her – an unsuccessful Jocasta who enjoys covering herself in symptoms and, as an adult, in lining herself with the sublime. 'In the symptom the abject (baseness) pervades me. I become (the) abject. Through sublimation, I hold/keep it', writes Kristeva, 'as

soon as I perceive and name it the sublime, a cascade of perceptions and words that open up one's memory to infinity is –
indeed, always has been – released. I forget the point of departure
and find myself transported to a second universe, different
(shifted) in respect to the one in which "I" am: delight and loss.'[15]
The life of the adult Housewife is interwoven with the abject and
the sublime, constantly alternating. She meets her abject double,
has visions, performs sublime and peremptory gestures, clothes
herself in sackcloth, is wrapped up in herself, either in the far-
reaching light ('eyes to the sky which was completely uniform
right up to the horizon and from the horizon, to her feet' [16]) or
once again in trunks or coffins. But both as a little girl and as
an adult, the housewife is brought back to herself, to her pre-
being, so to speak, by a recurring dream, or rather a nightmare:
the maternal egg which surrounds or expels her, the spider's web
of veins that suffocate or nourish her, the void that is around her
or hurls her from itself, she who never wants to be born. 'Instead,
suddenly, she realizes that the emptiness itself excluded her from
it: taking her by the shoulders, it obliged her to get up, sliding
along her sides, it abandoned her and put itself in front of her.
Well defined, with its boundaries ever more round and dense,
behind the threads which do not cease from crossing over one
another and from narrowing more and more.'[17] Here, facing up
to the maternal is literalized: born of the horror of the maternal,
she is in a void, hypnotized by the symbol of her very own
exclusion, huge or small, but, for her, always impenetrable. The
ultimate eroticism, that of mother-daughter incest, cannot be said,
if not by approximate, obsessive and phobic metaphors.

I have sought out perverse, fragmented examples of erotica –
texts which have slipped under others. Yet where everything is
said, nothing is said; this must be my excuse for not having
referred to Erica Jong or the more recent Angela Carter.

NOTES

This paper was first presented at a seminar on the female erotic imaginary, organized by the Centro Documentazione Donna and the Libreria
delle Donne di Firenze, Florence, 27–8 October 1984.

1 Anon., *My Secret Life* (1888–92?), ed. Steven Marcus, New York,
   Grove Press, 1966.
2 *Memoirs of an American Maîtresse*, n.d.

3 See, for example, Maurice Charney, *Sexual Fiction*, 'New Accents' series, London and New York, Methuen, 1981.

4 The practice of aphrodisia is investigated by Michel Foucault in *L'Usage des plaisirs*, Paris, Gallimard, 1984; translated into English as *The Uses of Pleasure*, tr. Robert Hurley, Harmondsworth, Viking Penguin, 1984.

5 Pierre Bourdieu, review of *L'uso dei piaceri*, the Italian translation of ibid. (Milan, Feltrinelli, 1984), *L'indice*, 1984.

6 Virginia Woolf discusses Behn in *A Room of One's Own*, London, Hogarth Press, 1929; the passage is reprinted in Virginia Woolf, *Women and Writing*, ed. Michèle Barrett, London, Women's Press, 1979.

7 Colette, *Il puro e l'impuro*, Milan, Adelphi, 1981.

8 Virgnia Woolf, *Orlando*, London, Hogarth Press, 1928.

9 Edith Wharton, *Estate* [Summer]. Milan, La Tartaruga, 1984; the erotic fragment published as an appendix to the Italian translation is part of the manuscript 'Beatrice Palmato', found in the Wharton archives at Yale University by Cynthia Griffin Wolff while researching for her book on Wharton (*A Feast of Words: The Triumph of Edith Wharton*, New York and Oxford, Oxford University Press, 1977); it has also been published by R. W. Lewis in *Edith Wharton: A Biography*, New York, Harper & Row, 1975.

10 Anais Nin, preface to *Delta of Venus*, London, W. H. Allen, 1977.

11 Marguerite Emery, *Monsieur Venus*, with a preface by Ginevra Bompiani, Rome, Edizioni delle Donne, 1982.

12 Paola Masino, *Nascita e morte della massai* [Birth and Death of the Housewife], Milan, La Tartaruga, 1982.

13 Julia Kristeva, *Poteri dell'orrore*, Milan, Spirali, 1981; translated into English as *Powers of Horror: An Essay in Abjection*, tr. Leon S. Roudiez, New York, Columbia University Press, 1982.

14 Masino, op. cit., pp. 14–15.

15 Kristeva, op. cit.

16 Masino, op. cit., p. 157.

17 Masino, op. cit., p. 229.

Chapter 4

A double-voiced silence*

Marina Mizzau

The word is double-voiced. Not only because it refers back to the 'already said', but also because it reflects the presence of the interlocutor as well as that of the speaker. Every word that is spoken meets on its trajectory the word of others, expected and foreseen, and is directed and determined by it.[1]

For this reason it seems to me that the specific communicative features of the female and the male should be sought within the realm of the discursive relation between the two poles of enunciation; for this interaction reveals differences which in an analysis of the two separate languages might well remain hidden.

In the man–woman relationship, as in other relationships but more so, and in differentiated ways, words are *for* the other, but also *against* the other. In the context of the couple we find the emotional situation mixed in with another dimension that has to do with inequalities of power; and this gives rise to a covert conflict which takes place in the realm of communicative relationships.

The relationship itself, its meaning and its rules, is the real and subterranean object of conflict, while the explicit aspect of the messages, at the level of 'content', becomes nothing but a pretext for implicit metacommunication on the relationship.[2] Communication becomes *oblique*: manifest intentions stand in for other intentions, the gap between signifier and signified can become such that what is said actually means the opposite. Refusals become offers, words of hostility are actually asking for love, the most harmless proposals become challenges, silences communicate complex messages, *what is not said prevails over what is said.*

A study of communicative modalities in the couple relationship

* First published as 'Silenzio a due voci', in *Inchiesta*, July–Sept. 1987. Translated by Sharon Wood.

helps us to identify the use of different forms of implicit or more generally oblique messages; naturally these are not only found in the couple relationship, but it is here that they take on a particularly intense significance and frequency. I give some examples here, ranging from those which employ more common linguistic and discursive mechanisms, through to less conventional ones:

a) use of semantic presuppositions which allude to other events: 'You *managed* to arrive late again?'; 'You could have done that *at least*'
b) use of conversational implications[3] which violate maxims of quantity, quality, relevance and mode. For example:
   – use of the general for the particular: '*nobody* loves me', 'you *never* listen to me'
   – vice versa, the use of the particular for the general, formulating a request or even a retort as a pretext for opening up discussion on general aspects of the relationship
   – saying the opposite, 'I hate you' for 'I love you', even ironically
c) substitution of the illocutive force of particular linguistic acts; for example, accusing instead of asking ('You don't love me' for 'Do you love me?'); or asking instead of asserting ('Wouldn't you like to . . . ?' for 'I want to . . .')
d) shifting discourse by introducing a totally different topic
e) as an extreme case of indirect communication we could indicate 'symptomatic' expressive forms (even hysteria, as somatic language)
f) and finally silence as a paradoxical mode of communication.

We know that to communicate implicitly means 'saying something without having to bear responsibility for having said it', so taking advantage simultaneously of the 'efficacy of the word and the innocence of silence'.[4] In the context of an affective relationship it probably means something more specific. Making a request indirectly means protecting oneself from the frustration of a possible refusal, especially threatening because acceptance of the request implies a confirmation on the level of the affective relationship. This results in a paradoxical situation, that the more the request needs to be satisfied, the more it becomes couched in an oblique manner and so risks not being understood. Moreover, since oblique communication generally elicits 'tangential' responses, responding only to the content of the message and ignoring, or pretending to ignore, the aspect of the relation, obliqueness starts to mushroom.

The modes and especially the functions of oblique communication are different for men and women. I hope the nature of these differences will emerge from the examples I give in this paper. But we can make the general point that they are connected to the different distribution of interpersonal power within the relationship.

Female characters of the nineteenth-century novel begin to outline a different awareness of the female situation. In them we find reflected a process – still ongoing – of woman's search for the word which will express her own reasons and motivations, in the face of and in spite of those of the male. In order to realize this objective the woman must give up the reassuring collusions which make her the holder of a false power, give up the 'feminine' weapons of simulation, seduction and hidden manipulation, weapons she has always used, encouraged by the indulgent gratification of the opposite party.[5] Only by renouncing what makes her an accomplice to her own subjection, only by going through conflict, can this clash with the man become a meeting, can the solipsistic coexistence of two narcissisms turn into a relationship.

But the word through which the woman, long relegated to silence, begins to express herself cannot always or immediately be articulated in a full, direct way. This word is often oblique; what is not said leaks into what is said; what is said is only the pretext, the symptom of a just but confused claim which has not yet found a way of articulating itself coherently. This word which is ambiguous and contradictory, but which claims much for itself, often verges on silence.

From these female characters in nineteenth-century novels, who enter into conflict with a man and what he represents, I have chosen the protagonist of a short story by Dostoyevsky, 'A meek young girl'.[6] 'A meek young girl' is the story of a relationship between a man and a woman in which silence is the principal weapon in the conflict. The plot is as follows: a pawnbroker meets a very young girl, an orphan who is so poor that she has to pawn her few possessions in order to be able to place an advertisement for work. The two get married. The consequence of their relationship – or is this an interpretation? – is that the woman commits suicide by jumping out of a window. The story, apart from a brief preface, is told in the first person by the male protagonist who is trying to understand and simultaneously refuses to acknowledge the reasons for this death.

ENIGMAS

> In the first place, from the very beginning, try as she did to restrain herself, she turned to me with an eager love, met me with delight when I came in the evenings, chatted to me (with that bewitching chatter of innocence!) about her childhood, her infancy, about her parents' home, her father and her mother. But I immediately poured cold water on these raptures. It was in this that my idea lay. I met enthusiasm with silence, an affectionate silence, of course . . . but, in spite of that, she soon discovered that we were unlike and that I was – an enigma. And that was exactly what I was aiming at!

From the very start of the story, of their relationship, the man presents himself as an *enigma*, he invites the woman to resolve the puzzle of his identity while simultaneously removing from her, by his silence, the means to do so. So he sets up a communication by opposites: he shows the most negative aspects of himself (his aridity, meanness, avarice and cowardice) while leaving her the task of discovering his positive side, the one which corresponds to the image he has, or would like to have, of himself. To show that he loves and to make himself loved, he refuses to give any demonstrations of love and rejects the ones she offers.

> I kept silent, was silent with her, in a special way, right until yesterdày – and why? Because I had my pride, I wanted her to find out for herself, without my explaining, but not from the tales of rotters either, so that she would *herself guess* this man's riddle and discover him! I wanted her to stand before me in entreaty for my sufferings – I was worth that. Oh, I have always been proud, I have always wanted all or nothing! It was precisely because I did not care for any half-share in happiness but craved it whole that I was forced to act like this then: 'guess and value for yourself.' Because if I had begun to explain to her and dictate to her, to crawl to her and to ask for her respect, you will agree, it would have been as though I were asking a favour. . . . And if it comes to that . . . if it comes to that, what am I talking about this for?

Here we are faced with an extreme case of indirect communication, which clearly has its origins in the need to protect oneself from the risk of the direct request, a search for confirmation and gratification of the self which has more value if obtained without openly exposing oneself.

The reasons for this man's cautious, defensive attitude emerge in part from the account the protagonist gives of previous events, which led him to take up his squalid profession: a clash immediately following his entry into the army when he refused to fight a duel which he thought stupid and futile, and more generally before that a life without emotional gratification ('Never and nowhere has anybody loved me'). The desire for compensation, in his pride and in his affections, reveals itself here in a form of behaviour which as well as being cautious is also sadistic and vindictive and so, inevitably, masochistic: the 'others' who have hurt and misunderstood him must learn to respect, understand and love him without any help from him, overcoming the obstacles which he himself puts in their way. He arrives then at the almost delirious notion that seeks to reconcile the sharp antithesis between his positive self-image and the negative one which others have of him:

> No, take a great-hearted exploit which is difficult, quiet, unheard, without brilliance, calumniated, which knows great sacrifice and not a drop of glory, where you, an exemplary being, are a scoundrel in the eyes of all when you are the most honest man alive – well, try to undertake that, no, you will refuse! And I – I have borne that burden all my life.

This addressing of the self-image to others pervades discourse. Even in this story built on a monologue, Dostoyevsky's style, as in all his novels, is 'dialogic' to use Bakhtin's definition; that is, closely tied to a conception of the individual which is such only in his interaction with others, and cannot be defined except through relationships with others. The other is within the word of the narrating I, which simultaneously anticipates the word of the other. This anticipation disintegrates and refracts the word, doubles it in a polemic with the real or imaginary other (sometimes the other self). In the words of the protagonist of 'A meek young girl' the other is seen as addressee – of challenge, justification, accusation, self-accusation, mystification: the addressee is sometimes accomplice, sometimes enemy. This other is not a neutral and indifferent listener, but an instance of those others who are guilty of having hurt and humiliated him, or are innocent and must testify to his innocence; it is the living wife who mustn't understand, the dead one who must. Within this 'multi-voiced word' the other is often not only confuted but disavowed in the attempt to neutralize its inevitable penetration into one's own consciousness. So we reach a paradox. The protagonist of this story, much like the one of 'Notes from underground', affirms his need of the other at the very moment he denies it, at the very moment he seeks from the other the confirmation of his own irreducible individuality. The paradox has existential roots, and comes from the impossible attempt to resolve the contradiction between the need for autonomy and the need for love, a contradiction which cannot be resolved but only recognized and accepted as such.

This contradiction comes out particularly in the couple relationship, and takes on within it specific characteristics linked to the disparity of sexual roles. If the imaginary recipient of the enigma is society in general, its real recipient is woman, and this is no accident. The request is made to the one whose historic function it is to accept in silence, to connive in a collusion designed to gratify the male I, to sublimate this image in a deforming and adoring mirror.

> And the woman who loves, oh, the woman who loves will justify even the vices, even the crimes of the loved one!

The man's power is determined by his success or failure in what defines him as a man, the values of the social sphere. The woman's (non)power is determined within what defines her as a woman, in other words her relationship with a man. So the man seeks in the woman compensation for the lack of social power; he seeks it by increasing the power he has over her – power which society confers upon him – enigmatically withdrawing from the relationship. A woman's only response to this is herself to seek to withdraw from the relationship, thus constituting herself as an enigma too.

This is perhaps what Freud did not manage to focus upon; failing to reduce femininity to the 'law of the same',[7] he speaks of the enigma of the woman ('You can see now that psychoanalysis is capable of dissolving the enigma of femininity'[8]). The 'enigmatic nature of woman', it seems, is the result of her narcissism – derived in its turn from penis envy[9] – and of her 'self-sufficiency' which makes her incapable of object-love, and it is here that lies her 'enormous fascination' for men, who are, on the contrary, capable of object-love.[10] But, we might wonder, how is it that this non-narcissistic man can love this woman who is interested only in herself and incapable of autonomous desire? How can he do it if not, *pace* Freud, because of his own narcissism, his own self-sufficiency, which makes him disinterested in the desire of the other, interested only in the affirmation of his self through power over an object which is not seen to be endowed with an autonomous thinking and desiring subjectivity? Isn't it the man's narcissism which is at the root of the narcissism of the woman, or at the very least are the two self-sufficiencies not related?

In the myth, Echo, condemned by the gods for talking too much, and sentenced to speak a copy of the other's speech, is relegated to silence. She cannot speak autonomously, and the only being with whom she wants to engage in discourse is Narcissus, whom she loves. But Narcissus, who loves only himself, never speaks to her. Both are condemned to silent infrasubjectivity. If Narcissus could forget himself, and speak to Echo, Echo could speak. But also, if Echo could speak on her own initiative, perhaps Narcissus could come out of himself and answer her.

A CONFLICT OF SILENCES

The paradoxical nature of a communication by enigmas also consists in the fact that the communication itself falls into the system of oppositions. The male protagonist in the story communicates that he does not want to communicate, he employs silence not only not to speak, but to make the point that he is not speaking. Silence becomes a refined and catastrophic instrument of communication and with this instrument the man tries to dominate the woman, forcing her to play his own game.

> Naturally I did not simply begin to speak of it or it would have looked as if I were asking for forgiveness for the pawnshop, instead I acted as through pride and spoke almost silently. And I am a pastmaster of speaking without words, I have spent my life in silent speech, and have lived through whole tragedies with myself in silence.

The word is an instrument of power. There is the power of he who says most and best (we will later see how, in the story, culture and the learned quotation are used by the man as a means of subduing) and there is the power of the person who says less. There is the power of nullifying the discourse of the other through one's own discourse, or through one's own silence.

One can dominate by placing the other before an enigma and changing the code for deciphering it; changing language every time the other approaches comprehension, modifying the context, shifting the meaning of words. And one can dominate more directly by offering the enigma without a code, when questions are asked or efforts made to solve the puzzle, offering only silence.

The act of silence disconfirms the other, denying them the means of defining the sense of their own behaviour within a relationship, within their own being.

'You guess, and value me!' But something unforeseen by the man happens. The response of the meek young girl is not an acquiescent one. She sets up in her turn a game of silences, silences which have more than the meaning of defeat. Still in silence, she makes gestures of rebellion: she goes out without his permission, she intervenes in the pawnbroking business in the client's favour, she meets a possible lover, she makes the gesture of killing her husband in his sleep, she confronts him with fits of silent fury. As here:

> She suddenly leapt up, began to shake all over and – what do you think – to stamp her foot at me; this was a wild beast, a fit, a wild beast in a fit. I was stupefied; I had never expected such an outbreak. But without losing control over myself, I did not even make any movement, I told her simply in the same calm voice that from that time onwards I would do without her participation in my affairs. She laughed in my face and left the flat.

This scene is almost a text-book case of the interpretation of hysteria (and psychic illness in general) as a form of indirect communication which asks the question while sheltering from the frustration of not receiving a reply, and at the same time permits the formulation of a request (for affection, confirmation, existential recognition).

Historically, hysterical manifestations have been considered an 'illness' typical of women. And it probably is, in the sense that the prohibition to communication has prevented women from expressing rebellion against repression and more fundamentally from becoming aware of the repression itself. Unease and rebellion show themselves in the only way which is socially codified if not accepted, through analogical and iconic modes. Faced with the woman's attempts at rebellion the man tries to nullify, and partly succeeds in nullifying, their meaning, interpreting them egocentrically so as to make them serve the purpose of the game he has set up. The failed betrayal, for example, (he appears and interrupts the encounter before it can reach its conclusion) is interpreted thus:

> Out of a hatred for me which was only fancied and fitful, she could in her inexperience decide to have this meeting, but when it came to the point, her eyes were immediately opened.

'Proud', 'rebellious', these are the terms used to define the woman; but these definitions, in the light of their context, appear as ways of exorcizing the opposition while making the game, of which the man thinks he controls the rules, more exciting:

> Proud! Well, I like people who have pride myself. Proud people are particularly fine when . . . well, when one no longer doubts of one's power over them, is that not so?

The most complex and significant example of how the man manages to neutralize her rebellions, turning them to his own advantage, is to be found in the episode of the revolver: following one of the many silent struggles, the meek young girl points the weapon at the man who is apparently asleep, but who in fact is only pretending to be so (this action is less comprehensible than ever: does she do it to really kill him, to prove to herself that she can do it, or, aware that he is conscious, to evoke a 'different' reaction?). The man's response is perfect within the order of the system he has constructed. By lying still and accepting death he confirms the image of his courageous self both to himself and also perhaps to her if she has guessed the truth, that he was not asleep (even if she had not realized this, his subsequent behaviour would make it clear). So the woman knows that whatever she does she will lose: deciding not to kill is a defeat, but even making the gesture is a defeat since the man, by choosing to die, deprives her of any space for autonomous initiative and once again places himself in a winning position. The situation can be defined in technical terms as a 'double-bind', a paradoxical situation in which the 'victim' loses no matter what she does. The consequence of this situation with no way out can be seen in the episode which follows: the illness which strikes the girl, an illness which can be interpreted as another mode of somatic communication, a way of asking indirectly what has become impossible to ask in any other way.

But towards the end of the story, the woman acts in a way which the man will no longer be able to neutralize, an action which, unlike her other failed attempts at rebellion, seems to put the man's whole 'project' into crisis. He realizes that the woman emerges from her silence only to sing, in his absence – as the domestic servant Lukerija informs him – and then in his presence too:

> Singing, and in my presence! *Has she forgotten about me?* . . . If she had begun to sing when I was there, she must have forgotten about me – it was this that was clear and terrifying.

With this action the woman seems to affirm her autonomy and thus her indifference; moving out of the system he has set up, away from the challenge of the enigma, she ceases to be an object and becomes a subject, the unreachable *other* in the eyes of the man, who cannot fail to realize his own defeat. Every effort to subdue her by constructing other games – he asks her pardon, he declares his love and asks for hers, he promises things will be different – fails. In her definitive silence the woman constitutes *herself*, for ever, as an enigma. The man still makes some effort to recuperate the suicide to his own advantage, or to empty it of any significance:

> Above all, it's hurting to think it was all an accident – a simple, barbaric, blind accident. There's the rub! I was only five minutes, just five minutes late! Had I come in five minutes before – the moment would have sped by like a cloud, and it would never have entered her head again. And it would have ended by her understanding everything.

While, amid the whirl of explanations he provides, some, like this one, seem to approach 'the truth' with more courage:

> She was frightened by my love, she asked herself seriously: shall I accept it or not, and she couldn't bear the question, and chose to die.

In fact the text allows us to interpret it in terms of relational pragmatics. The whole relation can be seen in terms of paradoxical communication: the woman is constantly receiving contradictory messages, and this contradictoriness cannot be denounced (it is impossible to metacommunicate about it) because it is the very condition of communication, the fundamental rule of the game (of the enigma). Therefore, whatever she does the victim cannot respond directly or adequately. The consequence is a reaction of absolute impotence and total mistrust in her own psychic capacities, a mistrust which also extends beyond the system of paradoxical communication, becoming the only response to any communication, even a fair one. In the context suicide becomes the only possible response, a radical response of 'withdrawal'.

The same type of interpretation can be formulated in terms which are no longer pathological but indicate conscious choice. Her action is above all the logical consequence of a relationship conducted right to the end in a way which is rigorously symmetrical. If the man by his behaviour renounced the system he had organized, and accepted his own defeat, this defeat would inevitably become a triumph as soon as it gave rise to acceptance by the woman of the new relationship offered. So suicide is the only way out, a rational response suggested by her awareness of the inevitability of the system, that the same patterns of their relationship would reassert themselves, or at least similar patterns of dominance and submission, if the woman were to give in. It should also be said that there is no other way out of the system, since the girl has no other means of survival less squalid than this, as has been made clear right from the start.

From this perspective suicide could be seen as a lucid and rational revenge: the holy image taken out of its frame and carried with her into death is not so much a witness to religious faith as a way of leaving him this ultimate sign of defiance, the frame which she once pawned.

This need for revenge does not in itself explain the radical way she puts it into action, unless we place it in a more complex context and refer to Freud's hypothesis that suicide is the shifting of the desire for the death of another. This hypothesis too is suggested by the text:

> But suddenly she came towards me, stopped in front of me and, taking hold of my hands (so recently!) began to tell me that she was guilty, that she knew it, that her guilt had been tormenting her . . .

THE SYSTEM

In this way the reductive, if partially correct, reading of the story in terms of executioner–victim is displaced by a reading which is much more complex. The relationship between the two, as all dyadic relationships, is structured as a 'system', to use the protagonist's own words.

Every interpersonal system 'forms itself' in the sense that it is largely circular: each individual belonging to the system acts as both cause and effect of the behaviour of the other. None the less this circularity is subject to different 'punctuation' by the participants who will, for example, locate the starting-point in different places.

When reading this story we ourselves cannot help partially falling into the error of seeing the person narrating in the first person as the initiator and principal manipulator of the game.

This view is suggested to us by the man himself, by his planning of the 'enigma' and its rules: silences, the frustration of shows of affection, and so on. But if we want to analyse this circularity correctly, we should leave aside the intentions elaborated by the man which might not be apparent to the woman and go beyond the facts themselves. The conviction as to 'who started it' is subject to the arbitrariness of point of view. Besides, the character himself seems at times to correct our perspective, suggesting that he is aware of being the victim of something which 'started by itself'.

> In a word, then, although I was quite content, I created a whole system. Oh, it almost created itself.

> So who started it? Nobody. The thing started by itself right from the very first moment.

Elsewhere he even seems to suggest the possibility that it was she who initiated the whole dynamic of enigma and silence. At the start he notes:

> As soon as she received her money she turned and went out. Always without a word.

At other moments the awareness of circularity seems to fall away and we see plainly the mystifying turning-around of the cause–effect relationship in the attempt to justify his own behaviour:

I remember she kept looking at me secretly somehow; and as soon as I noticed this I grew more silent still. It's true it was I who insisted on this silence and not she. She, on her part, broke out once or twice and ran to embrace me; but as these outbursts were feverish and hysterical and I wanted a firm happiness and her respect, I met her coldly. And I was right: every time after these outbursts we quarrelled next day.

Other times again, self-justification, the stubborn defence of the rightness of his own plan, in which, however, something was wrong, turns into a violent accusation.

That was my plan. But I forgot something or let something escape me. I did not succeed in doing something. But enough, enough. And who is there now to beg her forgiveness? It is finished and done with. If you are a brave man, be proud then! You are not to blame!

I shall speak the truth, I shall not be afraid to face the truth; *she* is to blame, *she* is to blame!

The symmetry of the relationship between them, tending towards conflictual equality and in some instances to competitive escalation, is documented by a dialogue – the only long verbal interaction between the two of them that we witness – which takes place near the beginning of the story. The woman has refused the man's offer of a higher price than usual for an icon she wants to pawn.

'Never despise anyone, I have been in straitened circumstances myself, and in worse than such, and if you see me now engaged in business . . . then after everything I've been through, it's . . .'

'You are avenging yourself on society, are you?' she suddenly interrupted with a rather bitter smile, which incidentally held a great deal of innocence (that is, she spoke in general, because she certainly didn't distinguish me from others then, so that she said it almost without offending). Aha! I thought, that's what you're like, another aspect of your character is coming out now.

'You see,' I remarked, half-jokingly, half-mysteriously: 'I – am a part of that part of the whole which wants to do evil and does good . . .'

She glanced at me quickly with great curiosity which was also very childlike:

'Wait . . . What thought is that? Where does it come? I've heard it somewhere . . .'

'Don't puzzle your head over it, Mephistopheles recommends himself to Faust with that expression. Have you read *Faust*?'

'Not . . . not attentively.'

'That is, not at all. You should. But I can see by your lips that you are laughing at me again. Please don't think that I have so little taste that I wanted to put my role as a pawnbroker in a better light by recommending myself to you as Mephistopheles. A pawnbroker will always be a pawnbroker. We know that.'

'You are very strange . . . I certainly didn't intend to say anything like that . . .'

She wanted to say: I didn't expect to find you were an educated man, but she didn't say it, though I knew she thought it; I had pleased her very much.

'You see,' I remarked, 'one can do good in every profession. Of course, I'm not referring to myself, I probably don't do anything except what is bad, but . . .'

'Of course, one can do good everywhere,' she said, giving me a quick and penetrating look. 'Everywhere, certainly,' she suddenly added.

It's worth lingering a moment over this verbal clash. The man is struck by the woman's profound refusal to accept his 'generosity', and interpreting her action as contempt, he seems to concede an explanation and justification ('If you see me now . . .'), so breaking in some way the rules of the enigma. The irony of the woman ('You are avenging yourself on society, are you?') puts her in a dominant position, despite his attempt to neutralize it ('innocently'). As a result the man finds himself on the defensive, and follows this with a renewed attempt to put her down by his exhibition of culture (the *Faust* quotation).

He takes advantage of this successful move – the woman falls into the trap, letting her cultural inferiority show through – and decisively regains his position of one-upmanship ('That is, not at all'). So with a 'metacomplementary' move of feigned subjection ('a pawnbroker will always be a pawnbroker') he strengthens his dominant position, but it is thrown into crisis again by the woman's final allusion, which can be read as ironic. The man's attempts to metacommunicate implicitly on the reasons for his way of life and of communication are blocked, in this dialogue, by the woman, whose role in setting up the conflict seems far from passive – to the point where she herself provides material for the accusations later to be made against her.

In these constant shifts of perspective, the story seems to change its appearance according to points of view, like an ambiguous shape. At one point it can seem that the woman is pulling the strings, that she is the absolute protagonist in this struggle between the sexes which she has controlled from the beginning and carried through to her paradoxical final victory. But it is not my intention to pursue this other reading, nor to underwrite it; only to suggest it as a possibility among the many different *possible realities* which this extraordinary story contains.

MULTI-VOICED MONOLOGUE

Many, but not infinite. The text naturally invites a plural reading and at the same time sets a limit. However much this is a first-person narration, a kind of inner monologue of a single character is, still following Bakhtin's terminology, a 'multi-voiced word'. Not only because of the presence of the absent interlocutor we mentioned earlier, but also because woven into it are the voice of the narrating I and, superimposed on it, subtly inserted into it, the commenting voice of the implied author. The image of the woman is formally circumscribed by the word of the character-narrator, and yet at times this image seems to free itself from the mediation of the narrating I, emerging into a perspective which is paradoxically discordant with that of the male protagonist.

The result is a story which is anything but linear; it is complex, contradictory, at times undecidable. The very title of the story makes the point: who is this woman 'meek' for? For the male protagonist, and not for the ideal reader the author has constructed, and endowed with a competence superior to that of the character?[11] At the same time, we might think that the two contradictory readings are located within the one contradictory perception of the man, and this is backed up not least by the recurrence of adjectives to define the woman in the course of the narration which are almost opposites: 'sweet', 'innocent', 'ingenuous', 'submissive'; but also 'severe', 'proud', 'rebellious' and so on.

This contradiction is anticipated in the 'Preface', where the 'Author' seems to keep his distance from the narrating character:

In spite of the seeming consistency of his narrative, he contradicts himself several times both in logic and feeling.

Yet straight after that, we read:

Gradually, he really does make things *clear* to himself and 'concentrates his thoughts'.

And yet we remain doubtful that this clarification has actually taken place, even at the end: the story seems continually to approach the truth only to shy away from it, and the motif of 'conscious ignorance' which according to Bakhtin[12] characterizes two-thirds of monologue seems to reappear up to the very end. And the 'Author', contradicting himself once more as he maintains his distance from the narrating I, seems to follow suit:

The truth is disclosed to the unhappy man rather clearly and precisely, at least for himself.

The effect of a gap between what the character tells us and what he tries to keep hidden from us, even while making us understand it 'involuntarily', is achieved by means of various techniques, among them what Bakhtin defines as the 'loophole word'.[13] Two examples illustrate this wavering between awareness and conscious ignorance:

And above all, I already looked on her as *mine* and had no doubts about my power. You know, it is the most voluptuous of all thoughts, when one no longer doubts.

But what's the matter with me? If I go on like this, when shall I bring everything to a head? Quickly, quickly – that is all not the point, O God!

In power, even when it is captivatingly disguised as love, lies one of the central concerns of the question: the man seems to get close to this awareness. But straightaway the process of repression, or of activating conscious ignorance, shows itself as he moves sharply away from the subject, and this happens every time that, as in this instance, he gets close to an unpleasant discovery.

Let us see another example of a critical gap in the character's words:

> I can't go to sleep. How could I? Oh, the mud! The mud I dragged her from! She should have understood, should have appreciated what I did!

Here the word 'mud' slips in significance through a sudden change of context: from the mud denoting the man's current situation we pass to the mud he has taken her from, and the shift in context permits once more a flight from awareness through recourse to an ennobling perception of the self who draws the other from the mud. Thus through the use of this loophole word by the narrating I, the 'Author' dissociates himself by denouncing his self-deception.

These waverings produce a disconcerting narrative paradox: the man's moments of opaqueness and conscious ignorance highlight the female character's traces of awareness, even though these are technically circumscribed by the male narrating I. So, to give just one example, when the man minimizes the woman's phrase 'You are avenging yourself on society, are you?', the ironic weight of this phrase takes on for us a profound significance which goes beyond the limits of comprehension of the character.

In conclusion then, this disconcerting story, with its ambiguity, the multiple levels of writing, the reticence which acts as an inexhaustible source of suppositions, leaves plenty of space for collaboration by the reader. I've taken advantage of this to put forward a reading such as the one I suggested at the beginning.

In the nineteenth-century novel the rebellious, destructive moment is nearly always given to the female figures. Anna Karenina, Madame Bovary, the two female characters in *The Red and the Black*, Effi Briest in Fontane's novel of that name, and countless others, attempt to subvert the constituted order, in the realm of the private, the family, relationships with the man. These rebellions, more or less lucid and more or less aware, are in a way doomed to failure: the suicides of these characters, or at any rate their self-punishment, mark the impossibility of finding a way out, the limited hope of becoming aware which cannot translate itself into a positive solution of the conflict given the absence of a responsive historical and social context.

The woman of this story follows the same path of destiny as the others, but she is at the same time a singular figure for the extraordinary ambiguity of her emblematic silence which, opposed by the silence of the man, can be read as the effect of cancelling the female in the order of discourse, but also as active refusal of the dominant code, subversion of meaning in a cryptic message which suggests its own solution, with tragic irony, to the other.

NOTES

1 For Mikhail Bakhtin's dialogical theory, see *The Dialogical Imagination: Four Essays*, ed. Michael Holquist, Austin, Tex., University of Texas Press, 1981.
2 Here and elsewhere I use the terminology and some theoretical presuppositions of relationship pragmatics, which goes back to Bateson and was then developed by P. Watzlawich. According to these writers, every message has two aspects: that of 'content', or the literal sense of what is said, and that of 'relation', which expresses the way every interlocutor sees himself and the other, how he thinks, how he wants to be seen by the other, and so on.
3 H. P. Grice, 'Logic and conversation', the William James Lectures at Harvard University, 1967, published in P. Cole and J. L. Morgan (eds), *Syntax and Semantics – Speech Acts*, New York and London, Academic Press, 1975.
4 Oswald Ducrot, *Dire et ne pas dire*, Paris, Hermann, 1972.
5 In making this comparison I am thinking of female figures of the eighteenth-century novel: Laclos' characters in *Les Liaisons dangereuses* are emblematic, especially Madame de Merteuil, who exercises the arts of 'diabolical feminine wiles' and carries them to the point of paradox.
6 Quotations are taken from the English edition in *Three Tales*, tr. Beatrice Scott, London, Lindsay Drummond, 1945.
7 Luce Irigaray, *Speculum of the Other Woman*, Ithaca, NY, Cornell University Press, 1985.
8 Sigmund Freud, 'Femininity' (1932), *New Introductory Lectures on Psycho-Analysis*, in *The Standard Edition of the Complete Psychological Works of Sigmund Freud*, ed. James Strachey, vol. 22, London, Hogarth Press, 1964.
9 ibid.
10 See ibid. and Sigmund Freud, *On Narcissism* (1914), in *The Standard Edition of the Complete Psychological Works of Sigmund Freud*, ed. James Strachey, vol. 14, London, Hogarth Press, 1957.
11 Umberto Eco, *The Role of the Reader*, Bloomington, Ind., Indiana University Press, 1979.
12 'The story 'A meek young girl' is directly structured on the motif of conscious ignorance. The hero conceals from himself and carefully

eliminates from his own discourse the very thing that is constantly before his eyes. His entire monologue can be reduced to his forcing himself to see and admit what he has in fact known and seen from the very beginning. Two-thirds of the monologue is defined by the hero's desperate attempt to get round what already internally determines his thought and speech as an invisibly present 'truth'. At first he tries to 'bring his thoughts to a focus' that lies on the far side of the truth. But all the same he is ultimately forced to gather his thoughts together at what is for him a terrible point of 'truth'. Mikhail Bakhtin, *Problems of Dostoyevsky's Poetics*, Manchester, Manchester University Press, 1984, p. 247.

13 For Bakhtin the word 'loophole' is enormously important for the whole of Dostoyevsky's work. By 'loophole of consciousness and of the word', Bakhtin means 'the retention for oneself of the possibility for altering the ultimate, final meaning of one's own words'. A technique used by a number of characters to avoid a previously admitted truth and so avoid the definitive definition of the self by the other; ibid.

Chapter 5

Language in the crucible of the mind*

Marina Camboni

What is an author's relationship to her subject represented by words in a text?

Is gender embedded in the text? If so, in what way?

In *Per una poetica della differenza* [Poeticizing the Difference], Myriam Díaz-Diocaretz responds to these enquiries, theorizing and then demonstrating – in her perceptive analysis of lyrical poetry – how gender is a formal element and how a work of art is necessarily linked to its social and historical context.[1] Basing her interpretation on Bakhtin's dialogic principle, she underscores the fact that every word is intrinsically bound to its previous contexts (and texts) and that whenever a subject – in this case a female subject – uses language, she is not only partaking in a social exchange, but at one and the same time evidencing and redefining patriarchal values.

Diaz-Diocaretz's investigation concludes with a proposal for re-examining the relationship contemporary women writers establish between their use of language and present-day literary, social and temporal codes, and for exploring the way in which daily life is transformed by the written word.

In full agreement with her, I want, however, to veer the analysis in another direction: above and beyond the context of literary production. I would like to focus on the very moment when words kindle an author's creative imagination; when the mental alembic transforms and appropriates experience and above all language.

In order to achieve this, I shall become, just for a moment, that ideal 'critic: detective and lover' described by Marina Cvetaeva[2] –

* First published as 'La lingua nel crogiolo della mente', in Myriam Díaz-Diocaretz, *Per una poetica della differenza*, Florence, Estro, 1989. Translated by Clarissa Botsford.

so as to be able to grasp to what extent texts by women project themselves beyond the present, and suggest new ways of viewing women, the world, and women's presence in the world.

I therefore propose a few starting-points for what I define as *projective* criticism, which might accompany and extend the scope of descriptive and systematic criticism. As in my other works,[3] my principal focus will be on the mind: centre of metamorphoses *par excellence*, where language, experience and mental images meet and transmute, opening up potential vistas, projecting the present beyond itself, revealing an infinity of possible worlds to subjects that never forget the fact that they are rooted in a woman's body.

Let me begin by quoting Virginia Woolf.

In her view, the mind co-ordinates and transforms messages transmitted by the senses:

> the reason, the imagination, the eyes, the ears, the palms of the hands and the soles of the feet, not to mention a million more that the psychologists have yet to name.[4]

Out of this apparently unscientific bundle of senses, Woolf draws a mind in which there is interaction – not exclusion – between physical and mental experience, and between these and that quintessentially human attribute: the imagination.

The mind connects within to without, reason and senses; it does not make everything abstract. The being that responds to this organizing whole cannot be satisfied by declaring *cogito ergo sum*.

Virginia Woolf, then, considers the mind a place where language is collected and recast. Gertrude Stein, on the other hand, sees it as the place where language – once its ties to tne world represented by it are loosened, once it is freed of all residuous attachment to objects – is finally distilled:

> Language as a real thing is not imitation either of sounds or colours or emotions, it is an intellectual recreation and there is no possible doubt about it and it is going to go on being that as long as humanity is anything.[5]

In 'Craftsmanship' Virginia Woolf asks herself where words live. 'Words do not live in dictionaries; they live in the mind', she answers: the mind is a 'deep, dark and only fitfully illuminated cavern in which they live'.[6] Words dwell in this cavern, ready to run to the rescue if summoned by thoughts or by other words;

emerging even if nobody has called them; clambering up out of the silent depths of the unconscious. The mind, in fact, is not just a cavern: it is also a well into which texts trickle their words, drop by drop, until it is full of language. Thus, according to her diary thinking becomes: 'slipping tranquilly off into the deep water of my own thoughts navigating the underworld; and then replenishing my cistern at night with Swift'.[7]

A submerged world in which memory organizes and redefines everything tossed into its deep sea.

Memory works in the mind like a 'seamstress', as Woolf put it in *Orlando*: 'and a capricious one at that . . . [she] runs her needle, up and down, hither and thither'.[8]

The mind not only accumulates information, it also displaces pieces of information, only to put them together again in an unsystematic way. So, for Orlando:

> Every single thing, once he tried to dislodge it from its place in his mind, he found thus cumbered with other matter like the lump of glass which, after a year at the bottom of the sea, is grown about with bones and dragon-flies, and coins and the tresses of drowned women.[9]

Unlike the semiologist Jurij Lotman,[10] Woolf considers the mind not so much a translator as a mechanism which deforms, dislocates and reconnects experiences, mixing up their languages and thus creating a new blend.

Language – in this rich mental universe – occupies the territory that lies between experience, thought and the unconscious. It is no surprise, then, that for Virginia Woolf the spoken (or uttered) word could never be reduced to a one-to-one relationship between sound and meaning. As far as she was concerned, Saussure's *signifié* and Carnap's 'mental image' could never be considered as a unit distinct from both speaker and receiver.

Words, for Woolf, are not the depository of what exists but of what may exist. They represent potential meaning; they are the moulds in which the signified is created by a continuous connecting motion between subject, object and language.

This concept was so important for Virginia Woolf that she lamented:

> Perhaps then one reason why we have no great poet, novelist or critic writing today is that we refuse words their liberty.

> We pin them down to one meaning, their useful meaning . . .
> And when words are pinned down they fold their wings and
> die. Finally, and most emphatically, words, like ourselves, in
> order to live at their ease, need privacy. Undoubtedly they like
> us to think, and they like us to feel, before we use them;
> but they also like us to pause; to become unconscious. Our
> unconsciousness is their privacy; our darkness is their light.[11]

To be unconscious means to allow words an inner experience, to
strip them of the acquired authority of their social significance,
and to let them assimilate, or become encrusted with, individual
episodes. It means to annihilate conscience (of everything: roles
and duties) for a while. It also means to cultivate the silence
which surrounds and nurtures words, the very silence out of
which a woman's life might surface.

In this space created out of silence, imagination has a role to
play in re-creating the conditions for the potentialities of language.

In the mind conceived by Virginia Woolf, memory is at work.
In Gertrude Stein's conception, to the contrary, it is forgetfulness
that governs words. For Stein, forgetting is a prerequisite for
staying in the present tense: losing memory is the only way to
make being and appearing coincide. The present in which things
happen – changeable and unpredictable – is a time of fullness:
language and writing are the instruments of 'an existence suspended in time'.

The annulment of historical time leaves Stein free to experiment
with 'new constructions of grammar' in order to achieve and
express 'this immediacy' capable of communicating the *sentiment*
of words over and above their *sense*.

A contemporary American poet, Kathleen Fraser, whose poetry
stems from the experimental tradition, once wrote: 'language
opened me up.'[12] This essential phrase – the springboard for a
poetic affirmation – condenses an experience at the very root of
her life as a writer into a metaphor.

Her words bring back to my mind a repeated (but long-forgot-
ten) childhood experience that could be summarized with the
words: 'language opened up to me.' On the stage of my memory,
the curtain opened on to an empty mind – like a huge screen in
a darkened room on to which a word in block capitals was being

projected. The word was suspended there for a while, then the letters started to move around, making various combinations in an anagrammatical dance.

This phenomenon, together with Kathleen Fraser's, illustrates how language can be created out of mental and emotional experiences combined. Language is a part of the world, a material object which is relived and reanimated in the mind, independently of its referential, social, or communicative functions.

Virginia Woolf's satanic s's in *Orlando*, or, in *The Waves*, her sentences which whirl through space in the shape of garlands or birds,[13] or the letters Mrs Dalloway gazes up at, traced by an aeroplane in the London sky: these too are representations of the material nature of language, of its capacity for evoking visions and transformations in the mind.

Such experiences – doubtless linked to a period of childhood in which the boundaries between reality and imagination are ephemeral – have their origins in an internal creative response to linguistic impulses.

In this context, language becomes a locus of freedom and play. It is a game in as much as one is free to construct 'possible worlds' or de-compose and re-compose knowledge.[14] It is a game in that it is a pleasure to play with words and enjoy their aesthetic, musical and rhythmic qualities. Last but not least, it is a game where the network of affection preserved in language is repeatedly relived.

This is the experience a writer recuperates, relives, or tries to re-create from scratch. It is within this act of creation and re-creation that I think we have to start looking in order to find out what is new and projective in women's writing, and to what extent this affects the reader, helping him/her see things differently.

Reading the works of Woolf, Stein, Sexton and Fraser (from which I have drawn my examples) I came across some key concepts which – because of their persistent appearance in contemporary women writers, and because of their internal differences – present us with a clear picture of constant aspects of the way the world–language relationship is presented.

For these writers, language is *possibility*: where the hypothetical becomes possible, where the constraints of a codified language, of a linguistic authority (as well as that of physics and the real world), of a social context, are the object of discussion.

For these writers, language is a *game*: detachment from the productive and reproductive obligations. It is freedom from preconditioned roles without escaping experience. It is a game which questions the rules of play.

'We are the words', Virginia Woolf once wrote in *A Sketch of the Past*, thus establishing a direct relationship between human beings and words. If *we* are words, the opposite must also be true; if words are *us* then they too must have a body and a mind.

The relationship between words is thus analogous to the relationships between people across space and time. Complexly loaded with memory, words can effectively be used to represent a mind. And yet, if we are to consider them people, then they have a body. And it is thanks to this body that words cannot be reduced to mere meaning. It is thanks to their corporeal nature that they establish among themselves an almost human relationship.

'How do [words] live in the mind?' Virginia Woolf wondered; and answered:

'Variously and strangely, much as human beings live, by ranging hither and thither, by falling in love, and mating together.'[15]

In *The Waves*, the process which brings forth expression out of silence is described from a bird's-eye view within the word-organ as follows:

The bar at the back of my throat lowers itself. Words crowd and cluster and push forth one on top of another. It does not matter which. They jostle and mount on each other's shoulders. The single and the solitary mate, tumble and become many. It does not matter what I say. Crowding like a fluttering bird, one sentence crosses the empty space between us. It settles on his lips. . . . The veil drops between us. I am admitted to the warmth and privacy of another soul.[16]

Words in the sentence mingle and match, but phrases and words in the dialogue connect people. In Woolf's vision, linguistic communication aims first and foremost at creating contact. Words are living beings which help connect the speaker to the listener in an acoustic continuum which creates communion first, communication next.

'Words, words, words / piled up one on another, / making a kind of weight of themselves', wrote Sexton.[17] Like Woolf, Sexton feels that words have an inalienable material quality. Poems can be held, like babies. They are pieces of reality with a form, a weight, a life.

Stein too considered language as above all substance – an object to manipulate and from which to extract ways of signifying which denied established linguistic and cultural codes. Suffice it to mention her *Tender Buttons* in which 'a carafe' becomes 'a kind in glass and cousin':[18] the link between the words in the phrase is brought about by the physical quality of the sound and by the echoes of sense associated with it. In her work, poetry can also be a sum of words set to a dance rhythm such as in 'Susie Asado':

Sweet sweet sweet sweet sweet tea.
   Susie Asado.
Sweet sweet sweet sweet sweet tea.
   Susie Asado.[19]

Her 'a rose is a rose is a rose', in detaching language from a referred world, rejects the ineluctable weight of culture. Words, in Gertrude Stein's writings, acquire 'the lightness of being'. Words, or the literary composition, represent the present tense against time. The lack of cultural and semantic memory registered in her works is a paradoxical exhibition of the material substance of language and of the silence that still lies within words, of the potential meanings which lurk there. Inside this sonorous body, open to infinite signification, Stein deposited the identity of an *American Woman*.

LANGUAGE (CULTURE, MYTH) CAN BE TRANSFORMED

The conviction that language (culture, myth) can be transformed was shared by the great women writers of this century: from Woolf to Rich, from Stein to H.D. But where precisely do these transformations take place?

Again Virginia Woolf offers us a dynamic interpretation of the mechanisms according to which language either endures or is renewed. In her writing she re-establishes a link between language and culture on the one hand, and nature on the other. In so doing she historicizes linguistic transformations, in a radical departure from contemporary structuralism.

A definitive example of this concept can be found in her last novel, *Between the Acts*. At the crux of a theatrical production, the words pronounced by the actors are suddenly blown away by the wind:

> The words died away. Only a few great names – Babylon, Nineveh . . . floated across the open space. Then the wind rose, and in the rustle of the leaves even the great words became inaudible; and the audience sat staring at the villagers, whose mouths opened, but no sound came.[20]

When words do not reach their destination, dialogue is interrupted, as are all human relationships, as is cultural continuity.

The silence brought about by communicative discontinuity in Woolf's dramatization demonstrates the extent to which language is the very substratum of existence, a cohesive force:

> . . . no sound came . . . Miss La Trobe leant against the tree, paralysed. 'This is death', she murmured, 'death.'
> Then suddenly . . . the cows took up the burden. . . . From cow after cow came the same yearning bellow. The whole world was filled with dumb yearning. It was the primeval voice sounding loud in the ear of the present moment. The cows . . . annihilated the gap; bridged the distance; filled the emptiness and continued the emotion.[21]

When human silence fills space in an allusion to death, a voice (of an animal, symbol of a female goddess) is heard from outside: it tells of an everlasting, omnipresent, active force – as if sound, or language, had a universal power more enduring than social communication, able to guarantee human links of affection and emotion.

In Virginia Woolf's view, language and culture are subject to a cyclical process of transformation. Language and culture are biodegradable: everything dissolves and returns to nature; and nature, in turn, becomes culture and language, thus uniting the natural world and the world of humans.

Whatever is new participates in the universal silence and linguistic force. The power of language as a social product is thus significantly reappraised, though the importance of exchange is once again avouched.

Women must be certain of this space, created from the silence of cultural language and from a universal and inalienable inner power. The female protagonists of *Between the Acts* are in fact associated with silence and emptiness. Though socially silenced they seem to have access to that silence which has potential for language – the same source that Heidegger considered to be the fountain of language.[22]

To be aware of the existing sources is a prerequisite for delving into the inner well-head of linguistic energy and learning to activate it. *But this awareness* can never override the recognition of the material and historic qualities of language: everything that is conserved in language is mortal, including patriarchal hegemony.

Stein too considers language to be the seat of possibility. In her last ironic novel/fairy-tale, *Ida*, the protagonist can travel 'on a train in an automobile by airplane and walking',[23] putting into practice all her possibilities – usually alternatives.

Ida's life and daily actions are logical paradoxes which nevertheless reveal how language can lead you to explore universes in which boundaries between what is possible and what is impossible are continually crossed, in which cultural and linguistic structures are propelled beyond the bounds of realism, and of logical possibility.

What Stein is looking for through her writing is not *identity* but *entity*: not what makes one identical but what makes one different. Thus language in the mind pursues the relationship of 'a human being to himself inside himself'.[24]

Exploring the world through language is always a bit of a *game*. A game which distracts from productive and reproductive work; a game which positions the creative ego at the centre of the board and impels it to play according to – and beyond – the rules.

Linguistic games are one of the most significant ways in which twentieth-century women writers have created their identities.

Gertrude Stein, queen of verbal games, gave one of her pieces the title *Identity: A Play*, which incorporated the pun on play and drama. A work of art was in fact for Stein the result of a mental game – free of the constraint of making sense – with no other aim in mind than to exercise her creativity.

In her writing, however, there is also an element of teasing the reader: her texts never live up to the expectations created and the reader is encouraged to adopt a ludic attitude towards language.

In her *Everybody's Autobiography* we read:

> I understand you undertake to overthrow my under-taking.
> I always did like that you did it like this:
>> stand take to taking
>> I youthrow my
> That was almost as exciting as a spelling match.

> That is all understanding is you know it is all in the feeling.[25]

This piece is an invitation for the reader to read anagrammatically, to invent a personal language, to play and have fun – to not take a literary text too seriously as a definitive version. It is an invitation to appreciate the full impact of meaning in the 'feeling' or sentiment of the words.

Stein's feeling is not so far from Woolf's emotion. Both indicate to what extent the sounds of words are able to provoke creative responses.

In a radio programme dedicated to the art of writing, called *Craftsmanship*, broadcast in April 1937, Virginia Woolf stated:

> Now we know little that is certain about words, but this we do know – words never make anything that is useful; and words are the only things that tell the truth and nothing but the truth . . . it is their nature not to express one simple statement but a thousand possibilities.[26]

The uselessness of words is what makes them ethical. With this apparent paradox, Woolf re-established the priority of the relationship between words and people and between play and language.

Anne Sexton agrees that games are one of the mechanisms for giving meaning to poetry.

> Busy, with an idea for a code, I write
> signals hurrying from left to right,
> or right to left, by obscure routes,
> for my own reasons; taking a word like 'writes'
> down tiers of tries until its secret rites
> make sense; or until, suddenly RATS
> can amazingly and funnily become STAR

and right to left that small star
is mine for my own liking, to stare
its five lucky pins inside out, to store
forever kindly, as if it were a star
I touched and a miracle I really wrote.[27]

Here word-play reveals an extra, possibly unintended meaning: language generates meaning, but its sense remains inaccessible if it is not left free to work, free to play. Play increases the range of meanings of words and things; it can also reveal a design hidden within chance (this is also true in Woolf's works).

Sexton's famous palindrome RATS/STAR illustrates the coexistence of body and intellect, of the material and the ideal, of a force which propels us towards death and a strength which holds on to life.

The truth of a word lies in the cohabitation of meanings within it. The coexistence of tensions within a human being is what this truth reveals.

Playing is – like the mirror-image of a palindrome – a way of creating silence, a way of distancing cultural impositions, a way of regaining mind and body (something that Adrienne Rich has clamoured for).

The truth mind and body extract from their knowledge must be clearly revealed; it must become an orienteering-compass. Starting with emptiness, with a void, Virginia Woolf can shape emotion and words into cohesive forces, presenting to the world at large her hypothesis which turns the hierarchy of values inside out.

Stein recognizes the fact that in a vision conjured up by reflection, 'a moment is not a moment and the sight is not the thing seen and yet it is. . . . That is what makes what women say truer than what men say.'[28]

Writing born from this vision represents a woman's rambling 'through space with the risk of getting lost in time'.[29] Roaming, with no boundaries and no rest-stops; 'wandering' like most Steinian women – from Ida to Melanctha – led here and there by an inexhaustible thirst for knowledge, by a rejection of the confinement of the home, of the constraints of security and identity. This writing (like Virginia Woolf's) proclaims its own social uselessness, its continuous winding up 'starting again and again', its communication of existence and desire. It has access to its own truth and makes it manifest.

To conclude then, the mental crucible in which experience is transformed into writing – as far as these women writers are concerned – does not offer a do-it-yourself kit, with instructions for women on how to use or modify language for their own purposes. It discloses how women can be themselves, which ultimately means how they can find their own linguistic space and tell the difference.

NOTES

1 Myriam Díaz-Diocaretz, *Per una poetica della differenza*, with an introductory essay by Marina Camboni, Florence, Estro, 1989.

2 Marina Cvetaeva, 'Un poeta a proposito della critica', in *Il poeta e il tempo*, ed. Serena Vitale, Milan, Adelphi, 1986 (1926), p. 15.

3 Works by Marina Camboni: 'Il gioco della mente: linguaggio e metalinguaggio in Gertrude Stein', *Letteratura d'America*, 1984, vol. 5, no. 22, pp. 5–34; 'H.D.'s Trilogy, or The secret language of change', *Letteratura d'America*, 1985, vol. 6, no. 27, pp. 87–106; 'Del cambiamento: Gertrude Stein', *Donnawomanfemme*, 1986, no. 3, pp. 56–72; 'Where words and language meet, or culture and language according to Virginia Woolf', *La Memoria*, 1989, no. 5, pp. 7–18 (Palermo); 'La lingua mi ha aperto: riflessioni a partire da un dialogo con Kathleen Fraser', in *Donne e scrittura. Atti del seminario internazionale* (held in Palermo, 9–11 June 1988), ed. Daniela Corona, Palermo, La Luna, 1989, pp. 151–70.

4 Virginia Woolf, 'A letter to a young poet', in *Death of the Moth and Other Essays*, New York and London, Harcourt Brace Jovanovitch, 1974 (1942), p. 224.

5 Gertrude Stein, 'Poetry and grammar', in *Look at Me Now and Here I Am*, ed. Patricia Meyerowitz, Harmondsworth, Penguin, 1967 (1934) (reprinted 1971), p. 142.

6 Virginia Woolf, 'Craftsmanship', in *Death of the Moth*, op. cit., p. 205.

7 Virginia Woolf, *The Diary of Virginia Woolf*, ed. Ann Olivier Bell, assisted by Andrew McNeillie, vol. 3, *1925–1930*, London, Hogarth Press, 1980, p. 33.

8 Virginia Woolf, *Orlando*, London, Granada, 1982 (1928), p. 49.

9 ibid., p. 63.

10 Jurij M. Lotman, *Testo e contesto. Semiotica dell'arte e della cultura*, ed. Simonetta Salvestroni, Bari, Laterza, 1980; see also Jurij M. Lotman, *Semiosfera*, ed Simonetta Salvestroni, Venice, Marsilio Editori, 1985.

11 Woolf, 'Craftsmanship', op. cit., pp. 206–7.

12 Kathleen Fraser, 'At odds: the dream of a common language', unpublished ms, 1985.

13 Woolf, *Orlando*, op. cit.; Virginia Woolf, *The Waves*, London, Granada, 1977 (1931).

14 Gregory Bateson, *Verso un'ecologia delle mente*, Milan, Adelphi, 1976 (1972).

15 Woolf, 'Craftsmanship', op. cit., p. 205.
16 Woolf, *The Waves*, op. cit., p. 70.
17 Anne Sexton, *The Complete Poems*, Boston, Mass., Houghton Mifflin, 1981, p. 563.
18 Stein, 'Poetry and grammar', op. cit., p. 161.
19 Gertrude Stein, *A Primer for the Gradual Understanding of Gertrude Stein*, ed. R. Bartlett Haas, Los Angeles, Calif., Black Sparrow Press, 1971, p. 57.
20 Virginia Woolf, *Between the Acts*, Reading, Berks, Triad Granada, 1978 (1941), p. 103.
21 ibid., pp. 103–4.
22 Martin Heidegger, *In cammino verso il linguaggio*, Milan, Mursia, 1984 (1959); translated into English as *On the Way to Language*, tr. Peter D. Hertz, San Francisco, Calif., Harper & Row, 1982.
23 Gertrude Stein, *Ida*, in *Look at Me Now. . .* , op. cit., p. 362.
24 Gertrude Stein, *How Writing Is Written*, ed. R. Bartlett Haas, Santa Barbara, Calif., Black Sparrow Press, 1974, p. 206.
25 Gertrude Stein, *Everybody's Autobiography*, New York, Vintage, 1973 (1936), p. 122.
26 Woolf, 'Craftsmanship', op. cit., pp. 199–200.
27 Anne Sexton, 'Busy, with an idea for a code, I write', *Voices: a Journal of Poetry*, 1959 (1953), vol. 169, p. 34.
28 Gertrude Stein, 'What are masterpieces and why are there so few of them?', in *What Are Masterpieces?*, New York, Pitman, 1970 (1935), pp. 91–2.
29 Luce Irigaray, *Etica della differenza sessuale*, Milan, Feltrinelli, 1985, p. 154.

Part II

Psychoanalysis

Chapter 6

Maternal role and personal identity
On the women's movement and psychoanalysis*

Silvia Montefoschi

THE DIALECTIC OF THE JUNGIAN MODEL

Since Jungian theory is inspired by the method of dialectical thought, it can constitute a possible theoretical base for the women's liberation movement or at least help in a liberating enterprise (and not only for women).

Jung's theory offers us an interpretative schema for the individual-collective dynamic which brings to light the problems of the masculine and feminine roles in our society while indicating how these roles could possibly change.

Let us review briefly the elements of Jungian theory essential to our discourse. I will present those concepts that structure the interpretative schema of Jung in so far as they relate to the human dynamic under discussion here.

Jung's inerpretative schema is articulated around the concept of *personality*, i.e. the individual's development through the rapport between the *Ego* and the *collective unconscious* and the *Ego* and the *collective consciousness*. This rapport is essentially dialectic because it is based in the need of the human subject to differentiate him/herself and to define his or her own identity, whether it be in reference to their own unconscious psyche that includes universally human and historically determined models of existence, or in reference to collective forms of consciousness, sanctioned

* First published as 'Ruolo materno e identità personale. A proposito di movimento delle donne e psicoanalisi', in *Nuova DWF*, 1978, no. 6–7. Only the second part is included here. Translated by Carol Lazzaro-Weis.

by the society in which one lives. These elements – the collective consciousness and the collective unconscious – tend to condition the individual into typical and thus impersonal modes of behaviour, endangering his or her uniqueness.

However, they constitute the foundation of his or her existence and, for this reason, the individual cannot live without them, but must continually confront them in order to recuperate his or her subjective liberty.

The dialectic operates on both the conscious and the unconscious levels. Thus Jung takes into consideration the two functions through which the Ego relates to the unconscious and to the external world.

These functions are the *Persona* and the *Animica*.

The Persona is the function through which the Ego relates to the personal world. It corresponds to the attitude that the subject assumes in response to his or her environment so that he or she can act upon it and adjust to it. The Animica function mediates the entry of the unconscious processes into the consciousness of the individual. It corresponds to the attitude the subject will assume in its relation to his or her own internal world.

Both these functions are necessary to the development of the individual personality because, whereas the Animica brings to the conscious level new possibilities for existence, the Persona enables the subject to express his or her existential meaning in the world. The total identification of the Ego with one or the other function will therefore impede development. Identification with the Animica and the subsequent refusal of the Persona (which happens when the subject recognizes him/herself only in his or her interior life and denies any value to all modes of social behaviour because they are contrary to his or her individual choice) blocks the dialectic of the subject with the outside world. Identification with the Persona and the complete rejection of the Animica (which happens when the subject can only recognize him/herself in his or her social role and thus does not understand his or her deep need for individual expression because it would be incompatible with the social role) leads the subject to limit individual activity to the social role imposed upon him or her by the collectivity.

HOW DOES THIS DYNAMIC OPERATE?

Since, in the relationship with the external world (i.e. society), the human being tends to identify with established values, the result on the level of the Persona is that he or she manifests a behaviour validated by society, whereas on the Animica level he or she finds ways to express all those characteristics of the personality that do not concur with models of institutionalized behaviour.

Hence the different names Jung gives to the Animica function, for a man and for a woman, since they will have different roles in the social context.

In a man this function is called the Anima. This feminine name is given because on the level of his Persona, a man will co-operate with those behavioural models that are considered to be masculine, while those characteristics that his culture considers feminine will be found on the Animica level. For a woman this same function has a masculine name, the Animus, since her Persona will adjust to the socially accepted feminine roles, and so those attitudes considered to be masculine are expressed in her Animica.

According to Jung, in fact, masculine and feminine modes of behaviour cannot be attributed to structural differences in the psyche; they are general human attitudes present at the same time in every man and woman. These attitudes are labelled masculine and feminine because in all cultures they have been seen in a differential manner and accordingly attributed to man or woman. Among masculine attitudes Jung lists activity, rationality and the capacity for control and self-determination. Together they constitute the formative principle of consciousness, the so-called male principle or *Logos*. Among feminine characteristics he includes receptivity, passion, availability, helpfulness and piety. They constitute the very principle of life, the feminine principle or *Eros*.

On the level of collective or social life the different modes of being of an individual, which can be defined as relative moments in the individual's changing rapport with the external world, become fixed in diverse and exclusionary modes of existence. Thus the masculine mode, the Logos, becomes the major structuring force in a man's conscious life, whereas the Eros, the feminine mode, structures the conscious life of a woman. The Eros, however, remains an unconscious possibility for men and the Logos functions likewise for women. And through the workings of the Animica, the Eros and the Logos present themselves respectively to the consciousness of men and women, proposing them modes of existence contrary to their conscious orientations, modes which they should incorporate into their make-up.

Already here Jungian discourse has broken with the typical organicist model that, when used on a psychological plane, regularly explains behavioural differences between the two sexes as a consequence of the structural difference of their psyches. Jung offers us an interpretative key to discuss the problem on a cultural level. In fact, once the dialectic between masculine and feminine is posited as an internal process of the subject in relationship to his or her social context, men and women, as *subjects of this process*, are presented as equal. Their differences in behaviour are explainable by the different ways one directs this dialectic in response to demands imposed by society.

The *feminine* and the *masculine* are represented first of all by the parental figures, in that the mother and the father represent for the child symbols or universal human figures that Jung calls archetypes. The child projects on to the parents attitudes that are its own, in that they are human, and projects them because in the first instance he or she experiences them in the relationship to the parents. To the mother, who responds lovingly to its needs, the child assigns the availability of basic instincts and an erotic viewpoint in life. To the father, who teaches the child to renounce the need for immediate appeasement in order to realize a finality necessary to the affirmation of its subjective presence in the world, the child assigns the ability to arbitrate events by controlling the instincts.

However, in order to differentiate itself from its parents, the child has to recover these projected attitudes, recognizing both of them as manifestations of its own existence. Only in this way will the child be able to create a personal identity; to recognize, if he is a male, his susceptibility to the Eros; and if she is a female, her ability to gain access to the Logos.

If this recuperation does not take place, the parental figures' symbolic efficacy will not facilitate the process through which the child becomes an individual; on the contrary it will become the main obstacle the child needs to overcome. The mother will remain the mediator of the child's rapport with its emotional and instinctual life and will prevent it from developing its Animica (which has precisely the function of mediating between the Ego and the unconscious); thus the child is stuck in a position of fear and inability to confront and come to terms with its own interior life. The mother remains for the child the mistress of the Eros and makes him or her a slave to the need for love. The father represents the possessor of the faculties of logic and control, and thus prevents the child from recognizing in itself its own ability to organize its life coherently. By remaining the representative of the Logos, the father keeps the child in the position of being incapable of self-determination. The child remains dependent upon an authority held responsible even for assuring his or her *subjective* survival in the world.

Once the child fails to recuperate for him/herself his or her own modes of existence, which keep being ascribed to the parental figures, the child cannot realize his or her own individuality and will search for an identity through identification. The man assumes the paternal stance as a behavioural rule, the woman the maternal equivalent, and each one, by identifying the whole personality with the Persona (one masculine, the other feminine), remains imprisoned in models of institutionalized behaviour and repeats these roles, denying him/herself any individual existence.

This situation is, according to Jung, at the base of all neurotic behaviour. It is the basis but not necessarily the reason for its development. As long as the identification of the Ego with the Persona, modelled on certain set roles, succeeds in keeping at bay or suffocating outright any attempt to transform the personality, the individual is not necessarily a neurotic but rather one who has adapted to the system. He or she is a *normal* person who will never realize the individual significance of his or her existence. Only when the individuating impulses break the rigid scheme of behaviour does the individual fall into a neurotic situation that could have a liberating effect.

To relate this discourse to social reality, one can say that this conflictual situation between the identification with a role and one's individuating demands, which can cause neurotic behaviour or can simply remain an existential condition, is found everywhere in our society. As for the social dynamic underlying this situation, one can only look for an answer in the behaviour of the parental figures within the familial and cultural context where this phenomenon takes place.

In the family unit, the maternal and paternal functions are

exercised as separate and exclusive roles in which the mother and father place their whole identity as well as the significance of their existence (at least with regard to the child). Thus when the child claims its autonomy, he or she must recognize the functions of both parents as being his or her own. The child must deprive their figures of all meaning; in other words, must destroy them without being able to ascribe an alternative meaning to their existence. This means that the child must undergo a sustained conflict, which is in effect the conflict that usually occurs in adolescence (at least in our society) and that clears the way for an individually significant and socially responsible life.

But in order to face this conflict the person must have already learned to deal with tension, must have already developed the mediating function of the Ego for his or her unconscious drives and emotional life, which, according to Jung, is precisely the function of the Animica.

And here the maternal role blocks the way. The mother, by continuing in her role as an overly indulgent satisfier of needs who can also reduce all tension, prevents the child from taking the necessary distance from its own emotional experiences to control and learn from them. The child cannot overcome the feeling that he or she is incapable of sustaining the tension necessary to learn from his or her own experience. The child then feels incapable of facing the anguish that accompanies any conflict on the conscious level. Thus, when, in adolescence, the first big conflict comes their way, children, male or female, can neither consciously face the pain involved in separating from their parents nor can they restore to their parents the chance to explore their own unknown destiny. Indeed, these children continue to identify with their parents and to sacrifice their own independence to them. And this happens precisely because of the position the *mother* has in our present society.

In our society, the mother dominates the family unit through the fulfilment of her maternal role. She constantly attends to the needs of others, helps them when they feel incapable and comforts them in their sorrow. The needier they are, the faster the mother rushes to assist them. She thus comes to think of herself as being necessary to the survival of others and she denies them the chance to become emotionally and physically self-sufficient. Within the family, on the affective level, it is the mother's values (the immediate satisfaction of desire), which prevail; whereas the father, who is also dependent, does not succeed in communicating to his children the affective foundation of his authority. Thus, he fails as well in his necessary role of assisting his children in the development of their social conscience. He becomes the symbol of a normative, impersonal and senseless authority. In the context of the family, it is thus the mother who, by affectively dominating the group, has the most influence on the children's individual and social destiny.

The woman identifies with the mother and accepts her mandate to perpetuate this appeasing and conciliatory attitude; perceived as the only acceptable mode of behaviour, however, this attitude prevents her from any self-expression outside of satisfying the needs of others. Since self-affirmation and creativity (which are human needs) are forbidden by the maternal mandate, a woman must stifle such tendencies in herself. In self-defence, she does this by investing within the family a thwarted creativity, and exaggerating her maternal role.

The man cannot identify with the mother and benefit from her actions, for that would mean losing his social identity according to the established social values. He continues to demand that the maternal figure (and all women) satisfy his needs and fill willingly all his affective voids. He remains in a totally dependent position *vis-à-vis* the woman; in order to convince her to distribute her 'gifts' to him, he internalizes feelings of his own fragility and incapacity to satisfy his own needs and desires. However, in doing so, he constantly runs the risk of falling prey to maternal power if he gives in to his affective side. He must defend himself against his own desire to be passively dependent and he does this by exaggerating the model of paternal power.

From the above, the following conclusions can be drawn: the domination of the mother figure results in the fact that the individual, by never reaching the ability to govern him/herself, entrusts to others the role of deciding for him or her. This in turn forces him or her to accept the sexually differentiated roles imposed by society through the parental figures who hand down from one generation to the next these male and female roles. Thus, there is no possibility here for the human subject to liberate him/herself outside of refusing maternal mediation, an act that would enable him or her to find in themselves the ability to control their own desires and needs. With this act, the individual empowers him/herself by taking power away from the mother, and, at the same time, liberates him/herself from the need to subjugate his or her existence to the law of the father. The individual thus liberates him/herself from blindly following social norms and claims the autonomous right to judge and question stereotypical roles, and to find new ways of existence that would permit women to use the Logos and men to open themselves to the Eros.

Returning to the question of women, who are really the principal object of this discussion, we conclude that the only road out of these dependent relationships and symbiotic chains is the one where the *sacrifice* of the mother in her is constantly repeated.

Only by liberating herself from the grip of the maternal sentiment can she reclaim a life that would both lead to her creative liberty of expression, and give back to the Other, man, that is, the liberty to be a *subject*.

Psychoanalysis as a practice constitutes a valid instrument to break this strong affective chain; but this is a topic to discuss at greater length elsewhere. Whereas now I would like to hazard upon another uncertain terrain in a more intuitive and less documented manner. I would like to shift the discussion of women's liberation from the psychological plane to a more specifically political level.

Since Marx considered the working class to be the last exploited class in the history of man, he believed that its liberation would free all humanity from exploitation. For Marx, to become conscious of one's own alienation is a way of understanding the essence of the alienation caused by the system.

The historical identity of the working class was, for Marx, to bring man to the 'kingdom of liberty'.

Marx does not consider the position of women in society from a revolutionary point of view for two reasons, one historical-objective, the other ideological.

The first reason is because women throughout history have never constituted a class. Their relationship to the employer (man, husband, or father) has always followed the pattern of a master—servant or owner–slave relationship. This position prevented women from ever having a class-consciousness or a knowledge of their own power. It also prevented them from recognizing themselves or from being recognized as a viable social and political force. The second reason for Marx's omission is that women have never been considered as active subjects within society. Even for Marx, history, which is itself governed by relationships of production, has been made only by men. Thus, he is able to conclude that the workers constitute the last exploited social class.

In reality, however, woman is found at the bottom of this system of exploitation and alienation precisely because her *activity* has always been confined to the realm of service and reproduction, while men were producing on cultural and economic levels. She belongs to the system of production in so far as she constitutes its foundation. She is the *sine qua non* of the system itself since the first division of labour reposes on her.

She thus represents the most exploited and alienated level of the population. She is more exploited than others because her work, which cannot be evaluated in quantitative or temporal terms, receives no economic recognition. She is more alienated because if, as Marx tells us, the cause of alienation is that man comes to conceive of his work (which is the expression of himself) solely as a means of survival, no one could be more alienated than she in the area of work: her work is *a priori* denied the possibility of being an expression of human nature since it is *a priori* excluded from the cultural level where men work. Women work on the animal level, defined by Marx as the level where survival is the only reason for working.

Thus indeed women constitute the last group (not class) to be exploited. And, by liberating themselves, they really can liberate humanity, for two reasons: first, by removing themselves from the division of the labour system, they destroy the base of the system itself; second, by coming to understand the dynamics of their opposition, women bring to light the essence of oppressive systems (Marx said this about the proletariat and it applies equally to women). Women occupy a key position in these systems because they transfer to man the affective roots of relational models of dependency – dependency between one who has the power to decide needs and one who lacks this power; dependency between one who has the ability to satisfy these needs and one who does not; dependency between one who produces and one who consumes. This model, coming from the mother–child relationship, lies at the base of all social relationships and is the foundation of the capitalistic system of production.

Thus women find themselves to be the human mediators of very basic models of exploitation and alienation.

The liberation of women from symbiotic, needy and interdependent states and their subsequent access to the position of the subject, and thus to discourse, culture and history (in Jung's terms, their liberation from maternal Eros to recuperate the Logos), are the keys to the liberation of humanity from the infantile, dependent instincts on which these mutually subservient social relationships are based.

PRAXIS

Psychoanalytical praxis, in so far as it is a dialectical instrument to transform consciousness, can link up with the women's liberation movement. In this transformation, women play a particularly privileged and central role.

Indeed, the object of analytical practice is the affective link to the model of symbiotic relationships. This link has its origins in the relationship that the individual has with the mother. The goal of psychoanalysis is to break up this affective conditioning.

In order to accomplish that goal, psychoanalysis must reproduce the mother–child relationship within the analyst–patient relationship. This is not an artificial operation but rather one which takes place naturally.

Let us see how this happens by looking at my own experience as an analyst.

At first glance, the analytical relationship appears to me to consist in the division of roles between the haves and the have-nots; the capable and the needy; those who act and those who feel. This division of roles appears to be the only possible method to establish a relationship. On the one hand, in order to enter into a relationship with me, the patient must have a problem he needs to solve, an affective void she needs to fill, a pain he needs me to comfort, a wound she needs me to heal.

The patient must need me because it is only by offering me his or her need to be satisfied that he or she can enter into a relationship with me. On the other hand, in order to justify my position as an analyst and my presence in this relationship, I need the patient to need me. Therefore, both of us, in order to justify our reciprocal interests and to endow the relationship with meaning, have to offer one another complementary needs to be satisfied.

One could say that this complementarity of roles and attitudes is part of the institutional division of doctor–patient roles. But in this particular type of relationship, that is, between patient and therapist, supply and demand do not refer to specific abilities of one of the parties to be utilized to satisfy specific needs of the other; what the patient is asking for from the therapist is not a technical service to repair a specific sector of his or her life. The patient wants the analyst to have a global concern for him or her as a human being, and the individual requests that the patient makes are ways of trying to incite the interest of the analyst. And indeed, the psychoanalytical method uses this fact to discover through the individual requests that the patient makes, and the way he or she does it, the affective relationship model that he or she is repeating (this is, in fact, the analysis of the transference).

For his or her part, the analyst does not offer to the patient a specific ability to cure a specific ill. The analyst offers an interest in the whole person of the patient and the knowledge of how to unleash the mechanisms of an interpersonal relationship. However, in order to be able to operate within this specific relationship, the analyst must present him/herself as an object of interest to the patient; the analyst's active interventions in response to the patient's passiveness can be viewed as part of the process of getting the other interested in him or her.

Therefore, the division into active and passive roles that takes place in the analyst–patient relationship does not seem to correspond to the division of roles that takes place in a typical commercial exchange relationship. Rather, this division seems to describe the only mode of behaviour that can give rise to and sustain an affective exchange in a dual relationship.

We must get to the root of this mode.

Upon closer observation, we see that it is actually the mother–child bond that reappears in the analytical relationship. Besides the dynamics of supply and demand defined by the institutionalized doctor–patient relationship, there is also an affective demand that can only be explained as being the reciprocal positing by the analyst and the patient of each other as the exclusive object of the other's interest. The patient proposes his or her neediness as the source of value for the analyst; the analyst makes him/herself appear to be irreplaceable. This is just what happens inside of the dual relationship to which society has entrusted its biological and social survival, the mother–child relationship.

In fact, in our society, where the survival of the child is the total responsibility of the mother, it is absolutely imperative that the child recognize in the mother the irreplaceable value of its life and thus that it become the exclusive object of her interest. It is also inevitable that, in return, out of fear of losing the total responsibility for her child, the mother posits the child as her sole object of interest and then convinces herself that no one can take her place in the child's eyes.

Here, love creates its own specific language, that of need and appeasement.

The affective bond between analyst and patient seems to repeat this language of love. This is also the case in many of the dreams that occur during the process of analysis. Dreams marked by symbols of the relationship of the mother, where the mother appears as the symbolic representation itself of this way of loving. A mode of symbiotic unity which protects one from life's contradictions, but which also denies life in its development.

The first problem then that presents itself in psychoanalysis is precisely this affective link to the model of the mother–child relationship and how one can dissolve it.

In order to dissolve this link, the analyst must precede the patient. The analyst's role is not to mirror the other's projections; he or she is as involved in the interdependent relationship as the patient. This could make one think that the analyst him/herself did not dissolve his or her own affective link to his or her childhood relational model, but things are a bit different here. If the mother–child relationship is indeed for all of us the first moment in the story of the establishment of interdependence, it is not its cause. Rather it functions as the model that shows up in all institutionalized relationships, including the analyst–patient relationship.

It is not only the patient who assumes a dependent stance in the relationship. For both parties, the establishment of dependency is the first step in establishing a relationship. Each tends spontaneously to satisfy the expectations of the other. What are posited as mutual expectations are in fact the two ways – active and passive – that human beings have to establish relationships; when one becomes fixed in an active role and the other in a passive one, a dependent relationship is established. Each one gives over to the other his capacity to be active or her wish for passivity, her strength or his weakness, his riches or her poverty. One gives over the capacity to give; the other gives over the need to receive. In such a relationship, giving and receiving establish a one-way movement between a have and a have-not, a producer and a consumer. And, since there is no real reciprocity, giving translates into invasion and domination and receiving means suffocation and loss of identity.

Until now both patient and analyst have fallen back into the same old relational model formed to satisfy mutual desire. The road the analyst must take to escape is the one that blocks the road to appeasement.

The moment the analyst takes the necessary distance from him/herself to recognize in him/herself the need to satisfy the desires of the other, he or she fills the position of the *subject* who, by making his or her own dependency the object of the enquiry, can refuse to satisfy it. In that moment, by freeing him/herself from the other's dependency, he or she also relieves the other from the obligation to be dependent: the analyst has shown the patient that he or she does need the patient's neediness.

This is how the analyst must precede the patient. By learning about their dependent relationship, they both learn that they have not negated the possibility of having a relationship by rupturing this symbiotic bond. Relationships do not have to mean our imprisoning one another in mutual dependency, if we learn to deal with the tensions that come along with the realization that the other is different from ourself.

In this way, both the analyst and the patient come to understand a new relational model, an intersubjective one, that is based on mutual presence. In this new model, expectations have changed. The dividing wall between active and passive behaviour crumbles. Feeling and acting, giving and receiving, are experienced simultaneously. Giving no longer results in deprivation for the giver but rather is an expression of new creativitiy. Receiving no longer results in cancellation for the receiver but rather is the discovery of a new mode of existence.

Therapeutic action, therefore, is to be located in the discovery of intersubjectivity. But intersubjectivity is both a tool and a goal. The breaking of the chains of dependency liberates the individual from the prison-house of his or her own reified image composed of the expectations of others and prepares him or her to face the contradictions in new relations where he or she will find a new identity. Intersubjectivity induces a transformation in the human subject; it motivates the human subject to embark on a voyage of progressive transformation. One must not assume that transformation takes place in a moment's time. The liberating moment we discussed here begins a process that lasts a lifetime. It is a process that leads to becoming human inside social relationships where interdependency, the sole relational model, will emerge again with every new encounter, to try again to imprison the individual who, in this privileged psychoanalytical model, has experienced the liberty to become a *subject*.

And it is in these constant negative encounters where the subject has to continue to try to exercise his or her liberty that psychoanalytical practice shows how it can become an important tool in the transformation of society.

The transformation psychoanalysis permits is not finished in that moment when the person comes to a fuller and more complete understanding of him/herself as an individual. Rather it becomes part of one's active formulation of relationships with the outside world, part of one's constant effort to change one's behaviour in the construction of objective relationships and part of one's commitment to change already existing relationships.

This description of praxis is a theoretical reformulation of my own experience; but one can find its basis already in Freud.

The Freudian psychoanalytical method, in so far as it calls for a development of a deeper level of consciousness in the individual, does allow for the *subject* to free him/herself from the dependency created by the projection of his or her needs on to the other. In so doing, the individual can become independent of those who have appropriated his or her projections. The individual under analysis learns to control the tension that results when needs are not appeased, through the experience of frustration that the analyst provokes.

But, in the Freudian method, the basic affective model that feeds interdependency is relegated to the past of the patient. It is not viewed, in the present, as the only affective model through which a person tries to construct his or her own identity in the society he or she lives in. Thus, the analyst does not recognize him/herself as an active component in the dependent relationship he or she is analysing but rather considers him/herself the reflection of a projection. Therefore, the analyst does not feel he or she needs to experience the frustration he or she will inflict upon the patient, the frustration necessary to distance oneself from one's own needs. The analyst believes he or she is outside the relationship, a subject divorced from the observed object; believes he or she is outside the dependency, and acts on the relationship from the outside; does not experience it internally. Therefore, although in the relationship with the analyst the patient should be learning to overcome the experience of dependency, which he or she feels as a part of the present situation, he or she is sent back to a dreamy and distant reality that does not explain to him or her the sociocultural reasons for their behaviour, because it is considered from a personalizing and ahistorical point of view.

Furthermore, in the Freudian psychoanalytical model, a distinction is made between a memory from our *past* and our present situation, between a fantasized experience and one that is adequate to *reality*. In doing so, it isolates the phenomenon (in this case the model of a neurotic relationship) from the relational context that produced it and denies it any social or historical significance. This is why Freud takes models of social relationships (which is what the Oedipus complex is) to be *natural* facts. He thus avoids viewing the problematic that reappears in any psychoanalytical relationship from a sociological angle and avoids discussing the active role psychoanalysis and the analyst could have in society.

In order to carry out a sociological analysis of the relational model that is both the object of psychoanalysis and the model upon which the psychoanalyst works, it is necessary to understand not only the social relationship we want to transform but also the relational model we are using to effect the transformation.

We have to analyse the analyst–patient relationship that we are using as a means to evaluate if and how we effect change.

In order to participate in this tranformation, the analyst must, however, recognize his or her participatory role in creating a neurotic relationship. This is possible only if rather than the transference being viewed as a repetition of something that happened in the past, and no longer concerns the present relationship of the doctor and patient, it comes to be seen as an actual experience taking place between them.

Such a definition of transference can already be found in Jung's 'psychology of transference' where the author interprets the successive phases of the transference relationship as a dialogue between the unconscious of one and the unconscious of the other (where the unconscious is no longer a past, but a plan for becoming). Transference is seen as their ultimate union and rebirth in their common project of mutual transformation. Thus the analyst transforms him/herself along with the analysant and together they transform the relational model.

Only with such a conception of transference can psychoanalytical praxis become a viable instrument with which one can transform the real; that is, mankind in its sociohistorical dimension.

We can now return to our initial question of how psychoanalysis as a praxis can constitute a valid cognitive, working instrument in the women's liberation movement. I believe this instrument not only helps woman's liberation but also shows her how to commit herself and learn to take responsibility for herself. It is the woman, inserted as she is in the social fabric, who prepares the affective terrain that hides the alienating norms of a system whose roots psychoanalysis has the duty to uncover. She is indeed the mediator of a relational model of needy interdependency upon which a whole social system was built. By giving in to the needs of others, she aids in the repression of the self-reflective and critical side of the human subject.

Her key position in a repressive system puts her in a privileged, if not the most central, position in the liberation movement. For, if this movement is to become a real liberation movement, it cannot just pertain to one category, class, or group of people. It must involve all of humanity.

Chapter 7

In search of the mirror
Fusion and differentiation in women's groups*

Maria Grazia Minetti

Let our movement finally find a collective body; let us make it live authentically. That is where I find my expression.[1]

Today the body is much talked about, and even more than that it is evoked and invoked in a whole range of activities; from animation, to a certain type of theatre, to all kinds of therapies, which adopt it as an object of manipulation or perhaps of knowledge.

Leaving aside the intrinsic value of each of these activities, this massive evocation seems to have all the hallmarks of the 'return of the repressed'. It is undeniable that the body, or perhaps we should say bodily experience, has been misrecognized and denied 'as irreducible and pre-sexual global datum, as that which is the cornerstone for all psychic functions';[2] it is therefore essential that such experience be studied and understood in the appropriate place, which is above all psychic.

In the course of my work as a psychoanalyst I have become convinced that bodily experience is the basis of a psychic structure: the 'bodily Self', first and foremost step in a more complex structure, the Self, which represents the narcissistic area of the personality. Today, even in non-analytical circles, narcissism is being increasingly mentioned; however, it tends to be regarded as the result of regression from object-love to love of self, more or less in line with the Freudian position which conceives of a single evolutionary line for the personality from primary narcissism to object-love. I want to make it clear straightaway that

*First published as 'Alla ricerca dello specchio. Fusione differenziazione nei gruppi di donne', in *Memoria*, 1982, no. 3. Translated by Sharon Wood.

when I speak of the narcissistic area of the personality or the Self, I mean a part of the personality which has its own processes of structuring and evolution, as distinct from the development of object-drives and object-relations. The substance of my position is close to that of authors such as Kohut and Grunberger, who postulate the existence of two evolutionary lines for the psyche: one which goes from primary narcissism to object-love, and another which goes from primary narcissism to mature narcissism.[3] My reflections on the 'bodily Self' presuppose the distinction of these two evolutionary lines.

So I will not be speaking of the body, but of aspects of the 'bodily self', which in my opinion can be traced not only in the early development of the child, but in all situations in adult life which result in a momentary destructuring and transformation of the Self; or to use a more common expression, sociological rather than psychological, every time that problems of 'identity' arise. My hypothesis is that even in group situations where these problems arise, narcissistic needs are mobilized, analogous to those encountered in individual development and bound up with the structuring of the bodily Self. I say simply 'analogous' because I want to make it clear that I am not trying to compress different experiences one into the other. I am simply trying to look at certain group experiences, particularly groups of women, with a perspective that, while it does not claim to be exhaustive or the only one possible, promises at least to be very suggestive and to deepen our understanding. I am interested in creating an interpretative bridge which will allow us to understand certain aspects of feminist experience, to recognize what narcissistic needs this experience has or has not fulfilled.

I do not propose to trace a history of women's groups, nor will I quote too many, since my main source is my own experience, the thread of my own thinking. My intention is not to offer a complete treatment of the subject, nor to identify causal sequences, but in relation to the problem of narcissistic needs, to evaluate the sense and significance of an experience. I am convinced that by concentrating our attention on narcissistic needs rather than on conflicts tied to object-drives, we can come to understand aspects which until now have been inadequately investigated even though they are extremely important.

PRIMARY FUSION AND THE 'COMMON SKIN'

For a long time after birth, mother and child constitute a single system; they *are one*. The fusion or con-fusion of mother and child follows a very complex, non-linear evolutionary process, whose main points can be expressed by the difference which lies between *being and feeling one*, and *feeling two* in a relationship; put another way, we might say that the baby passes – in early childhood – from total, passive fusion to a more partial and more active fusion, in which its Self is no longer identified simply with the mother, who then becomes an 'Object-Self'.

In the initial situation of 'being one', mother and child have the same 'skin', it is she who lends her body in order to give existence and meaning to the baby's scattered, disordered, and senseless perceptions. Her way of talking to the child, feeding it, holding it in her arms, lulling it to sleep, cleaning it, the fact that she treats the child as a whole person when it isn't yet, constitute the first psychic matrix for the formation of a sense of *being*, which will gradually enable the child to feel itself to be inside a skin, to be whole, to have an inside and an outside, to be the body *which is* before it knows *who* it is. This sense of *being* comes before everything else, before knowing how to *do* anything. Winnicott says of this:

> However complex the psychology of the sense of self and the establishment of a sense of identity can become as the baby grows, there can be no sense of self other than on the basis of establishing a relationship in the sense of *being*. This sense of being is something which precedes the idea of being one with, because without identity there can be nothing else. Two separate people can *feel* themselves as one, but here . . . the baby and the object *are* one.[4]

What has happened then, when women choose separatism and gather together in search of a collective identity?

In the beginning what counted above all was being together, belonging to the collective, or the small group, or the 'movement'. It was talking together, finding ourselves, or rediscovering ourselves; being, existing. In our talk of our mothers, our past lives, we found it difficult to grasp perhaps what we were simply living through; a common 'skin', a *being one*, undifferentiated parts of a whole, a single and complete body. The essence of belonging was 'being' that collective or that group. Speaking to each other, finding each other, touching each other were almost like maternal caring, the magical incantation of the mother's voice, who calls us by name and gives us existence even before we are capable of recognizing ourselves. What I am suggesting is that the constitution of feminist groups mobilized a whole web of needs connected to feeling *that* I am even before knowing *who* I am. These needs 'must' be satisfied or else we risk disintegration and annihilation, and their satisfaction requires an environment which will sustain the illusion of being a smoothly functioning whole; an indispensable premiss for future differentiation of individuals. To this end a strong sense of belonging is necessary.

I certainly do not think that all the psychic problems at work in women's groups were situated at this very basic level, which concerns the sense of being. It is likely that we cannot even think of a 'chronological' succession, as for the child, as if the history of women's groups could be read like a linear process, a development from the sense of being to the sense of self, as is precisely the case in the infant's psychic development. 'Before' and 'after' serve here more than anything to bring to light the internal logic of psychic needs, predominant each in its own time as they seemed to me, like actors on the stage at any given moment. Besides, it is important if we are to think clearly on this to 'blind ourselves to other points in order to shed light on just one', as Freud's famous remark goes.

There is another point which we should clarify. Although the analogy with infant development might prove useful, it seems better to me to speak of 'fundamental' or 'basic' psychic problems, rather than of 'archaic' or 'primitive' levels. I believe that these problems recur, sometimes harshly and painfully, every time that in adult life there is a transformation of the Self and hence a destructuring of the previous integration, not to mention the fact that a human being carries around for the whole of life these so-called 'infantile' or 'primitive' problems and needs. It is important that these needs be recognized as legitimate, rather than stigmatized. As far as the experience of women's groups goes, each discussion of it involves an 'interpretation', and I well know that each such interpretation can be felt as an offence, a reduction, a rupture of the sense of totality; and it is this rupture which not only the small baby but each one of us experiences, in some circumstances, as a threat to our own sense of being whole. In writing this paper I have myself often had to face a narcissistic wound to my need for totality, for a total adhesion to the experience shared with other women. But I am convinced that however partial this effort to understand, it can lead to an advancement, even if a painful one, in our way of thinking.

Coming back to the problem of belonging, I think that the need to be *that* group, *that* collective and/or the 'movement', has for the most part been satisfied, for a time at least. *Autocoscienza*, which functioned to trace similarity in diverse experiences, probably formed the connective tissue where to feel this sense of belonging, the fusion into a single body. *Autocoscienza*, and not simply the fact that we were all women, is to my mind precisely what made it possible to live this experience of fusion; and I think that this peculiarity of women's groups with respect to any type of mixed group should be understood in all its importance, and looked at closely. The significance of such an experience should not be undervalued in a culture such as ours which has lost any moment of initiation and in which, because of changes in the institution of the family, the child is thrown into a precocious process of 'autonomy' which prevents him/her from experiencing fusion as something which need not be suffocating and from which one can emerge without a violent wrench. Something which one can go out of and back into, and still maintain a sense of self; for, on the other hand, this sense of self cannot structure itself in the absence of a vital and beneficial experience of fusion.

As we shall see, the experience of fusion in women's groups has only partly worked; in particular, it has not allowed the 'going out' without a harsh and traumatic break. To understand better the problems encountered, however, I must go back to the 'analogy' with the baby.

FROM A 'COMMON SKIN' TO BEING A SEPARATE BODY: THE CENTRALITY OF THE MIRROR FUNCTION

What does it mean to come out of fusion without suffering a violent wrench?

As far as the baby is concerned, the extremely long and complicated development from a 'Self-skin' totally fused with the mother to the discovery and consolidation of one's own limits is stimulated and sustained by the very process of growing up. The more the baby acquires co-ordination and differentiation of its own functions (sitting up, discovering the various parts of its own body including its voice, holding objects, walking, eating by itself) the more it experiences contradictory states of mind; from pride to the fear of losing what it has gained, to the terror, sometimes, of being broken into pieces, a terror reawakened by its greater knowledge and differentiation of the various parts of its body. In this phase, the mother must be able to modulate her own response of support and narcissistic confirmation of the baby, respecting its needs – of both autonomy and fusion – in a delicate alternation of 'being what the baby has the capacity to discover' and 'being herself while waiting to be discovered'.[5]

This alternation is connected to a particular function which Kohut denominates as 'specular', consisting in mirroring the affirmation of the baby and its exhibitionism of its own body. The baby needs above all to see itself recognized, admired and confirmed in the process of growing up, and so to construct its own 'self-esteem'. The essence of the specular function lies then in the 'participation' in the baby's narcissistic pleasure; this enables the baby to structure isolated experiences of physical and mental functions into a whole, and also to draw pleasure from individual parts of the body and their functions, or from individual mental activities, as parts of a coherent and solid whole.

These manifestations of admiration of and participation in the baby's expression of its different abilities must clearly be realistic, in suitable proportion to the importance they have for the baby itself. Kohut and Wolf say of this that the essence of a healthy matrix of the Self in the baby is a mature and supportive parental Self, in harmony with the changing needs of the baby; a shared flash of joy can mirror the baby's grandiose exhibitionism and just a moment later if the baby has become anxious or over-stimulated by its own exhibitionism, the parental Self will harness this exhibitionism, adopting a realistic attitude with regard to the baby's limitations.[6] The possibility of exhibiting one's own capacities, displaying one's own body and being given a suitable and realistic response allows the establishment of a global Self, separated from the rest and an autonomous centre of initiative. It can happen on the other hand that this 'proud exhibition of the Self which blossoms in the baby'[7] encounters parents who do not give a suitable response (either excessive or insufficient), thus hindering the baby's process of 'personalization' which Winnicott talks about, that sense of being a real and whole person (an intellect-psyche-soma unit): 'feeling oneself to be real is more than existing, it's finding a way of existing as oneself.'[8] I insist on this point because I believe that for my argument it is important to understand the significance of the specular function.

At this stage I would like to put forward the hypothesis that the structuring of women's groups, having satisfied in part at least the need tied to the sense of being, has encouraged the emergence of other narcissistic needs linked to the individual participant's need of self-affirmation, with the correlative manifestations of aggressiveness, exhibitionism and omnipotence. Unfortunately these emotions are often little tolerated and stigmatized as unhealthy; it is not understood that it is precisely the missing empathetic response to the needs which they express, which cuts them off from the totality of the Self and makes difficult their psychic elaboration: thus they are perceived as 'intolerable' and at times 'acted out'. But more of that shortly.

As fusion into a single body made women able to carry out functions previously delegated to men – such as organizing demonstrations, publishing journals, promoting radio broadcasts, making legislative requests and proposals, and so on – within the groups there mushroomed the undeclared need to find space for the expression of individual differences. One example of this need is given by the following statement from Clara:

> In a previous time I saw clearly the necessity for and function of the collective and of *autocoscienza* . . . as a tool for the constitution of our own identity *in relation to* women; to as many women as possible. . . . It is no longer enough to verify myself with the women who are near me. . . . I want the chance to confront more women, because from more minds, more emotive situations, more women's bodies, more things are born. . . . I need a collective moment on the product of our individual efforts, I need to feel each woman's need and effort to communicate with me and with other women, *I need this to grow and to discover my own name.* [emphases added][9]

Unfortunately this kind of need could find no response in that individual differences were seen as a threat to the one body and its totality, rather than as an expression of its richness and complexity. In order to tolerate these outbursts of aggressiveness, the manifestation of privileged relationships within one group, or the entry of 'new' women who often brought real generation conflict with them, in order to elaborate the presence of lesbian loves, as well as all the different modes of being a woman, a change in our way of being together was necessary, and perhaps in particular a change in that famous *autocoscienza* which had been one of the founding pillars of the groups themselves, their connecting tissue. What had previously been a question of recognizing ourselves as equal, discovering common problems and paths (a process culminating in '*donna è bello*', 'woman is beautiful'), had to turn into the real possibility of recognizing ourselves as different. This mirroring function proved impossible: what happened was the end of the collectives through a progressive crumbling apart, an emptying of meaning.

The possibility of recognizing diversity was compromised by various factors. First of all, diversity appeared as a sharp outburst of unconscious needs, which required the group to bear an excessive emotional weight, experienced as a laceration of the sense of being, of globality, of achieved cohesion. The failure to elaborate the loss of the initial totality and the emergence of new needs led to the end of the collectives and to a temporary loss of this sense of being together: in this phase, speaking of collectives and *autocoscienza* gave a sense almost of nausea.

Before reaching this point, what attempts were made to deal with this crisis of cohesion (achieved through *autocoscienza*, which constituted the imaginary common 'skin')? I would say that in substance two types of attempt were made. There was on the one hand the effort to reconstitute the lost fusion; and on the other, the effort to fall back on a fragment of past experience in order to adopt it as a substitute for the shattered globality. An example of the first type are the stories each group told about themselves in *Differenze*, a journal which far from representing the arena in which differences could be confronted out in the open from within the collective, became the place in which the group speaking about itself tried to rediscover its lost fusion and solidarity. An example of the second type is to my mind groups which were established on the basis of particular 'areas of competence' – women poets, psychologists, etc. – or 'diversity' such as lesbians; the failure to mirror these 'areas of competence'; and specificity means the disintegration of the joyous experience of

being a whole Self; often both child and adult are forced to fall
back on a fragment of their own experiential unity or of their
own body in order to feel alive.

One thing should be made clear. The acceptance and mirroring
of differences should not be thought of as an uncritical and generic
'yes' to everything. The suitable and realistic response I referred
to above holds good not only for the baby. I am sure that the
difficulty women in collectives had in saying a clear, reasoned
'no' to the other was often the symptom of the impossibility of
defining their mutual limits, and this is the same as the impossibility of mirroring, due to the anguish unleashed by the loss of
fusion. The great difficulty in saying 'no', and the corresponding
violent expulsion or massive denial of everything which was felt
to be unacceptable, was quite a common experience in women's
groups; and obviously I am speaking here of expulsion as a
psychological mechanism and not as a concrete procedure. This
expulsion happened indirectly, rather than as direct and motivated
aggression. The reality was that some women 'migrated' from
one collective to another, others shut themselves up in silence or
in sleep, others simply left. The groups for their part closed
themselves off to newcomers or, if they remained open, they
often exhausted themselves by getting bogged down in frequently
destructive dynamics between the 'old' and the 'new' women.

When *autocoscienza* revealed itself as unable to carry out the necessary specular function and so lost its cohesive and reassuring
character with regard to differences, which up to that point had
been projected on to the 'male' outside, there emerged the anguish
born of finding ourselves among women, equal but devalued.
What had been a factor of growth (being equal among equals)
now became a factor of paralysis, not *because* of being among
women, but because of the evoked phantasm of a lack. What had
given a sense of plenitude and totality, now reduced to one factor,
if an important one, among many, came to have a devaluing
connotation. If we are all almost worthless, what can we recognize in each other? Although there was more than the occasional
flash of insight on this point, the whole problem remained more
or less unconscious while still causing feelings of acute anxiety.
To my way of thinking, one reaction to this anxiety, and indeed
a sign of it, was for women to shut themselves up in ever more
rigid and abstract ideologies, or idealizations.

I have often been surprised to notice in analysis how women who had been given a huge momentum in their personal growth by contact with the movement, then remained tangled and tied up in a grand-sounding but sterile bog of ideological, schematic affirmations, and this in spite of their own vitality and intelligence. In general I have found that the need to shelter behind idealizations (not to be confused with ideals) of this type is an attempt to inflate a Self which is emptied or threatened with fragmentation or collapse. Unable to live out a suitable experience of self-affirmation, of recognition of their own abilities and differences, and finding no space for personal display or expansion, exhibitionism is satisfied by inflating an idealized collective identity, a rigidly constructed net of 'musts'. In the place of an ideal or a goal against which to measure oneself, a grandiose idealization is set up, with which there is a fictitious sense of identification and under whose weight one risks being crushed. These idealizations and ideologisms are more than simply hot air; they feed on real problems, they have their own 'logic' and their own 'rationality', and this is precisely why they are so dangerous; they show a rupture in the unity of the intellect-psyche-soma, a very painful situation in that the 'psyche is "seduced" by the intellect, breaking the intellect's original and intimate relationship with the soma'.[10] Bodily experience, emotions, feelings, desires and needs are all denied and masked by ideological affirmations. Having a child or an abortion, loving a woman or a man, getting married, splitting up, living alone and so on become what we must or must not do; either all the private is political or it is not dignified with existence. We have a particularly significant example of these paralysing idealizations in the whole business of the concept of autonomy, independence and liberation within groups.

The possibility of realizing ourselves no longer *through* the man, the capacity for real emancipation achieved by women on the one hand, and on the other the creation of even more extensive psychic autonomous nuclei, had given rise to an ideal image of liberation (as a goal to aim for and measure ourselves against) which was valid as long as the expectation of personal fulfilment (still absorbed in simple *being*) was maintained. When the outburst of personal needs and ambitions threatened this sense of being, the goal transformed itself into an intellectualized idealization and was theorized as total 'self-sufficiency' – with the result that it trampled over and denied the need for dependence and the real chances for autonomy which actually existed.

Split off from the body, the mind looks down at it from above and considers its needs to be something vulgar, futile, reactionary, or shameful. This split wipes out the chance of integrating opposing feelings and emotions or even tolerating them, it denies the needs of the body as inferior, to the point where the body's only way of expressing itself is through arrogance and intellectual exhibitionism. Of course the defence *from* change, which was seen as catastrophic, through ever more grandiose idealizations could not work for very long: like the giants with feet of clay, these idealizations collapsed under their own weight, and I believe that the failure to recognize what was happening contributed to the decline of the collectives through 'exhaustion'.

I would not claim that this decline happened only because of the processes I have tried to outline in this paper. However, I do believe that the violent rupture of the common 'skin' and the failure to make space for individual characteristics and their relative need for recognition, not only represented a cluster of difficult problems relevant to the destiny of women's groups, but were a determining factor in 'how' their ending was experienced: exasperation, saturation, or, at times, excessive indifference prevented a common sense of sorrow. To my mind the so-called 'return to the private' which has been so heavily criticized in political terms represented rather a reaction to the anxiety of fragmentation caused by the crisis of fusion.

Although the work of mourning has been left up to individual women, it is certainly an important sign that since the end of the collectives, more groups have begun to spring up in a number of places. These initiatives are still too close to us, still too *in fieri* for us to be able to see clearly what they are: however, they are both a sign that the previous experience was not entirely lost and, probably, a significant way of responding to unsatisfied needs and to the narcissistic wound. I think it is important to stress that these initiatives have in common that they are 'cultural'. This fact keeps bringing to my mind a bizarre fantasy, that they are the expression of an attempt to turn to the 'father' in order to get what could not be obtained from the 'mother'; speaking of father and mother, of course, in a metaphorical sense.

The fact of being all women and feeling all 'equal-devalued' just when fusion was being lost made it impossible for the group to adopt an effective maternal mirroring function. The mother, though invoked, was never there; there was never a symbolic mediation which could make possible the workings of a maternal function, especially the specular one. Among equals it is difficult to bear differences, to recognize the other's need if one cannot recognize and tolerate one's own lack, just as it is difficult for a child to admit that his or her sibling is different, and knows how to do different things. If one does get to this point, it has to be by going through all the pangs of jealousy and envy, and in a group these feelings are even more difficult to deal with. The rupture of sisterhood, and the possibility of turning the initially vital complicity into solidarity and recognition of multiplicity, implied all these feelings of pain, creating a situation which required the group to personify for all participants that urge to differentiation which conjures up – between mother and daughter – the phantasm of the wicked stepmother. What was needed was a mother who was also able to take on this role: 'Mirror, mirror, on the wall, who's the fairest of them all?'

For reasons which I think I have shown, the mobilization of similar levels of competition within women's groups could be neither contained nor elaborated. This is particularly dramatic because it is precisely the mother who must acknowledge the daughter's chance of becoming in her turn woman and mother, and in a way very different from her own. The attempt to get this acknowledgement from the father might appear to be easier given the mediation of 'culture' which already establishes some distance, but in certain senses it cannot possibly succeed. If – metaphorically speaking – it is the father who legitimizes the daughter, he can only legitimize her to be *like* the mother: in other words he cannot give a genuine acknowledgement of individuality. Thus the need for recognition risks being continually evoked and continually eluded. We should be clear that the need for recognition does not exclude that for legitimacy; both needs should be satisfied, but it is important to recognize their different natures.

On an individual level, of course, the function of recognition, and the urge to growth, can come from both parents. However, the parents can acknowledge their children's right to be different from what they themselves would like only if, in their own personality make-up and capacity for elaboration, they can, *first of all*, be separate individuals, apart from their children; and as we know, this happens only rarely. In society today the crushing presence of unilateral cultural models, the devaluation of individual differences (side by side with a contradictory and exasperated call to 'be yourself'), the lack of significant stages which make it really possible to become ourselves, to take account of our own abilities and our own limits, to discover our own desires, to get in tune with our own needs, are all factors which objectively reduce the space for a real recognition. Women have dramatically had to face this problem: instinctively they have managed to create a structure which allowed them to satisfy a part of their own needs, those tied to the 'sense of being', but for all the reasons I have tried to illustrate here, they have been unable to satisfy those tied to 'being oneself'.

It is possible that the attempt to overcome some of the difficulties by turning to the 'paternal' realm of legitimization will encourage new ways of thinking. In any case, it will take a lot of time and patience, and a great effort of thought, and for this reason I hope my attempted analysis and my invitation to recognize individuality and to elaborate our narcissistic needs will prove of some use.

NOTES

1 Graziella, *Sottosopra*, 1974.
2 D. Anzieu, 'Le moi-peau', *Nouvelle Revue de Psychanalyse*, 1974, vol. 9.
3 B. Grunberger, *Il narcisismo*, Bari, 1977; H. Kohut, *Narcisismo e analisi del Sé*, Turin, 1976; H. Kohut, *La guarigione del Sé*, Turin, 1980.
4 D. W. Winnicott; see his *Playing and Reality*, London, Tavistock, 1971.
5 ibid.
6 H. Kohut and E. R. Wolf, 'The disorders of the self and their treatment: an outline', *International Journal of Psychoanalysis*, 1978, vol. 59.
7 ibid.
8 Winnicott, op. cit.
9 Clara, *Sottosopra*, 1974.
10 D. W. Winnicott, *Dalla pediatria alla psicoanalisi*, Florence, 1975; see his *Therapeutic Consultations in Child Psychiatry*, London, Tavistock, 1971.

Chapter 8

The female animal*

Silvia Vegetti Finzi

Premiss: 'Sacred in origin is that which we have taken from the animal kingdom, the bestial.'

(Engels)

Before I really start, I want to refer back to the discussion which took place this morning in order to confess a fault: in my research I have used all the cultural instruments at my disposal; it is neither spontaneous, nor immediate. It is, I hope, a scholarly piece of work. If not, then this is due solely to the limitations of my own academic skills. I have used philosophical, psychoanalytical and historical tools and also my therapeutic experience as an analyst, working with little girls. I believe that the immediate, the originary and the concrete, which have been called upon here, run the risk of banality unless they are invested by critical and historical research. I do not support either therapeutic or cultural impatience. Long periods of time, and a lot of patience, are necessary in order to reach that tiny glimmer of truth which may be attained on completion of a lengthy investigation.

During the discussion, Viola Papetti said something important: speaking about some of Nin's erotic writings, she said she thought that these writings were not so much a moment of liberation and authenticity, but rather an unveiling of herself which the woman offered to masculine voyeurism; that it was a carrier of contents which the man then incorporated into his own schemata and into his libidinal economy. In fact, the mere expression of our instinctual fantasies, of our erotic imaginary, is

* First published as 'L'animale femminile', in *I labirinti dell' Eros*, Florence, 1985. Translated by Giuliana De Novellis.

of very little use, unless it is accompanied by a shared collective project.

A collective political project means finding a subject. I do not believe this subject to be the individual woman; it is not enough that each of us should consider her own erotic imaginary, together we must give ourselves objectives, share thematic journeys.

The collective female subject is not a biological given, it is not something which already exists, but a slow and laborious construction; as Luce Irigaray told us when she last came to Italy, a woman's subjectivity requires both love among women, and love for women's cultural work. Therefore, as women participating in this conference, you should examine these lines of research, and not expect a finished product. Moreover, I think you will be able to see for yourselves, at the end of these two days, which elements of subjectivity, that is, of common themes and relationships, of collations in the feminine imaginary, are also present. Without there being, among us, a tradition of scholarship, an institutional mode of working together, we have discovered correspondences and reflections of topics, of contents, and of affinities of methods; precisely those empathies which go beyond intentionality. This happens because there now circulates a women's knowledge which must, however, be informed by a political project, on pain of being expropriated by masculine culture.

I would like to graft whatever is new in my proposal of work on to a tradition of philosophical research which has been in existence for many years, and, in particular, to take part in the current debate on Michel Foucault's last two books concerning the genealogy of the modern subject.[1]

This is so that what I am about to say will not seem arbitrary, absurd, or presumptuous. I am putting forward, in fact, to the collectivity of women, an investigation which uses the archive of culture, but which subjects it to a different look, to a point of view which positions itself on the side of the object rather than on that of the subject.

Cultural tradition, as we know, is androcentric, it gives back to us the representations that the subject man has given himself, but silences the objects of his knowledge: the woman, the child, the slave, the animal.

Nevertheless, we cannot unthinkingly adopt the principle that everything which is known about woman can be reduced to what man thinks when confronted with her.

For man, woman is not an inanimate object, similar to the things in nature. Woman is his 'other', someone who returns his look, who subjects him to a judgement, even if only supposed.

I do not share those simplistic narratives of the feminine which unfold as a series of dominatory practices of men over women.

Two considerations refute it: the first is that man constantly tends to discipline the feminine, inscribing it in his social plan, but he does not intend to give up what is, in some ways, a joint relationship which he needs for his own existence. The greatness of man is strictly dependent on the greatness of the look of the other.

If woman were domesticated like an animal, completely compliant with his orders, she would leave him without alterity, without a hearing, in that solitude that we experience in the company of an animal.

Second, woman has always resisted 'normalization', she has never completely entered the place assigned to her by the masculine economy. At the same time, though, she has not expressed an autonomous and alternative representation of herself. At least, not in the deliberately communicable and transmissible strong forms of masculine culture.

How, then, can we outline a feminine outside these co-ordinates? It entails making the silence speak, saying the unsayable, at the risk of reluctantly projecting our own image.

Nevertheless, if subjectivity means history, we need to produce an archaeology of the feminine beginning precisely from those residues which have not been assimilated by the dominant discourse, from all that remains of the real deposited in the imaginary, from that which the masculine discourse on woman presumes.

If speaking the feminine presents itself as an 'endless lingering', it means that something remains unresolved, that the question is never closed once and for all. Feminine desire, which works by provoking in the other the question 'What does the woman want?', makes her exist as a subject despite her position as an object. The feminine enigma, the 'black continent', to use Freudian metaphors, functions as an interrogation which disrupts the hierarchy of pre-established positions, investing them with the dialectic of desire.

Interpreted thus, the feminine, instead of a place of continual dispossession, is configured as a site of unpacifiable tensions, as a constant bid to put opposites in relation with each other.

Much has been done in recent years to reconstruct the effects that culture and institutions have had on woman, on how they have represented and regulated her body, her image, her roles.

The feminine, from figure of nature, as romantic culture had understood it, has revealed itself to be a product of ideology and its apparatuses.

For this turning-point we are indebted first to Marxist culture; and second to the historiographical perspective inaugurated by Foucault; not forgetting the historico-philosophical anthropology which goes back to Vernaut, and Althusser's critique of ideology.[2]

In his latest two books – *The Uses of Pleasure* and *The Care of the Self* – Foucault modifies the trajectory of his investigation, shifting it from the reconstruction of social practices which fashion behaviour, to the administration of the self, to what he calls the 'arts of existence'.

By this, Foucault means 'those intentional and voluntary actions by which men not only set themselves rules of conduct, but also seek to transform themselves, to change themselves in their singular being, and to make their life into an *oeuvre* that carries certain aesthetic values and meets certain stylistic criteria'.[3] In some ways, Foucault abandons the history of repression to embark on a history of sublimation.

In psychoanalysis, sublimation requires that the instincts (drives) operate a change of object, to be invested in socially valorized aims. With regard to the economy of pleasure, which requires the immediate discharge of tension, it means the deferral of satisfaction, a removal as well as a change of object, the suspension, in short, of the whole process to the uncertainty of its realization.

But not only that; according to Freud, sublimation requires that the libido, originally focused on the object, be withdrawn on to the ego and transformed into narcissistic libido, then to be, in a second instance, reinvested on a substitutive object, and desexualized.

It is a psychical dynamics which evidently requires the management of sexuality in the sense of limiting, first of all, libidinal expenditure. Foucault does not use this problematization but he observes, through medical and philosophical texts, the introduction of self-restraint into the valorized image of man which is

produced in classical Greece in the fourth century BC and in the
first two centuries AD of the Roman Empire.

In the absence of moral norms or social taboos, we witness a
self-limitation of desires with a view to self-mastery.

Foucault makes his intentions quite explicit: he is not writing
a history of behaviour, but of cultural self-representation.

As far as behaviour is concerned, anthropology has taught us
that any social organization is based on a series of prohibitions.
Thus, self-restraint, to a greater or lesser degree, is coextensive
with civilization. The instincts which are not ordered and hier-
archized, in as much as they are partial and anarchical, are always
socially disintegrating. Every society fosters, for its own existence, the moderation and regulation of sexuality. But not every
civilization represents itself through the limitation of this capacity.
Homeric divinities, for example, draw their excellence from their
ability to pursue excess, to disregard the practice of limitation.
Zeus's sexuality is regulated neither by marriage, nor by rank,
nor does it stop at the barriers of the species. Cronos' oral avidity
does not spare his children. The wrath of the gods is destructive,
their rivalry boundless, their vanity inexhaustible. Heroic morality transfers this valorization of excellence through the practice
of excess on to mankind. The feminine participates fully in this
economy of immoderation: goddesses act out their passions without the slightest restraint, they too, like male gods, excel in the
unlimited exercise of good and evil. But whereas ancient goddesses are allowed to take part in the banquet, to sit at the
common table, the ethics of austerity, pursued by the master of
desire, does not involve women, does not concern them, and
overlooks them.

The free man who affirms the mastery of the self through the
exercise of limitation, is alone in front of the indifference of his
acts. Instinctual renunciation thus concerns not the manner in
which sexuality is exercised, but only the quantity. What is feared
is the unrestrained exercise of pleasure, not its practice. This
stylistics of the self does not hold good for woman, who is
controlled by social norms and not by a sense of inner duty. The
feminine participates, as we have seen, in the economy of instinctual excess through the figures of the goddesses, and will also
participate in the universal morality founded by Christianity
which holds good *erga omnes*. She is, however, expulsed from the
self-regulated economy of moral subjectivity.

The sexuality which the Greek intellectual of the fourth century BC intends to manage is exlusively one of penetration of the other. Being penetrated equals being subjugated, being the object of the master's sexuality.

Self-imposed austerity institutes the subject of sexuality and subjects that sexuality to the primacy of reason. No longer subjected to the unseemly storms of passion, ancient man can say that he is free in himself, is master of himself before being master of the world. The administration of the self is homologous to the administration of society. In *Civilization and its Discontents*, Freud states that as regards sexuality, *Kultur* behaves like a 'people or a stratum of its population does which has subjected another to its exploitation'.[4] Instinctual renunciation furnishes energy first for self-valorization, and then for sublimation. Subjectivity invests that libido, removed from the object, in itself, thus obtaining a narcissistic surplus-value; it projects it on to substitutive objects, receiving in exchange a greater social value. In this way, the mastery over the self justifies that over others, and vice versa. The woman remains excluded from this joint libidinal and social economy. She is relegated to the walls of the *oikos* (domestic space) and, at the same time, abandoned to an unmanageable sexuality. Excess, which is connaturalized with her nature, closes the social space around her and leaves the instinctual one unbounded.

Self-restraint is presented as an exercise of power and of freedom, which, as such, becomes the sole right of the human being who is male, adult, free and idle.

The woman, who is not free, cannot practise self-government. Her sexuality condemns her to ethical impotence. The effects of this sanction are so long-lasting that we find them in the theoretical apparatus of psychoanalysis when Freud asserts that women have a less powerful superego than men, less ability to sublimate, weaker social interests and a poor sense of justice.[5]

Moral inferiority is seen as an effect of psychic debility, as a necessary consequence, while the events which have determined both one and the other remain in shadow.

We have thus delineated a genealogy of masculine subjectivity and, at the same time, the exclusion of the feminine from this collective experience. However, the woman has been neither reified in her animal-like position of object, nor put under child-like guardianship. She has made her way to subjectivity, understood as submission to practices of subjection and as the exercise of freedom within strict rules. It is a journey to be completely reconstructed; a history of the sublimation of feminine sexuality which takes her biological and historical specificity into account.

EXCLUDED FROM THE ECONOMY OF PLEASURE

The question Foucault has helped me to formulate is the following: Why was woman, with whom man shared, even if in separate spheres – to one the *oikos*, to the other the *agora* (public space) – the economy of the *polis* (city, state), not invited to participate in the management of sexuality, in the stylistics of desire, with which man was constructing his new image?

Because – is the answer that I am trying out – Greek culture felt woman to be the bearer of a sexuality radically different from masculine sexuality; one marked by excess. According to Aristotle, there are three figures of excess, those which are discharged from the rational circle of the city and the logos: the tyrant, the undertaker and the woman.[6]

In as much as it was unlimited, feminine sexuality could not be moulded, channelled and managed from the inside, but only controlled by rules and enclosed. Women's very bodies contained, according to Plato, an animal of uncontrollable cravings: the womb. This animal longed for nothing other than to make babies, to produce issue incessantly, in accordance with a sexuality which was completely autonomous as regarded the intentionality of the body which contained it.[7]

It was an impersonal vital force, geared towards a productive aim, which employed both sexual partners for its own ends.

We cannot, however, understand the dual concept which, in ancient culture, connoted woman (animality and immoderation) without bringing into play an evolutionary and always evaded perspective.

When Freud lists the three narcissistic wounds which modern man has inflicted on his ideal image, he states that the second one is that produced by Darwinian theory, which has excluded him from divine descendance to include him in the genealogy of the animals. Man, he observes, denies this uncomfortable kinship so much that he uses the names of animals to stigmatize the most ignoble vices, and to wound his enemies. Only children, he concludes, are willing, in fairy-tales and in play, to identify with animals.[8]

The effect of this collective repression has been an indifference which has all but cancelled what is, for the woman, a fundamental event: the loss of oestrus.

It is true that there is very little available knowledge on such a remote event, but that does not entitle us to forget it. If its cause evades us, its effect can still be evaluated.

Alone of all the mammals, the female human is not subject to the laws of heat. Oestrus constitutes a relatively brief period of pro-creativeness, receptivity and attractiveness of female mammals, which usually coincides with a coextensive period of fertility.

The sexuality of animals in the wild is only reproductive, or, rather, aimed at reproduction. It can, however, lose in captivity the rules which govern it, when deprivation leads to stereotypes such as incessantly pacing back and forth along the same track. Among the artefacts of captivity one also finds the loss of the synchronicity of oestrus; animals can then copulate with infertile females even during menstruation. Now, since the diffuse recur-rence of oestrus leaves no doubt as to the fact that it represents the original condition of mammals, it may be presumed that the ancestors of humankind may have been suddenly deprived of it. I cannot here go into the system of hypotheses that have been put forward on this subject. I am interested only in taking up the question which Donald Symons asks himself in *The Evolution of Human Sexuality*, 'Are human females always in oestrus? Never in oestrus?'[9]

The Greeks would have had no doubts as to the first hypo-thesis, while current scholars of widespread female frigidity would opt for the second. This is because they are probably talking about two different things.

But, going back to origins, we must note that menstruation is the only observable event in the woman which denotes the reproductive cycle. As such, it is a vestige of a broader member-ship with the astral cycles.

On this subject, Franca Basaglia writes:

[Woman], prey to the species, carries within her body a continous possibility of life. She is fertile earth and like the earth participates in the mystery of nature: menstruation and procreation are obscurely linked to the cosmic cycle by which she is possessed. . . . Man's battle with nature, then, also includes her; she who embodies and contains his fears. The man will no longer be afraid of himself, of his own animal nature, if he can recognize it in her, so that he can overcome his own fears by observing her.[10]

And, I would add, by exorcizing her.

We can assume the existence of an ahistorical time in which the human female lived in total synchrony with nature, but we can speak of 'woman' only by cutting her off from this originary membership. Woman is, thus, a domesticated animal. This conjoins her sexuality indissolubly with capture and captivity. But 'loss of oestrus' does not only mean loss of synchrony with the cycles of nature, with the seasons, with the phases of the moon, but also estrangement from her own body, and from her desire which no longer manifests itself through a system of univocally decodifiable signals. It means the cancellation of the instinctual images which regulate reproductive behaviour: recognition of the partner, precognition of childbirth, the proto-mental image of the cub, the nest, the automatism of suckling the young, the initial steps of maternal care. An internal theatre – whose structures are preformed – closes down and leaves the way open to the social processes of learning.

Woman emerges from this upheaval sexed by a natural force which is only partially regulated by natural cycles. She is the site of a process which, although it needs her, floods her with its imperious necessity. For the woman, writes Gladys Swain, the externality of the body is manifest, patent, incontestable. To escape from the dominion of the laws of nature does not mean, for her, the conquest of liberty, but only substituting the control of society for that of nature.[11]

Her body, always available for mating, is felt to be a threat and, as such, is enclosed within the concentric circles of the great common laws of religion, of the city, of the home.

The subject of reproductive sexuality is not the person but the species.

It is indifferent to the dimension of individual well-being. The reproductive processes pursue their own ends, even if it means the death of the biological organism in which they are lodged. The female pays a higher price to reproduction than the male, in terms of vital energy. Thus the loss of that protection which is constituted by sexual unavailability multiplies her energy expenditure to excess. One need only think that the more evolved apes have no more than five offspring in their lifetime. Permanent availability for copulation which opposes adaptation with regard to her biological survival, seems determined in the human female by the necessity to cement the couple bond, to keep the male bound to her.

While, in terms of reproductive success, the interest of the male is to copulate with as many females as possible, that of the female does not gain any profit from the multiplication of partners.

She needs, instead, not to conceive offspring which cannot be raised, she needs to induce the man to help her and the offspring, to maximize the return on her favours, and to minimize the risk of violence and of abandonment.

Non-reproductive sexuality (mating also in infertile periods) seems functional to the constitution and the perpetuation of a social bond: that of the family. Whether or not the female obtains a natural orgasmic pleasure from copulation is very controversial because experiments on higher mammals have produced conflicting results. Probably, for the woman, orgasm is a cultural acquisition. On the other hand, the problem is not fundamental because, as we have seen, the availability of both fertile and infertile mating, which is the effect of the elimination of oestrus, is functional to her survival and to that of her offspring.

There is, thus, an accord between natural benefit and social interest. The woman's deafness to the hormonal stimuli which inform the phases of the reproductive cycle estranges her from her body and consigns it, thus objectified, to the administration of society. Going back to the situation in classical Greece (with a leap which I hope you will forgive) one finds that a series of ceremonies accompanies the stages of female sexuality,[12] almost as though society were replacing the loss of the instinctual regulation with a religious regulation. Let us also remember that the number of pregnancies was limited by a series of prescriptions which suspended sexual intercourse at certain times of the year. A whole series of norms governed marriage, legitimated heirs, punished adultery (of the wife), allowed the disownment of sterile women, and protected the dignity and honour of the free woman.

Her behaviour as a daughter, wife and mother was governed by external norms which did not require her internal consent, and controlled by the fear of losing the benefits of her status. The status of the free woman, in Greece, is identified with her household, with the space of the *oikos*, unit of production and preservation. Generating legitimate offspring and preserving her husband's wealth, these were her task and her value.

The Greek woman did not *have* a social function, she *was* that function. It is difficult for us now to imagine an existence which does not take into account that form of self-organization and self-perception which we call person. Attributing to ancient woman a modern sexuality, understood as a set of individual potentialities, as the demand for freedom and for pleasure, seems an inappropriate projection of our own ideals.

We have to force ourselves to think differently; in this case, of a sexuality which coincides with the exercise of status. Simonides compares the ideal woman with the bee, which, as we know, is practically devoid of sexuality, completely inscribed within a collective goal, devoted to the workings of the social apparatus.[13] Woman belongs not to herself but to the family organization: first to the father, then to the husband. The most detailed tract on woman's *paideia* is found in Xenophon's *Economics*, a book which sets out to outline the principles of good management of the estate.[14]

It is precisely within the sphere of economic skills that Xenophon places the problem of the relationships between husband and wife. We are thus presented with the ideal case of the 15-year-old bride who must be trained to collaborate with her husband in managing the *oikos*. It is interesting to note that a reciprocal relationship between the married couple is never discussed. Separated by a total dissymmetry (the man is master of himself and he commands, the woman belongs to him and must only obey), they find a common ground in the management of the household. The household divides their space into two spheres of competence: to the woman the internal, to her husband the external; the begetting of children articulates domestic time.

Marriage is the sharing of goods, of bodies, of lives. As far as the sharing of bodies is concerned, it is based on the natural attraction of the sexes and needs no artifice. But at this point an implicit question arises: 'How can the wife remain an object of desire for the husband, how can she be sure of not being supplanted, one day, by a younger and more beautiful woman?' However strange it might seem, it is once again the management of the household which constitutes the decisive element. The government of the home, with its harmony of gestures, its dignity of command, its variety of tasks, guarantees the lady a beauty which is the very reflection of her position. The well-bred woman, the bee-woman, flourishes in the harmony of the home, thrives on domestic living. The indolent woman, however, sinks to the state of the alluring strumpet. To the one, the light of the hearth, to the other, the darkness of night and of the forest.

This arrangement of feminine diversity, this joint management of the estate and of the wife, is so gratifying that nothing would justify a preoccupation with the use of her pleasure and desires.

The field of pleasure, furthermore, extends beyond the conjugal relationship.

In the harangue *Against Neaera*, attributed to Demosthenes,[15] the author formulates a famous aphorism: 'We have courtesans for our pleasure, concubines for the care of our person; wives to have legitimate descendants and a faithful custodian of the home.' Pleasure is thus attributed to the courtesan, but it is exclusively a matter of the man's pleasure, of the pleasure which the woman must procure him, not share with him.

And yet this apparently pacified world in which everyone is prepared to keep their place is disturbed by a feminine pathology, by a disease which strikes the lady of the *oikos*: hysteria. On the one hand, it is attributed to malformations of the womb, on the other hand, to an excess of the feminine desire to reproduce. The appointed cure is coitus, a regulatory act capable of reactivating menses, of fixing the wandering womb, of inducing a harmonizing pregnancy.

The sexual act, then, is prescribed as a *pharmakos* for a sexuality which, by virtue of its hyperbole, escapes the regularization of society.

We see, here, how feminine sexuality hinges on submission, on fear, on constriction, on guilt and on expiation. The site of this conflict is the body; a body not psychologized, not represented, not felt as self-owned, as an image of the self, as harmony between the internal and the external.

It is not because of the inadequacy of diagnostic methods that hysteria, in antiquity, was only an organic illness. It was such because it took place exclusively in the body, in a body which, as we have seen, did not participate in the economy of subjectivity.

In this way, woman in antiquity is like a tamed animal, psychologically different from man because inscribed in another register, in the unpersonalized conjunction of nature and culture. Her status is twofold: elevated social function, and animal sexuality. Economic management avails the first, normative repression and reproductive sexuality the second.

Meanwhile, the free human being, male, adult, protagonist of subjectivity, focuses on (not with woman but in the pederastic relationship) the act of self-mastery through the interior precepts of pleasure.

In erotic relationships with boys, future citizens, inheritors of the government of the city, it was necessary to abstain from those acts which would lead them, through excess and passitivity, into an undignified position. It was necessary, therefore, to carry out a practice of courtship, a moral reflection, a philosophical asceticism which would preserve the subjectivity of the love-object. While the man–woman relationship was regulated by natural attraction, the man–man one had to be administered by an *ars erotica*, that is, enclosed within a game of refusals, of reluctances and of evasions, which tended to delay it as long as possible; but also in a process of exchanges which determined when and under what conditions it was appropriate that it should happen.[16]

Within the art of the deferral of pleasure is fulfilled the economy of sublimation which would gradually allow the sexual relationship to be transformed into a moral relationship: from true love of the object to true love of truth.

The lover becomes a master of thought, the beloved a disciple, in a correspondence which passes through a deciphering of the self, a hermeneutics of desire, an auto-transparency of erotic fantasies.

Nothing of this for the woman, who remains enclosed in a double web; on the one side, residues of astral time inscribe her within the calendar, on the other, the social norms and rites of the city prescribe her functions.

There is no room at all for a dynamics of subjectivity, for the employment of the narcissistic energies which it requires.

There is a contrast, as Freud observes, between love of the object and love of the self.

The woman in antiquity was almost totally inscribed in the register of objectual love, since such is the demand of the maternal function. A succession of pregnancies involves a total expenditure of energy which impoverishes libidinal availability for other investments. Edward Shorter's *A History of Women's Bodies*[17] documents the biological wretchedness of the woman, much heavier to bear than her economic dependence and her social subordination. Her reproductive task imposes itself as a necessity even to the detriment of her very survival. The incidence of death in childbirth certainly did not function to deter other pregnancies.

Thus woman was blindly subjected to the natural and social impositions which joined together in privileging reproduction over her own survival.

In this way, her sexuality which we had seen as conjoined to capture and captivity, is connected, through inscrutable ties, to another will, to a faceless, wordless imposition.

Freud says that femininity is a mystery, but there is one thing which he will not renounce: the coincidence of femininity and passivity.

Passivity assumes different forms: obedience, reception, subordination to that other who is the husband, and to that great, neutral Other which represents man's mastery over nature.

Ancient woman was subject to the symbolic and, as such, she participated in its field of activity, but not as a subject since she lacked the power to take her distance from its impositions.

Just as in Kafka's *Penal Colony*, the law is engraved in her flesh, written on her nerves, but it is not possible for her to decipher it; she follows its command without ever understanding either its letter or its meaning. For this absence of herself to herself, she is excluded from wielding the *logos*. Her voice is pure *phone*, not speech; because speech demands a subject of discourse. Plato is sorry that women cannot sit as fellow guests at the symposium, but he says that if they were invited, they would run away shrieking.[18] Whoever is not a subject in discourse, does not know how to say 'I', cannot even be a subject of desire and of pleasure, as we understand it.

We can think of something similar to this by calling up the impersonality of the *id*, its necessitated libidinal economy.

In the ancient world there existed neither an ethics nor an erotics of the feminine: woman was wholly on the side of need and her excess could, and had to, be managed by containing and penetrating it.

Only with Christianity would the woman be called upon to share the masculine ethics. The mother of the saint would play a determining role in his biography.

With the sanctification of the feminine, finally, the doors of

moral excellence, of self-realization outside her natural reproductive tasks, are opened to her.

Like man, woman would participate in the supernatural, erect
herself above her originary condition: ascesis represents the
manner of her sublimation, the convent is its place. Something
happens with the diffusion of feminine monasticism, there comes
about an event whose historical import is difficult to evaluate. A
large number of young women, for the first time, escape from
the biological cycle of fertility. They keep their vital energy and
their objectual love for themselves.

LOVE IN ITSELF AND FOR THE SELF

In the silence of the cloister, in a time regulated by rules which
are devoid of content, for the first time, woman measured herself
against herself.

To begin with, she escaped from the care of the home, from
the repetition of domestic tasks, from the need to see to everybody's needs.

The institution took on the responsibility for her material needs
like a huge maternal body within which she could be at once
mother and daughter.

Her tasks were limited, not all-encompassing like her domestic
ones.

The time of meditation left her space for herself, the rule of
silence curbed idle chatter and encouraged her to listen to herself.

In the relationship with her love-object, God, woman found
that distance and that closeness which allow the management of
desire, and allow it to be thought of in terms of feeling. The
libidinal saving, provided by chastity, furnished the energies
which are necessary to the process of sublimation. Once removed
from its natural investments, the libido can turn back on itself,
become narcissistic energy. Woman could thus rediscover her
body as a source of desire and of pleasure. The energy which must
be channelled into the form of the self is, however, overflowing,
excessive, difficult to manage within an individual economy.

It is a question of neutralizing a sexuality which is geared to
the species and inscribing it in the narrow confines of the person.
In the dynamics of psychologization, reproductive libido, like a
swollen river, drags with it the debris of its original destination.
Corporeal images, removed from the predetermined process of

instinctual behaviour, torn away from their organic hinge, emerge as drifting psychic content.

The visions of female mystics present us with a luminous image of the instinctual baby, of the child of the female body which precedes every social elaboration, thus revealing the erotic journeys of the body. They show us, incarnated in the divine husband, the great Other which dominates feminine submission, which perpetuates it as an end in itself, independent of any external aim, of any natural necessity.

The great mechanism of social domination loses its presumed natural necessity and reveals to the woman her own profound complicity.

The moment she lost her generative sexuality, she was afraid of being annihilated together with it, no longer existing. She evoked an imaginary scenography with substitutive effects. The nuptials with the divine bridegroom, the ring, the veil, the cutting of the hair which stands for the renunciation of virginity, the stigmata, the hysterical pregnancies, the attacks of convulsions which mime childbirth, are all ways of expressing, within the machinery of acting and games, the impossibility of renouncing reproductive sexuality and the economy of the species.[19] At the same time, though, in the very act of pretending, the body learns to contain excess, and the psyche to manage the sublimated *eros* by expressing it in the symbolic.

In some ways, the disturbances of the body (pains, amnesias, hallucinations, wounds, anorexia, insomnia, anaesthesia) which characterize mystical experiences can be inscribed in the taxonomy of hysteria. Hysteria, this inconstant, polymorphous illness, changes status: from gynaecological disease it becomes psychosomatic anguish.

The term 'psychosomatic' reveals the uncollocability of mystic 'jouissance' which Lacan thinks of in terms of excess, of the *plus-de-jouir*.[20]

Excess in terms of the psyche, excess in terms of the relationship with the object, God, in as much as it evades possession by the mystic, her will to knowledge and to power, throws desire into the desperation of powerlessness.

The incommensurable grandeur of the object, in turn, reverberates on to the subject of love, thus aggrandizing it. The mystics dared to address the pontiff, to give orders to the clergy, to break the enclosure of the convent with frequent journeys, to speak, to write, to be the protagonists of their own lives, to make their mark on history.

It was said that ecstasy made them beautiful, that death caught them in a moment of eternal youth, that pain did not bend them but elevated them.

In reality, what can be observed, for the first time, are the effects of narcissistic investment and of sublimation. The sublimation, however, is still incomplete, either because of a lack or because of excess. The civilization of the female body does not produce that ideal figure of the sage, does not result in that economy of mediateness in which we can recognize the stoic. The very language of the mystics contains something redundant, excessive, difficult to channel into the bounds of codified discourse.

The same is true of their pleasure. On the one hand, it is attained through the body which experiences it, while on the other hand it escapes the power of that body. Ecstasy comprises a coming out of the self, a loss of awareness, a dispersal of the mind which leaves the body at its own mercy.

The process of the individualization of sexuality leaves a residue which cannot be assimilated; the vestige of a remote instinctuality. Therefore, feminine subjectivity is always imperfect, because it has never found a way of experiencing itself as mastery of the self and of the other.

Man's eroticism with other men has created a series of paths by which the libido can project itself and withdraw itself, can simultaneously invest the self and the other in a game of symmetries and of deferments which tends to compensate for the constitutive dissymmetry of every amorous relationship.

Woman, on the contrary, projects on to the love-object an unbounded libido which desires the other, the One, God; a love-object so large that its boundaries and its dimensions are lost. Which is why the woman in love is always a visionary and a madwoman.

There is nothing left for her but to wait, passively, beseechingly, a restitution of her love under the sign of benevolence. Freud notes that the woman is dependent on the love of the other, that she can never really oppose herself to the objects of her first affective investments because she is afraid of losing their favour.

Therefore she remains an eternal child. Elsewhere, however, he says that the 'real woman' is the one who keeps her libido in herself, who encloses herself in the self-sufficient circle of her narcissism, like a cat.

These two figures, the one who bleeds herself dry in loving the object, and the one who encloses it completely in herself, are two extremes; two provocatory images of what is, instead, a complex feminine economy.

Libido is always twofold: on the one hand it belongs to the ego, on the other hand it is tied to the object. Only, for the woman, it is not a question of the same sexual energy. Her natural energy runs through her but is directed towards the production of the object, as such it floods her from everywhere; the sexuality which flows to the ego, feels, in turn, the effects of this originary 'excess' and never closes itself in managing, equally, the love of the self, and the love of the other.

While masculine eroticism has 'politicized' the sexual relation through a form of negotiation of the desires and the pleasures, feminine eroticism remains in the sacred sphere of dominion and of violence.

The theatre of feminine erotic immoderation stretches out in the imaginary, between the psyche and the body. Only in this dimension does the woman feel able to express her fantasies. Social reality constricts her, it continuously disappoints her. Musatti says that every woman hides a Madame Bovary.

Bovaryism is the attempt (analogous to Don Juanism) to transport the code of unconscious desire into reality. While Don Juan wants all women, Emma Bovary wants the one true man. Two forms of immoderation which are born of the impossibility of thinking, in the sense of inscribing it in one's own representation, originary sexuality, not yet regulated by morality and by ethics. Freud writes, in *On Narcissism*, 'the individual does actually carry on a twofold existence: one to serve his own purposes and the other as a link in a chain, which he serves against his will, or at least involuntarily. The individual himself regards sexuality as one of his own ends; whereas, from another point of view, he is an appendage to his germ-plasm, at whose disposal he puts his energies in return for a bonus of pleasure.[21]

Putting one's energies at the disposal of a vital force so indifferent to individual well-being has meant that, for centuries, woman lived under the sign of masochism. Accepting sexuality meant preparing herself for the violence of coitus, for the suffering of pregnancy, for the pains of childbirth, for a premature death.

Now, the withdrawal on to the self of reproductive sexuality, as we have said, drags these elements along with it, and makes feminine narcissism different from masculine narcissism, closer to the death instinct.

If cultural creation is the symbolization of bodily fantasies, then woman's creation will be much more difficult and arduous than man's because her fantasies are more unmanageable and polymorphous.

Hysteria which for centuries has shaken our bodies, in the shape of a gynaecological illness, of mystical seizure, of demonic possession, of magnetic vapours, of neurological spasms, of organ-discourse, seems to have been placated.

The contrast between the two types of sexuality, the specific and the egoistic, has by no means been resolved, it is only that the place in which it is managed has been moved: from the body to the psyche, from the gesture to the imagination.

The new question of the hysteric is not 'What do I want?' but 'Which sex do I belong to?', which erotic economy should correspond to the feminine position?

Exhausted by this conflict which undermines her very identity the new visionary seeks a cultural expression of her fantasies which would introduce order and regulatory laws into the chaos of heterogeneity.

A large part of the imaginative production of recent years (science fiction, video games, horror films) can be read as a dispossession of the feminine imaginary, as a commercialization of her interior objects. In a way, the exploration of the unconscious – mostly feminine – inaugurated by psychoanalysis, has provided new materials to a by now already depleted masculine creativity. Woman speaks unconscious sexuality better than man because she suffers it directly, without the mediation of an erotic deontology.

Let us take a book which we know to be written by a woman, like *Histoire d'O*.[22] It contains more truth about feminine sexuality than many love stories.

First of all, it immediately appears as theatre of the imaginary, as a rewriting of that 'theatre of cruelty' which mocked eighteenth-century knowledge and medical practice on women. In the imaginary, two positions are immediately established.

For a certain time, O. has managed a self-sufficient and inaccessible narcissistic sexuality. She has obtained her pleasure by stealing the libido of the other: her lovers have been driven to ruin and to death.

The attempted suicide of her admirer leads her to the realization that the object which is not affectively invested, which is not recognized as necessary to ourselves, disappears. Sadism, with which she had so cruelly denied herself, is then transformed into its opposite: masochism, through which she offers herself totally. Complete submission to the desire of her lover, René, is, however, just as destructive as her former denial.

While the narcissistic withdrawal of the libido on to the self makes the world disappear, as in psychosis, its total projection on to the object annihilates the ego.

O., as the closed circle of her initial indicates, seeks a pacification of the feminine conflict, a definitive way of managing its impossibilities, a severing of its inextricable knots.

First, she goes out of the place of conflict, abdicates her subjectivity, and every form of organization and of autonomous recognition of herself.

O. does not have an autobiography, a family story, a history.

She leaves a presumedly real situation (her work as a photographer), to enter the dimension of the imaginary.

There, she dematerializes, becomes a phantasm among phantasms. Her body does not have the organization of the organism, it is only an empty shell pervious to every penetration.

This phantasm of the feminine places itself in what it thinks is the place of masculine desire, that of absolute possession, of control without residues.

But this is only what women presume masculine erotic desire to be, a desire to which they give their own economy.

Don Juan does not want all of one woman, but all women. This is O.'s mistake, that which leaves her alone in front of a lover who does not share the desire she attributes to him. Confronted with the vortex of unbounded masochism, the man recognizes, with horror, the incorporating maternal desire, the deadly invitation to fusional unity. The sublime instinctual sacrifice tends to assume the horrific face of the Medusa. The lover, in fact, responds to O.'s offer by backing away from her, by handing her over to others, by sharing her with his friend in a homophilic situation which eludes a total contact with the object.

On O.'s side, there is no eroticism, but only unconscious sexuality, subjection to the impersonal element of the twofold sexual

chain. Her availability has the immoderation of the specific reproductive sexuality, but does not share either its natural or its social
rules: it is a force which is empty of contents and of methods,
mortal rather than vital.

Eroticism, the political art of desire, is solely and completely
masculine. This dis-fusion dichotomizes the nature–culture link.
But we are dealing with a de*cap*itated nature, estranged from its
constitutive rules, which cannot hold the animal woman nor
recognize it. For what is the natural place of sexuality which is
not aimed at reproduction, of an *eros without telos*?

The uncollocable O. gradually comes to situate herself in the
no man's land of perversion, in the dimension in which artifice
attempts to act as a substitute for irreparable loss. But since O.
has lost herself, and has never possessed herself, she has made
her body into a fetish. It is an auto-erotic fetishism where the
body-thing covers the void of a non-existent subjectivity. A body
which is fashioned like a manufactured article (chained, tied, constricted in corsets, knots, strings and collars), becomes a com-
modity fit to be circulated among (masculine) bodies.

O. tries to take the other through her apertures, which are
wide open to ingest, but the other flees from this assimilative
capture.

In refusing O.'s offer of a fusional love of the maternal kind,
René respects the incest taboo, while her desire remains that of
knocking down every fence and every barrier, of living the other's
sexuality without difference, restriction, or deferment: the tomb
of desire.

And yet the feminine imaginary of the reader participates in
O.'s desire.

Like her, the reader invests with desire the flight from freedom,
captivity, the process of domestication and of training. Almost
as though one wished to relive actively what was once suffered
as an external violence. This is a paradox of the unconscious: to
duplicate an evil in memory, in games, in rites, in dreams, to try
out an 'encore' which makes us feel in control of the event rather
than at its mercy.

In this way, traces of past events which are excluded from the
archives of intentional memory are freed; inscribed, though, in
those delirious formations which exercise an extraordinary power
over us. 'They owe their power', writes Freud,[23] 'to the element

of *historical truth* which they have brought up from the repression of the forgotten and primeval past.'

In conclusion, what, then, is the fragment of truth embedded in the delirious sexual events which happen to O.?

First of all, the irreconcileability of the love of the self and of the object, of the libido geared towards self-preservation and the one aimed at reproduction, of the imaginary and the symbolic. A constellation of incompatibilities which demonstrates how feminine subjectivity, that is, the attempt to keep such antinomies unified in a self, is configured as the site of a permanent conflict.

On the other hand (and here an apparently immoral book is revealed to be moralistic), it shows how every attempt to appease the contradictions within the omnipotent logic of the imaginary is doomed to failure.

The events in O.'s story can be read as the reluctantly projected images of the history of her subjection. Her desperate submission to the Law (because the desire which is managed by males is presented as such) unravels the bonds which used to fascinate her. Every ethical, social, or natural justification fails, and domination is revealed in all its violent arbitrariness.

It is thus a journey of revelation which, however, is never transformed into an experience of liberation. Recognition of the law must, in fact, be accompanied by an ability to take one's distance, to subtract and to disavow. Otherwise the fatal machine will kill in its vice-like grip.

O., who does not want to live the conflict between submission and freedom, between obedience and insubordination, who severs all the links which articulate the imaginary in the web of the symbolic, far from finding herself, loses herself.

Transformed into that enticing strumpet★ which Xenophon so feared, without either social status or biological function, she is dragged, nude and masked, to a nocturnal orgy.

The myth, often called upon by feminists, of being themselves, of following the immediacy of desire, of seeking a natural authenticity, is, here, mocked in the most cruel way.

There is, in fact, no authenticity, no naturalness, no earthly paradise, for the female human being, torn, from time immemorial, from herself.

There is only management of the conflict, administration of

★ The Italian word *civetta* means both 'strumpet/flirt' and 'owl'. [Translator's note] the impossibilities, accounts of the over-determinations, the practice of those few degrees of freedom stolen, little by little, from a biological and social destiny.

To reconstruct our history is an indispensable but dangerous project because it places us in front of the masculine symbolic, in front of its apparent neutrality, impersonality and necessity; or even in front of our fantasies, marked by submission, or by our desire, offered, from time immemorial, to the desire of the other.

We need a great collective project, an achieved social subjectivity, to cross through all this without getting lost, to construct, as Bion paradoxically says, *a memory of the future*.

NOTES

This paper was first presented at a seminar on the female erotic imaginary, organized by the Centro Documentazione Donna and the Libreria delle Donne di Firenze, Florence, 27–8 October 1984.

1 Michel Foucault, *Histoire de la sexualité*: vol. 2, *L'Usage des plaisirs*, Paris, Gallimard, 1984, translated into English as *The Uses of Pleasure*, tr. Robert Hurley, Harmondsworth, Viking Penguin, 1986; vol. 3, *Le Souci de soi*, Paris, Gallimard, 1984, translated into English as *The Care of the Self*, tr. Robert Hurley, Harmondsworth, Viking Penguin, 1988. These two volumes follow vol. 1, *La Volonté de savoir*, Paris, Gallimard, 1976, translated into English as *The History of Sexuality: an Introduction*, tr. Robert Hurley, Harmondsworth, Penguin, 1981.

2 In Italy, this renewal of studies on the history of culture has produced many interesting works; e.g. S. Campese, *La donne e i filosofi, archeologia di una immagine culturale*, Bologna, Zanichelli, 1978; E. Cantarella, *L'ambiguo malanno*, Rome, Editori Riuniti, 1981; S. Campese and S. Gastaldi, *Madre Materia, sociologia e biologia della donna greca*, Turin, Boringhieri, 1983; and see 'Nuove Antichità', special issue of *Aut-Aut*, July–October 1981.

3 Foucault, *The Uses of Pleasure*, op. cit.

4 S. Freud, *Civilization and its Discontents*, in *The Standard Edition of the Complete Psychological Works of Sigmund Freud*, 24 vols, ed. James Strachey, London, Hogarth Press, 1953–73, vol. 21, p. 104.

5 S. Freud, *Femininity*, in *The Standard Edition*, op. cit., vol. 22, pp. 129, 134.

6 Aristotle, *Politics*, 1, 5–9; see the 'Everyman' edn, London, Dent, 1912.

7 Plato, *Timaeus*, 91; see the Penguin edn, Harmondsworth, 1971.

8 S. Freud, *A Difficulty in the Path of Psychoanalysis*, in *The Standard Edition*, op. cit., vol. 17, pp. 140–1.

9 D. Symons, *The Evolution of Human Sexuality*, New York, Oxford University Press, 1979.

10 F. Basaglia Ongaro, 'Donna', in the *Enciclopedia Einaudi*, Turin, Einaudi, 1978, vol. 5, p. 75. See also F. Basaglia Ongaro, *Una voce. Riflessioni sulla donna*, Milan, Il Saggiatore, 1982.

11 G. Swain, 'L'âme, la femme, le sexe, et le corps', *Débat*, 24 March 1983.

12 S. Vegetti Finzi, 'La maternità negata. Alle origini dell'immaginario femminile', *Memoria*, 1981, no. 7, p. 45.

13 See M. Vegetti, *Il coltello e lo stilo, animali, schiavi, barbari, donne, alle origini della razionalità greca*, Milan, Il Saggiatore, 1979.

14 See Foucault, 'The wisdom of marriage', in *The Uses of Pleasure*, op. cit., part 3.

15 Demosthenes, *Against Neaera*, 122; cited in Foucault, *The Uses of Pleasure*, op. cit.

16 Foucault, *The Uses of Pleasure*, op. cit.

17 E. Shorter, *A History of Women's Bodies*, Harmondsworth, Penguin, 1984 (1982).

18 Plato, *Laws*, VI, 781 C–D; see the 'Everyman' edn, London, Dent, 1960.

19 B. Craveri, *Sante e streghe. Biografie e documenti del XVI e XVII sec.*, Milan, Feltrinelli, 1980; St Teresa of Avila, *Il libro delle relazioni e delle grazie*, Palermo, Sellerio, 1983; St Teresa of Avila, *Vita*, Milan, Rizzoli, 1962; see the English-language edn of her works, 3 vols, tr. E. A. Peers, London, 1963; R. Rossi, *Teresa d'Avila*, Rome, Editori Riuniti, 1983; J. C. Schmit, *Mort d'une hérésie*, Paris, Mauton, 1978; J. Michelet, *La Sorcière*, Paris, 1867, translated into English as *Satanism and Witchcraft*, tr. A. R. Allison, New York, Citadel Press, 1939; E. Macola, 'Il godimento mistico', *Freudiana*, 1982, no. 1, p. 19.

20 J. Lacan, *Encore: Le Seminaire XX, 1972–3*, Paris, Seuil, 1975.

21 S. Freud, *On Narcissism: an Introduction*, in *The Standard Edition*, op. cit., vol. 14, 1957, p. 78.

22 P. Reage, *Histoire d'O*, new edn ed. J. J. Pauvert, Paris, Hachette, 1954–72.

23 S. Freud, *Constructions in Analysis*, in *The Standard Edition*, op. cit., vol. 11, p. 269.

Part III

History

Chapter 9

Premiss: a figure of power and an invitation to history
Epilogue: to room nineteen*

Gianna Pomata

PREMISS

From the text of the abortion bill passed in the Chamber of Deputies on 21 January 1977:

> The doctor, having listened to the woman, carries out according to his conscience and his science the health checks that he thinks necessary, having respect for the dignity and freedom of the woman.[1]

Dignity and freedom on the one hand; conscience and science on the other. A moral aura shrouds the female figure while the rational competence is centred on the role which, for the past few centuries, has been referred to only in masculine terms.

The relationship between doctor and woman is defined as an interaction between a minor to be protected and a competent person in charge. It is a game of rights and duties, at first sight: the right to ask for control over one's own body, where one's 'physical or mental health' may be at stake; the duty to ensure that this control takes place in conformity with a body of knowledge which is recognized to be objectively sound and technically efficacious. The association of the doctor's science and conscience, which is both obvious and revealing, tells us that it is in fact a relationship of protection. Incorporated into an institutional role, science and conscience are put at the service of those who have, one presumes, neither the one nor the other and are therefore

* First published as 'Premessa: una figura del potere e un invito alla storia', in *In scienza e coscienza. Donne e potere nella società borghese*, Quaderni aut-aut series, Florence, La Nuova Italia, 1979. Translated by Judith Kelly.

supposed, if not to obey passively, to comply with its rational equivalent, that is, persuasion.

The asymmetry between the two figures formulated in the text of the bill is obvious, that is, between the woman to be protected in her 'dignity and freedom' and the benevolent male figure who stoops down to her service. In this asymmetry there is a hidden power: the decision, formally left to the woman, is in short ascribed to the one who has the competence not only actually to put this decision into effect but, above all, to make it possible.

Abortion is in fact determined exclusively by the field of medicine, even before it has been decided upon. This occurs not simply when, as in Italy, grounds of health are the only ones legally permitted, and not simply because only the co-operation of the doctor can put the woman's decision into effect; but above all because, in general, abortion is assumed from the start to be a medical matter. Knowledge of the body and protection of life do not lie within the competence of actual individuals, except in a minor and dependent way, but rather with the anonymous subjectivity of scientific knowledge and with the officials who symbolize this. The request for an abortion has to be screened medically because it is by definition understood from the start only according to medical criteria.

It is not the power to decide, to impose his own will, which the law gives to the doctor; however, the power is such that it reduces the power of decision attributed to the woman to an empty parcel. It is the power which a guardian has over a minor, thinly veiled by a contrivance of duties and rights: it is true that the guardian has only duties, the minor has all the rights; but who defines the rights of the minor, who defines the danger from which she must be protected and the 'good' which she must be guaranteed? The guardian knows what is 'good' for the minor and has the know-how to carry it out. The power of protection is based on the ability to ensure for the minor the right to a 'good' which is determined and defined by the guardian himself: in our case 'the physical and mental health' related to the 'social value of motherhood'. So the doctor's power is that of defining the area of realities and values within which the woman's rights can be considered, even before they can be exercised. It is a power which is inextricably intertwined with knowledge, a knowledge publicly recognized as valid, and at the defence of a moral and social order which both recognizes itself in and expresses itself through this knowledge. It is a power which is both science and conscience, objective knowledge and moral vigilance. It is a conjunction of power and knowledge – which can be termed 'power-knowledge'.

Compared to the nominal right to decide attributed to the woman, this is a power which has behind it the massive support of institutionalized knowledge; compared to every female 'body' and 'psyche', this is the power of defining them and ensuring their 'health'; compared to the poverty and frailty of lives, this is a power which the law delegates as that 'protection of human life' that the bourgeois state undertakes as its own positive task, with a will of total management for its own ends.

This 'power-knowledge' is surrounded by a halo of moral authority; in the features of this power which is both science and conscience, science and conscience blend together.

We are used to thinking that women's status as minors in this society has been mainly determined by moral institutions which are in decline, by a transitory form of conscience, i.e. bourgeois morality. Moreover, we have always thought that the conscience of this class was a different thing from its science; the former being repressive and ideological, while the latter is positive and rational. Now we find science and conscience intertwined in the figure of power which keeps women under protection. In this duty to protect, in this right to be protected, is there a vestige of paternalism? And yet, paradoxically, this patriarchal vestige intertwines with the more rational, more modern figure of authority: the doctor who regulates and protects human life on the basis of scientific knowledge of nature.

We have also thought that the women's movement may have been and may still be essentially a movement to claim rights: previously a right to the vote and to education; now to the control of our own bodies. We used to think that the acquisition of a right meant the acquisition of power, a step forward as regards a power characterized fundamentally as that which forbids and represses. Now we find ourselves facing a figure of authority which certainly forbids or permits, but is not characterized so much by these negative actions as by the positiveness and the range of its radius of action. Not an intermittent authority, like that which steps in to prohibit or to allow; but an authority which would like to be the tireless conscience, the unceasingly vigilant gaze which never lets go its hold on reality. Authority is here first of all a power which knows; which defines reality; which separates it into normal and pathological; which produces a reality fitting its own definitions. Knowledge here is not contemplative, a passive description of empirical reality, but an active intervention, the construction of models to superimpose on reality, so that one can anticipate its moves and control it.

It is often said that the women's movement is above all a movement of revolt against patriarchal order. In this sense, the women's movement would be the last offshoot of the bourgeois struggle against absolutism, the final emancipation. Woman would be the last 'minor' to achieve the maturity prescribed by the Enlightenment as the goal of human development.

It is as though the main figure of authority were the paternal and its basic form of exercise were despotic will. We have been so fascinated by the bourgeoisie beheading their king that we have not noticed the figures with which bourgeois order has surrounded us, the doctor and the teacher, the scientist and the judge, figures which fill the void left by the beheaded king, or by the dispossessed capitalist, in the name of an authority legitimized as being rationally indisputable. Not that the beheading of kings or the dispossession of dispossessors are at an end, far from it. But perhaps we have been too busy deposing our small domestic tyrants and eliminating private property as the root of every form of oppression to notice the multiform and elusive nature of bourgeois power.

This applies especially to women. Their 'minority' is not simply the vestige of a patriarchal society which preceded the capitalist order, and which the progressive logic imprinted by the bourgeoisie on the course of history would deprive of any reason to exist. If there is something that the bourgeoisie has innovatively created, something which did not exist before it, it is not just its proletarian antagonist but also a crowd of beings marked by a new specificness, the woman and the criminal, the child and the madman. Beings identified by medical and biological norms, even before moral and social ones; redefined and, in a certain sense, re-created, beginning from a scientific definition which imprisons them. Perhaps the realities which seem to us part of the solid foundation on which the order of the world rests are only the concretion, which at first sight seems solid but is in fact brittle, of a recent onward flow of history. What is more solid, at first sight, than the reality of 'woman' with its correlated ideas, the 'woman question', 'women's condition', 'women's oppression'? It seems to weigh heavily on a good part of history, and to begin to free itself only with the Age of Enlightenment. But is it not perhaps the opposite? Perhaps woman has become a 'question' only when, under the spotlight of practical reality, women were focalized as a distinct object, and therefore as a new and specific object.

This cultural product of the bourgeoisie, 'woman', took action at every tremor in social stability, appeared at every cracking in the crust of bourgeois order, and away from the bright glare of revolutions has got on with her unceasing, unrecognized and intense activity which is that of a lower and subordinate culture.

That which is usually called feminism is in fact a very strange movement. At first sight, it is easy to catalogue it. It has been considered, for example, the fringe which attaches itself to the progressive movement of the time: to Enlightenment and to Jacobinism, to liberalism and to utopian socialism, to Marxism and to recent student anarchism. The presence of women – it has classically been said – is the sign which attests the 'maturity' of 'every historical innovatory movement'.[2] So it is said once again that feminism is linked to 'the great thrusts and democratic struggles which constitute the basic plot of contemporary history'.[3]

Indeed, apparently, feminism itself has believed, from time to time, that it is a democratic battle for political and civil rights, a secondary front in the class struggle and, above all, the extreme expression of a deep-founded mistrust of the area of the 'private': the area that the bourgeoisie had originally created as its own specific sphere, defining it – be it the market or the family – as a space free of power, and indeed to be protected against its possible interference. The classic manoeuvre of the opposition to the bourgeoisie has been the 'politicization' of ever wider areas of this 'private' sphere. The class struggle had 'politicized' the market and the sphere of production; feminism, it is said, has 'politicized' daily life, the worlds of emotion and sexuality. If at one time the 'despotic power' of capital over labour was revealed as being the cornerstone of bourgeois democracy, today it is revealed that the personal is political, and what is private, rather than being separate from that which is public, is produced and controlled by it.

But we are trying to understand the meaning of the feminist metaphor, 'the personal is political'. The classic opposition to bourgeois power used to take at its word the declaration of the bourgeoisie that it had no part in public power, and tried, consequently, to turn this neutral power against the bourgeoisie itself. For this opposition, the 'politicization' of new areas, their opening up to political debate and to public surveillance, used invariably to be seen as a positive step, as a setback for that partial power, the bourgeois power, hidden in the anarchy of the 'private'. But the feminist reuniting of public and private, its 'politicization' of the personal, has another meaning. 'Politicization' here is not understood as a positive programme, to be carried out, but simply as the discovery of an already existing link, a link not to foster but, if anything, to denounce.

What in fact makes the metaphorical expression of sex as 'politics' click? An analogy. In the world of sex one again finds the aspect of domination, of organized violence, of power ritual, which characterizes the world of politics, as an area of oppression and dispute. Thus a relationship of similarity between politics and sex comes to light, a relationship of affinity between 'public' and 'private'.[4]

Metaphors often betray these secret blood-relationships, these unconfessed family likenesses between things, and they indicate hidden and unorthodox links. The feminist metaphor of political sex reveals the relationship between two worlds on the surface so far apart: the world of sex as basic instinct, natural, wild energy, and the world of politics as reasoning, planning, rational decision.

It is difficult to say on what the suspicion of their relationship is based, against the apparent diversity of the two terms. Perhaps it is the suspicion of a common origin, the suspicion that sex as basic instinct may be the child of a power which in the public dimension takes on the aspect of rational planning. It is a suspicion which moves us to address a new question to the history of this power and of women. But one can draw an immediate conclusion from the feminist metaphor: it does not imply that the personal, or the sexual, is an area to 'politicize' but is a political area from the very beginning. It does not imply that politics is rational control of a wild anarchy but is a field of action for power, an area in which the effects of power are recorded.[5]

But then, for feminism, turning public power against the relationships of force which exist in the private sphere is an impossible hope, if between them there is complicity, continuity and homology. For feminism, there is no opposition but rather similarity and bonds between that which appears in private as vestigial authoritarianism, a survival of patriarchal power, and that which asserts itself in the public sphere as growing rationality. The history of the assertion of this public power, with its regulatory and rationalizing ability compared to private anarchy, with its modernizing presence on the ruins of the 'traditional' world, appears from the feminist viewpoint as the history of a power which is ever more articulate and effective in its ability to discipline, to impose order and civilization on undisciplined and barbarous populations, among whom – the very symbol of decay, of obscurity – are women.

From the feminist point of view, the progressive vision of history, with its linear and positive image of the great processes of 'industrialization' and 'modernization', is not convincing: it is almost, I would say, impossible to perceive. Under our eyes, this image dims and grows confused; from the clear-cut ouline of a process of unquestionable positiveness with well-known contours, it becomes the incomplete and disconcerting vision of a process which for us is most unclear. We know nothing, or very little, of the meaning which it had for women; of the part, passive and active, which women have played in it. From this point of view, evidently, the assertion – apparently so innocuous, in its banality – of a connection between feminism, the condition of women and historical progress can be deceptive. It implies in fact that female liberation may have been the by-product of a necessary social evolution and that the coming to power of the bourgeoisie may have marked for women, if not an actual improvement, at least the premiss for an improvement. The shackles of the pre-capitalist world, continues this thesis, were more oppressive for women than for men; but inescapable and substantially linear like the development of the productive forces, the recognition of women as being free individuals, free contracting parties in the democratic society of the social contract, would come about. Progressive against its will, introducing women into the sphere of production, the bourgeoisie – one concludes – cannot cease to carry forward the development of the productive forces.

A variation of this story explains the delays and the reluctance with which the bourgeoisie carries out its progressive task. After the bourgeoisie seizes power, its point of view ceases to coincide with the universal interest in progress. Only the corrective mechanism of class struggle will then spur on a class forced to repudiate its own ideals, in order to defend its own power. Only a new class, which in its turn is the bearer of the general interest in liberation, in the development and the conquest of nature, can summon up, against the bourgeoisie, its very legacy and, with the elimination of class divisions, can resolve the 'woman question' rejoining the two sexes in a sole working individual, the disciplined and responsible person of planned socialism.

The two stories clearly have a lot in common: both presuppose, in the first place, that the shift from the pre-industrial world to capitalism marks for women, if not an immediate improvement in their condition, the very basis of any possible improvement. Both also presume that women have been introduced into productive activity through the industrial revolution and that their traditional activities were confined to the domestic space. Lastly, both see the reproductive activity as a natural function, defined in biological terms, and therefore as a necessary, non-eliminable, decisive factor of woman's role in any society.

All these premisses are wrong and misleading and must be abandoned. They refer to a conceptual framework dominated by evolutionism and functionalist determinism. Up to now the history of women has been seen through this opaque screen. A legacy of the nineteenth century, which is still as noticeable in Marxism as in the functionalism of the social sciences, this interpretative grid projects into the past that which is perhaps the product of recent history: the detailed description of a general condition of women through a 'biological function', the definition of the reproductive activity as a 'bio-social role'.

It is no accident that feminism itself has more often been theorized in an anthropological-biological key than a historical one. On it this evil legacy also lies – it also turned to biology rather than to history in order to account for female subjection. But, from the nineteenth century to the present day, women's inferiority and specificness have been codified in the very framework of biological evolutionism and on the basis of presumed constant factors which are anthropological in nature. In this framework, history has served simply to provide data which can be pigeonholed in a matrix which has been set out beforehand. Anthropology certainly does not immediately mean biological reductionism, but it implies none the less a framework of discourse which favours general scientific hypotheses rather than a comparison with that fluidity lacking fixed values, which is the very field of history. So feminism has fallen into the temptation of rewriting the general theory of human evolution[6] from its own point of view, and of turning to history only to revive matriarchy and witchcraft by way of counter-myths. But to rewrite the history of evolution as her-story, to talk of a thousand-year-old oppression rooted in biology, means remaining inside the scientific practice which has invented woman, which has claimed to discover in nature a species defined, in is historic destiny, by its physiological characteristics. It means to believe that this scientific construct, the 'femina biologica', this being, 'homo oeconomicus', which is just as abstract, may have always existed and may be retraced in history, if one wants to.

Perhaps, it is necessary to be nominalist and to voice aloud the suspicion that 'woman' does not exist, that it is a name given to the solid appearance whose consistency we would like to test by giving it a good shake; a name given to a host of stories that we would like to free from a forced cohabitation; or to a closed space whose boundary line we would like to blur; or to a net whose knots we slide between our fingers asking ourselves when and how were they knotted, and thinking: then it is possible to undo them.

So to address history could mean to see with one's own eyes that 'woman' does not exist, except in the extent to which a historically defined form of power, that which we have called 'power-knowledge', has invented and built her. But it also means to discover instead that women have existed and that they have left a mark. Women were present while 'woman' was being created, and their activity, their way of understanding themselves and their experience, has interacted with power in complex and sometimes unpredictable ways, whose complete richness must be retraced.

But we will not go in search of the women who have taken part in the various progressive movements of European history; we will not measure the female groups who little by little formed part of the historical vanguard of the moment; we will not even try to write a unitary history of the women's movement that, as has already been done for the history of the working class, becomes part of a progressive pattern of a thrust ahead, of civilization. At least for women it is legitimate to mistrust a history which systematically uses and abuses the concept of a vanguard. A poet who was an expert on metaphors has written that the concept of a vanguard is military and male, it is a 'macho metaphor'.[7] If women's history has a function, it is that of insistently reproposing the dissatisfaction that we have felt for some time with the whig version of history, the history that searches for and sees in the past the very anticipations, the vanguards, of that which it has overcome and today controls.[8]

Women's history could have a twofold critical significance. In the first place it forcefully reproposes that the great reforms of the age of the bourgeoisie, the spread of the 'enlightenment', the development of the sciences and of medicine and their entry into popular culture, must not be seen only as a positive process of improvement of the means of life. Women's history exposes the ambiguous aspects of this process, its character of introducing discipline and control, the closing off of spaces of popular and female autonomy.

Besides, women's history can serve to reconsider the concepts through which we understand industrialism and capitalism. These concepts are usually based on the contrast between 'traditional' elements and 'modern', innovative elements; they can be brought up again for a discussion by comparison with women's history, where the distinction between traditional and modern is confused and problematic. What is traditional and what is modern about women's condition? What is an anachronistic survival and what is a recent institution in the structure of their subjection?

With respect to women, power certainly has a paradoxical and disconcerting character: it at times appears as an archaic survival and at times as pure rationality. The history of feminism, correspondingly, typically appears as the problematic research of the adversary, the pursuit of an imaginary, multiform and elusive power, which from the transparency of the political struggle withdraws ever further into the obscurity and indisputability of natural law. Characteristic of feminism is the necessity of identifying power on many levels, the awareness that, beyond the explicit law which one must confront, other laws and other adversaries remain to be discovered and defeated.

Feminism and this enigmatic power are linked. A separate female movement, perhaps, is typical of the bourgeois world just as the notion of womanliness as a specific nature and as an isolatable type is typical of the bourgeois world. If the proletariat is as old as bourgeois power on the means of production, the social category 'woman' is born perhaps together with another form of power, a power of definition and of control based upon scientific knowledge, a 'power-knowledge'.

If we try to reconstruct the process through which 'power-knowledge' has asserted itself, intertwining with other forms of social power, we find that, with it, 'woman' as a sexually defined social type is gradually formed; that is, the category through which science and conscience are able to put women under guardianship.

EPILOGUE

There is a short story by Doris Lessing, 'To room nineteen'. It is the story of a married woman who has made a 'good marriage', a successful marriage, who has a nice house and lovely children, and who begins little by little to withdraw from all this, while realizing that she is the living nucleus of it, its support structure; while realizing that she cannot cease to exist even for an instant, because it will fall to pieces around her. So she begins to withdraw, under this imperceptible but constant pressure, and once a week she goes to sit for a few hours in a hotel room, where she finds relief because the pressure is suspended and once more she has time all to herself, a blank space which is not cut into by anything, by any duties or demands, and she enjoys the freedom of not having to prop up even a particle of the world.

It is difficult to understand from what form of oppression the woman in room nineteen is seeking relief. Never has authority been so invisible or, if it has shown its face, never has that face been so ordinary and innocuous, so capable of fitting perfectly, like a mask, to our own face, of blending with our own identity. An attempt to distance ourself from authority, to express our difference as compared to its definitions, can begin with the inability to sustain this daily mask, with the search for a place where we can let it fall, where we can be another person or, simply, be ourselves.

Anyone who has experienced the relief that even a temporary and uncertain refuge can afford, with regard to the pressure of a life which drains; the delights of any rest from a life in which rest is not allowed, because it is not defined as work but as pleasure, knows how precious is this asylum, where one can eat, sleep and sit down without being asked to maintain a role. Room nineteen is the anguished projection of women's old desire, 'a room of one's own',[9] a place of freedom, rest, sincerity, and where we can take stock of ourselves.

To ask for a room of one's own – we have been told[10] – is indeed the expression of a wish, but it is also a demand for control. In fact it is simply the demand for a place of rest and repose, an area in which to recover one's strength, a spot from which to view the world freely and clearly and once more to find purity in it, by means of our senses. A room of one's own, for women, is a reserve of moral and intellectual energy, the basis of their intellectual independence and their self-respect, as it also is of their personal relish for life.

To ask for it is not to ask for a form of control. A room of one's own is instead the desire of someone who does not wish to control anything, not even their own identity: of someone indeed who does not want to have a fixed and defined identity. To have a room of one's own is to ensure oneself the possibility of movement, of metamorphosis. To ask for it means to try on one's own behalf to give life a margin of manoeuvre and unpredictability; it does not mean to ask power, yet again, for the concession of a right or of an official space.

If the new women's movement distinguishes itself from that of the suffragettes, it is precisely because it no longer thinks that power has denied rights to women or has closed spaces off to them. Rather we think that power has defined and built 'woman' and has created and assigned a specific space for her. We have tried to identify the site of this internment. But the space of internment is not our room, just as we are not 'woman' as defined by power.

Among the problems of the new feminism there is also the need to identify and, indeed, to create and sustain difference between 'woman' and women, between the artificial objects constructed by authority and real experiences, between life as defined by biology, for example, and the positive multiplicity of lives. In the watchwords for reclaiming ownership of our bodies, of sexual happiness, of life, the awareness is implicit that neither the body, nor happiness, nor the life that we ask for are those defined by power, but rather a body, happiness and life which elude its definitions. Today we have not only irreverence but also scepticism towards the power of science and conscience, the power which affirms its own reality and its own standards of judgement as the only possible. We are sceptical of its definition of reality, because we can see differences which it is unable to see: the difference between the life which it claims to safeguard, for example, and that which we understand as life. We are sceptical of the image of itself which power projects when it establishes its power to protect life. Rather, we see in this protection a threat to our lives, an attempt to define and administer their pleasure and fertility. And we are even more sceptical, but, above all, irreverent towards that professional conscience which, on the request for abortion, is responsible for protecting our 'dignity and freedom'. We know that, precisely because of their professional impartiality, the doctors assure the functionality of abortion to the present system of family and sexual norms; that abortion is allowed in defence of these norms and not in defence of women.

In denying deference and consent to power-knowledge we also advance a different perception of reality. The natural place for the women's struggle seems today to be alongside movements which impede and limit the scientific definition and direction of life, which try to kindle the sense of the unalterable complexity of what would be restored to order and uniformity.

The past, this place of difference, is precious to us precisely because of this; because it is the place from which we originate and which, on returning to it, we always discover to be incomparably richer than the image of it which we have treasured. It is a tangle of many threads of which we have been able to unite only a few; it is a place of possibilities, which, when rediscovered, even if very gradually, proves to be more varied and more spacious than our own imagination and thus reveals the limits not only of our own definitions, but also of power's. Going back to the past, trying to perceive its difference, we broaden our world and our space. The past too is our room, shifting and open, full of windows, from which we can view unexpected, changeable landscapes.

Searching in the past for what women used to say and do, for what has crushed them and for what they, in their turn, have moulded and expressed, what they were afraid of or loved, we can perceive not the fixed identity of 'woman' but the multifaceted nature of this identity, and the impossibility of reporting her as a single concept or a single history. But to do this we must also change some frameworks of importance in our way of looking at history. Above all, we must perhaps reacquire the sense of and the liking for the individual, against the predominant importance which we usually grant to social structures and institutions. The variable and multiple richness of women's identity is particularly contained in their experience of life, and one finds it more in the course of individual lives than in the vague corps of movements, classes, or institutions.

From the individual we can certainly learn something even about large movements.[11] But, above all, individual history can give us material for reflection and imagination which enters straight into our life. The history of the individual does not mean the history of the unrepeatable, of that which, because it is unique, cannot be reproduced in our experience and can therefore tell us nothing. If biography is perhaps, traditionally, a genre which mainly accentuates an experience which is specific and unrepeatable, there is another traditional genre which plays instead on another aspect of individuals, their exemplariness. This genre is the story. A story captures our attention precisely because, although telling of a single and unrepeatable happening, it opens it up, so to speak, for the listener, asserting above all the exemplary character of the story, its value as advice and instruction, of the widening of the boundaries of experience of those listening to it. The story of the individual is an instructive story. By means of the story we learn to compare our experience to that of others, we learn, therefore, in the ordinary, everyday sense of the word.

It is mainly because of this that, without believing in 'woman', it is worth telling women's history: to learn from this, as from a story, possible styles of life and experience, to imagine other identities and to forget the one which power has imposed upon us.

Detachment from the identity imposed by power, the unease which leads to room nineteen, has at first sight the inarticulate nature of an escape into silence, of a self-destruction which leaves no messages behind. As if that of 'woman' were the only possible identity. It is true, woman's self-destruction is carried out under the sign of a deep distrust towards words. But it also creates words which, in the fragile perfection with which they depict the changing situation in which we find ourselves, tell a truth and deserve to remain.

I do not trust the spirit. It escapes like steam
In dreams, through mouth-hole or eye-hole. I can't stop it.
One day it won't come back. Things aren't like that.
They stay, their little particular lustres
Warmed by much handling. They almost purr.
When the soles of my feet grow cold,
The blue eye of my turquoise will comfort me.
Let me have my copper cooking pots, let my rouge pots
Bloom about me like night flowers, with a good smell.
They will roll me up in bandages, they will store my heart
Under my feet in a neat parcel.
I shall hardly know myself. It will be dark,
And the shine of these small things sweeter than the face of
    Ishtar.[12]

These 'last words' of Sylvia Plath express not only the contemplation of her own death but also a hidden desire for survival and metamorphosis.

NOTES

1 Article 3, subsection 2 of the bill, as reported in the Italian daily press.
2 Antonio Gramsci, *Il Risorgimento*, Turin, Einaudi, 1966 (1949), p. 169.
3 E. Santarelli, 'Il cammino delle donne verso l'uguaglianza', *Rinascita*, February 1961, vol. 18, no. 2, p. 329.
4 Kate Millett, *Sexual Politics*, London, Hart-Davis, 1969.
5 On politics in this sense see Michel Foucault, *Surveiller et punir*, Paris, Gallimard, 1975.
6 For example, S. Firestone, *The Dialectic of Sex: the Case for Feminist Revolution*, London, Cape, 1971.
7 Charles Baudelaire, 'Mon coeur mis à nu', in *Oeuvres posthumes et correspondances inédites*, Paris, Quantin, 1887.
8 For a review of whig history in another context, see R. M. Young, 'The historiographic and ideological contexts of the nineteenth-century debate on man's place in nature', in M. Teich and R. Young (eds), *Changing Perspectives in the History of Science*, London, Heinemann, 1973.
9 Virginia Woolf, *A Room of One's Own*, London, Hogarth Press, 1929.
10 By Gilles Deleuze in his postface to J. Donzelot, *La Police des familles*, Paris, Editions de Minuit, 1977, p. 220.
11 On the return to the individual in history see R.C. Cobb, *Reactions to the French Revolution*, Oxford, Oxford University Press, 1972, p. 117. An exemplary historiographic use of the individual is that of Carlo Ginzburg, *Il formaggio e i vermi. Il cosmo di un mugnaio del '500*, Turin, Einaudi, 1976.
12 Sylvia Plath, 'Last words', in *Crossing the Water*, London, Faber, 1971.

Chapter 10

On 'mothers' and 'sisters'
Fragments on women/feminism/ historiography*

Annarita Buttafuoco

Je m'interroge sur l'énigmatique relation que j'entretiens avec la société présente et avec la mort, par la médiation d'activités techniques.

(Michel de Certeau)

I have chosen the phrase of a male historian, arbitrarily taken from the context of weighty pages, to open my 'fragments', because it seems to me that it summarizes the problems on which it would be necessary to dwell for a slightly more thorough analysis of our relationship with historical knowledge than any that has been done up to now. If my choice appears provocative then I have hit the mark, in the sense of having made clear right from the beginning the critical opinion which guides my studies and which comes from the conclusion which I have reached by reading the works produced by feminist historians (myself included, of course). That is, that the theoretical reference points which we still have are those drawn up by male historians.

This is a simple observation and in itself the fact does not 'shock' me; rather I am worried that, in denying it (as one generally tends to do in the name of an originality which is more proclaimed than substantial, at least at the present state of our thought and production), we continue to avoid a strict and accurate analysis of the 'debts' contracted with male knowledge. Basically, I am worried for two reasons: on the one hand because I think that the attitude of denial of such debts reveals an implicit fear of not having in one's hands adequate counterweights to put on the scale; on the other hand (but in fact this follows on from

* First published as 'Di "madri" e di "sorelle" . . . Frammenti su donne/femminismo/storiografia', in *Nuova DWF*, no. 15, 1980. Translated by Judith Kelly.

the former) because by doing so we impoverish or deny the full value of our theoretical-political intuitions which are on the contrary a resource to develop and put to good use.

In the face of male historiography – which in the meanwhile is maturing and evolving thanks in part to our own critical presence – we do not start out with an attitude of equality, of mature awareness of the reciprocal contributions that we would be able to exchange, but rather yet again with an attitude which seems to me to be one of substantial subordinacy and which finishes by blocking our capacity for independent analysis.

Nevertheless, I do not claim (although I confess that I would like to be able to do it) that here I am setting off to calmly construct an on-a-par association – loyal, reciprocal, positively critical – between the already numerous crowd of feminist historians and the army of male historians. All the more so since, obviously, neither the one group nor the other is reducible to compact, homogeneous line-ups, without internal differentiations. Actually, I think such a 'pacification', even if it were possible, might mean that we would be reduced to silence with the small reward of a general amplification of history with the 'compensatory' introduction of women. Personally I still prefer the heated debate, given that, as I mentioned, it is becoming more aware and mature. I prefer coming to a standstill, braking or even skidding, to the peaceful journey on the main road that others could mark out for me, in order to . . . 'take me home'.

With these comments I would like to try to delineate briefly the issues which in my opinion would need to be reconsidered by us, without any claim to exhaust them all or to give strict instructions.

Following the outline that I have chosen, Michel de Certeau's phrase,[1] the first problem which I find myself facing is that of the relationship that historians engage in, between the actual society in which they *live*, and *death*. The relationship of human beings with the past is marked by two extreme features which the historian has the task of putting together by setting in motion the memory process; thus restoring to that death – which has already happened and is for us untenable,[2] since it recalls the inevitability of our own death,[3] which must still take place – the life which it had been, by means of *our own life*.

This involves a judgement on our life and then a selection of that which we are willing to find about ourselves or to find different from ourselves in the men and women who have gone before us. By saying 'we' I mean to denote the society in which historians work and which they interpret, through the filter of their personal sensitivity and capacity of perception, the specific traits on which they measure the experience of past societies for affinity or for differences.

The net into which one weaves historical knowledge is that of memory[4] which extends its threads into the 'void' of amnesia. Selective amnesia and memory are in fact at the root of the relationship between human beings – as national, ethical and social groups, etc. – and their history; historiography is that 'technique' which is prompted by its specific status to devote itself to dissipating amnesia and cultivating memory. However, it too acts in a selective manner, leaving some experiences in limbo and bringing others to light, according to the personal and social 'point of view' which orientates the researcher. In this way amnesia and memory also acquire a history of their own for they bind themselves to the individual intervention of the historian, as well as to different social and political moments during which a certain type of relationship between the past and the present is required by human groups.[5]

The manipulation of collective memory (and of amnesia) has in fact constituted the terrain on which the struggle for power has been largely played, as the various social groups emerging during the course of the centuries engaged in it: the attempt to wipe out the memory of the *ancien régime* by demolishing its insignia and the need to re-establish historical time through the invention and introduction of a new calendar to take place of the Gregorian one, on the part of the French republican revolutionaries, is the best-known example and it well expresses the will to control and direct collective memory.[6]

The process of selection of the traces, their actual wiping out (directly, or indirectly, by attributing value to features of human experience that do not include them), or their rediscovery, are brought about also through the use of historiography, which can be the servant of the dominant group or become a tool of the rebels.

It is not, however, so much the instrumental or ideological use of the historiographical technique that I would like to stress here; neither am I interested in the age-old and by now taken for granted problem of the non-objectivity of history, in the sense of its 'understanding the present by means of the past and understanding the past by means of the present',[7] an expression which indicates, more clearly than an entire treatise can, the relativism of this discipline whose fields of research are orientated by the present, that is, from the point of view of the observer, and not from that of the observed.

The present/past dynamics, in fact, interests me rather for the third dimension which opens up and which is rarely considered when one ponders the meaning of history: that is, that the choice of which features of the past to illuminate through historical observation is determined by a present which already poses a hypothesis of the future.

History studies change, but it can 'recognize' alterations because it perceives their development and the elements of continuity: proceeding like this it can identify the trend of future developments.[8] Moreover, modern-day society asks the past for confirmations of its own, conscious or unconscious, hypotheses of future development that it has already chosen anyway, because it questions history on specific sections of experience and not on the comprehensiveness of the questions which the present could pose (here, I think, is also an obstacle to the dream of a 'total history').

For example, when Marxist historians began to study in depth the events of the sans-culotte movement, during the French Revolution, they were driven to this not only because their interest applied itself to the rediscovery of the modern roots of the class struggle, but also in order to examine on what structural and ideological foundations that movement developed and in what sphere it was defeated, so as to investigate the potentialities of the contemporary class struggle and the resources of resistance put up against it by the system.

I do not mean to reduce historiography to a sort of 'strategic' study; I am anxious, however, also to point out the cognitive and forward-planning aspect of historical research in the political sense. In particular, from the point of view I am taking up here, that of a feminist historiography, I would like to understand if and to what extent our relationship with women's historical experience, the knowledge that we are laboriously putting together – which is orientated by our present as women and feminists – might be marked by the need to prepare a possible future, for which we are already trying to build a meaningful (I am not saying 'positive') image of ourselves and of our movement. I would further like to understand what type – if there is one – of collective planning ahead persuades us to 'make history' today; that is, to combine ideas and techniques for a knowledge which is concerned neither with an analysis of the individual self (as it is in the case of psychoanalytical therapy), nor with the study of 'broadened' selves, groups of individuals who feel bound to a vast and consistent range of common features (as in the case of the 'practice of the unconscious' and of the little groups of *autocoscienza*): a knowledge which needs to overcome the barrier of the death of women who have gone before us and of their movements. This is a knowledge which tries to retie the thread of the memory that Ariadne lost or that Theseus broke after having made use of it to get out of the labyrinth.

This is an enigma (the question of who is responsible for the loss), which first must be unravelled, I believe, to pick out interpretative outlines in our research; because between these two opposite poles – that of an autonomous vs a violently imposed loss of memory – stands, in a precarious balance, the double-image that has so far directed feminist historiography, and on which we build our identity for today and propose it for tomorrow.

'Memory', writes Jacques Le Goff, 'is an essential element of that which is now usually called the individual or collective "identity", the "feverish and anxious" research of which is one of the fundamental activities of individuals and of society today.'[9] And again, commenting upon a study on the significance of the 'family album',[10] Le Goff observes: 'The father is not always the portraitist of the family: often it is the mother.' And he wonders: 'Should one see this as a vestige of women's function to preserve recollection, or as a conquest of the group memory by feminism?'[11]

Memory-identity; woman as guardian of recollection; feminism and conquest of memory: we are at the heart of the problem. Everything revolves around the first pivot: memory-identity, but precise objects and subjects are added to it: women and feminism.

Women's identity seems to have been constantly defined by others – by men, charged in different guises with this task as priests, philosophers, doctors, scientists, politicians; more than any other human group, women need to build a memory which might be self-identification and value-attribution. It is not, however, 'women' in the abstract who need to set about the problem, but rather feminists, in other words those women who for various social reasons (the economic condition, the possession of cultural tools and so on), have developed an analysis of the mechanisms of sexual oppression and hypothesized its overthrow, through specific political practices (*autocoscienza*, separatism, etc.).

Granted that the process of knowledge is triggered off by awareness, however diffuse, as is the case for feminism, and that no feminist historian – at least I hope not – thinks of keeping her specialized knowledge and her acquisitions in a locked drawer, far from other women, in her study or in a university department, the problem still remains that the historiographical research until now[12] has been articulated as coming from a 'place of socio-economic, political and cultural production'. That is, it implies

> an environment limited by specific determining factors: a liberal profession, a place of study or a teaching post. . . . Therefore it is subject to conditioning, linked to privilege, rooted in a specific situation. It is in relation to this situation that methods are elaborated, a topography of interests is created, and one organizes *dossiers* and questions to put to the records.[13]

Which means, in our case, that the definition of the field of research is determined by our being *historians, women and feminists*, with a specific position in society and with specific interpretations of the social destiny of women in history, according to the inter-pretation each of us gives to the causes of sexual oppression and to the ways that, inside the various parts of the movement, we single out for overcoming such oppression. By this I mean that the idea of *women*, as well as that of *feminism*, shows the effects of the various formations and the various practices which each feminist historian has experienced in the movement.

These differences are already present in the definition of women's historical memory. In the researches carried out so far, according to the political viewpoint with which the researcher started, and in particular according to her definition of the histori-cal object/subject woman and of her social destiny as a victim of oppression or a rebel, we found ourselves facing either a white, opaque magma – 'that must have been the colour of time, of the white time of long years without history'[14] – or a seething of signs which are still vivid even after being expunged by male historiographers. That is, we have on the one hand denounced the wiping out of women due to oppression, and we have on the other hand instead perceived in the female historical experience pockets of resistance and of refusal of imposed roles, which expressed themselves in all kinds of ways. The magmatic rebelliousness of popular uprisings led by women; conscious, organized revolt in the emancipation movements; individual refusals which, however, because they were widespread phenomena, became signs of 'social unrest' (prostitution, criminality, hysteria: experiences all marked, among other things, by a maladjustment to sexuality as it was imposed).[15]

Apart from researches about the liberation movement, which I will come back to, in both cases (wiping out or presence) the female memory–identity has only been retraced as it was 'spoken' by people other than women:[16] doctors, police officers, priests, who while condemning the deviants describe to us the 'standards' which the others, presumably, stick to. So research has had to penetrate the gaps in male argument and, often, it has not been borne in mind that it was an oblique, indirect research, that women's memory–identity was not there, except through mangled evidence given to the judges or in hospital files.[17]

The urgency of covering this void in historiography, of flinging ourselves into probing in the libraries and the archives in order to find that lost thread, has allowed us an accumulation of data and of indispensable information without which it would not even be possible, perhaps, to put the further questions which will move us forward. But, on the other hand, by proceeding, as we have done, without at the same time closely examining the very meaning of the research, without defining more accurately theoretical fields and methods, we risk obstructing our own interpretative categories which become absolute and atemporal: 'in history as elsewhere, a practice without theory necessarily ends by falling, sooner or later, into the dogmatism of "eternal values" or into the apology of an "out of time" [intemporel]'.[18]

So, to go back to women's historical memory, we are still at the crossroads: one wavers between anxiety at its loss, above all when one refers to the experiences of the emancipation movement which seem to recur exactly the same after decades or even centuries; and the voluntaristic glorification of a link which unites us all through time. Perhaps the moment has come to probe further on this point.

What is the memory of which women would have been the

custodians, as a widespread cliché states, unexpectedly approved of without further comment, in passing, by Jacques Le Goff?[19] Is it a matter of a 'social' memory, which preserves the recollection of meaningful facts and events of the group (family, relatives, neighbours . . . society)? In such a case, how much of this memory is 'female'? Is it not rather the *task of remembering* which is 'female', in the sense of the preservative role historically attributed to woman and of which she is once more the bearer not for herself, but for the group? Or must we think in this case – searching for female memory 'in a pure state' – of sedimentary layers of historic memory, as if it were a matter of biological memory? In such a case, can the hypothesis be put forward of a 'gender' memory, which mainly passes through the repetition of physical experiences (menstruation, pregnancy, childbirth, sexuality)?[20] It is obvious that these questions – only lightly touched upon – open up to many other questions; they aim mainly to spotlight the underlying political knot. That is, briefly: who are the women wiped out of and ignored in male historiography (at least this fact seems established!) whom we want to bring back to light by 'going over with a lead pencil the outlines of a rubbed-out, but well-delineated, drawing, which no one has ever worried about'?[21]

If the longing to re-create our past induces us to reply 'Every woman', we are deceiving ourselves, we are denying that even we necessarily operate a selection, as men have done with regard to women (and with regard to other men who, because of their economic position, race, religion, etc., have not been considered, until very recently, worthy of 'going down in history'). It is not so much because of the impossibility of finding the sources, which anyway has its own considerable weight, as for the need, on the one hand, of identifying ourselves and, on the other, of self-justifying our presence and our struggle. The 'lead pencil', in fact, can retrace only the outline of lives and experiences recognizable through an affinity with or a difference from our own, and *proposable* to awareness.

Here is the crux of the political problem; for in defining the requirements that we are making in order that the women of the past can emerge from limbo, we precisely require to define our own image.

An area widely explored has been that of so-called 'women's culture', the culture of private life, of domesticity, to indicate the ability of women to create structures of resistance to oppression.

The concept was originally based on that of the 'culture of slavery' elaborated in the historiography of black people; but it has very soon had to detach itself from it, since the examination of sexual oppression implies the construction of a more precise methodological paradigm. Indeed, as Gerda Lerner warned in one of her first theoretical papers, women cannot be defined by race, class, or ethnic group; although they are part of racial groups, classes, ethnic groups, their oppression is *sexual* and crosses all these boundaries.[22]

The concept of 'women's culture' has proved very fertile to overcome a historiography which used to see women as victims perpetually subordinate to male domination. However, the emphasis put on the structures managed by women in the private sphere, the emphasis on the separateness between the two 'spheres' (the domestic sphere dominated by the feeling of love and solidarity between women, and the public sphere dominated by competitiveness between men) has moved some women historians to stretch their analysis too far. So, for some of them 'separateness' appears to mean 'separatism', in the meaning that we today give to a political practice consciously chosen;[23] others see in the domestic sphere, in which the 'female culture' was developing, a world of quite improbable 'perfect happiness'.

To read some of these studies, it seems that women – previously seen as ghosts, shades, women lost in the hell of oppression – were instead all very happy, independent, tied to each other by a love which could freely be expressed in a world in which the males 'put in a rather dull appearance', to use the expression of an eminent scholar like Carroll Smith-Rosenberg who, although being the leader of this historiographical trend, does not fall into the error of generalizing the phenomenon beyond the field defined for her by the documents that she is analysing.[24]

Other researchers, on the contrary, have become increasingly acritical in the study and interpretation of the private female sphere. Born from the desire to point out and to value women's historical experience beyond its 'high' moments, to show that there was never silence – or that the silence had its own language as meaningful as the writing of a polemical pamphlet or a speech from the platform – the interest of the hidden, familiar, daily world of women has often translated itself for feminist historians into an attitude of what I would call 'emotional adherence'; that is to say, an empathy evocative of features of female behaviour which appear more deeply marked by emotion, or, rather, by women's ability to build independently from men an individual and collective identity based on emotion itself.

In the period which generally is examined in these studies and which goes from the end of the eighteenth century to the beginning of the twentieth century, when a long phase of gradual transformation of the family structure and of social relationships in general developed, the network of interpersonal relationships is seen as a 'gender-based social structure' with its own internal laws, impenetrable from outside.

The point of view which guides these interpretations seems quite close to that which in the early days of the movement induced more than one researcher (mainly historians and anthropologists) to search for an era of lost 'matriarchy'; or to that which, overcoming a series of not irrelevant historical elements, moved others to read the phenomenon of witchcraft as an expression of a world of women based on the rhythms of nature. Although it is given the name of 'women's culture', often and willingly the experience of American women between the eighteenth and twentieth centuries is seen as the result of a 'natural' relationship between women, not polluted by male culture or history.

Instead it is necessary to note that research carried out on the same historical period makes it clear that the 'female world' was heavily thwarted by male intervention; a discourse which was both investigative and at the same time *prescriptive* of 'female nature', established, by means of philosophy, religion and science, the criteria of 'real femininity' to which women had to stick. As Barbara Welter opportunely states,[25] the invention of 'true womanhood' was not an independent and self-enhancing invention by women; it was imposed by the male sociocultural structure and was directed, not by chance, mainly at white middle-class women who were not necessary as a workforce outside the home. Besides this, the physical intervention must be considered: there exists a vast literature – it too orientated by problems debated in the movement – on male violence exercised against women at all social levels:[26] a sign that the 'spheres', separated as they were ideologically, were certainly not happily isolated from one another.

I do not mean to repropose a victimistic historiography, but the shift of some American historians towards a sunny optimism about the female world, about solidarity and about the transmission of female values, seems to me excessive, or at least judgements like the following appear hurried: 'the segregation of women in a separate education system, specifically defined through their women's life, reinforces the female awareness which characterizes the domestic sphere',[27] or even: 'female domestic culture furnishes the basis for the widening of female activity in the public world dominated by males. The moral superiority attributed by the ideology on femininity legitimizes their efforts at organizing themselves collectively to promote social causes',[28] where it is clear that one plays too much with words like 'awareness', 'organization', 'social cause', without previously defining the social and political meaning which is attributed to them.

In *Feminist Studies* Ellen Du Bois attacked the acritical use of the concept of 'women's culture', too often described as a romantic experience of a lost world, uprooted from the rest of society. The discovery and the high valuation of a female identity which is autonomously built, beyond the image and the models imposed on women by male thought and social organization, have a historiographical and political value, according to Du Bois, on condition that one does not aim at hiding the internal contradictions experienced by women themselves, both in the relationship among themselves, and in that between them and society as a whole. If then, as Smith-Rosenberg does in Du Bois's opinion, one denies full significance to the rights movement and the suffragist movement, maintaining that they are of very little importance both in American politics and in women's history, one arrives at the absurdity of denying the very thing one meant to prove: the ability of women to resist oppression. According to Du Bois, this leads to a 'depoliticized' historiography, academic in the worst sense of the term, because one denies the links between the process of construction of awareness and the expression of this in an exquisitely political project, that is, one of communication and of external intervention.[29]

Smith-Rosenberg's firm reply underlines that if indeed there is a need to clarify things, it concerns not only the words 'awareness' and 'feminism', but also the different political points of view – about the movement and in general – which move the historians to emphasize one feature of female experience rather than another. For the emphasis put by Du Bois on the political can mean a subordinacy to a traditional point of view which denies the basic acquisitions of women in the movement, which have widened and redefined the political nature of the experiences of solidarity and love, beyond their programmatical transposition in a project of confrontation or of dispute with the institutions.[30]

The point of the debate expressly concerns the construction of a new political historiography, in the sense of a history of emancipationist movements, and the contribution that can be made to such a historiography by social history, in particular by the discovery of structures of relationships between women which are not directly political.[31]

However, the problem that again arises concerns our attitudes as feminist historians and the attitudes of women who are our field of investigation; of whom, I repeat, we read the signs that we want to read, in search of their (our) collective identity.

'Awareness of the past does not mean nostalgia', warns Pascal Werner,[32] yet in the analysis of 'women's culture' women historians have carried out exactly this operation: but it has turned out that solidarity between women, assumed as a categorical imperative by our movement, must be built up politically, rather than being a naturally constituent element of the relationship between women. If for a large part of the movement (I am thinking mainly of the Italian movement, whose more 'political' characteristics have allowed it, in my opinion, to 'withstand' the impact of this progressive awareness) the analysis of the 'differences' beween women constitutes a further point of strength, other parts have perceived the need to refind in the past that which the present did not offer in desired terms. From here derives, on the one hand, the interest of certain investigations, on the other, the voluntarism in the identification of a reality without internal fissures.[33]

The example of the historiography of women's political movements, can better than others clarify what I mean when I underline the selectivity of our intervention. Once again I will refer mainly to studies carried out by American feminist historians. In the USA, as elsewhere, male and female historiography has sometimes dealt with the emancipation movements of the past, generally in connection with the emergence of new women's movements. The criticism of those old studies has been severe, and in its developments, as well as on the basis of more recent research, it is possible to check the correspondence between the 'phases' of the contemporary movement and the questions put to political historiography. Aileen Kraditor, for example, denies any emancipationist thrust to the demand for the vote, as in her opinion it remained linked to the reactionary defence of the female role in the home, with no general political request;[34] whereas Freedman sees in the debate on 'female values' advanced by many leaders of the emancipation movement in the nineteenth century a conscious choice of 'separatism': moreover, she maintains that forsaking this strategy, and above all 'women's values', in the 1920s, brought about disintegration of the self-awareness of women with the consequent loss of their collective strength.[35] Du Bois, in her turn, finds that the critics of the reactionary nature of the emancipationists are superficial, because they measure the radicalism of their requests by today's standards, while for her the request for the vote, the request for 'citizenship', opening the way to clear-cut roles not based on the family but based on the individual relationship between women and the state, was 'in the nineteenth century, the most radical programme possible for female emancipation'.[36]

I could give numerous examples, but those which I have chosen seem to me enough at least to indicate how, in a phase of downright refusal of emancipation by the contemporary movement, the problem was to deny any continuity between this and nineteenth-century movements, which often sacrificed important parts of their 'most feminist' demands to enter into men's sphere of action on the conditions imposed by the latter. The need to justify our strategies – for example, separatism – has instead led to an 'imitative' reading of our experience: finally, it seems to me, Du Bois's attempt to measure the experience of the past on its 'realistic' facts points to the need to consider the difficulty of the adventure which we are living not alone, but in a world in which women are not *Woman*; in which there exist general political strategies, social and economic structures, and problems which are born of generational gaps which we cannot ignore, turning to 'nature', or to no better identified 'mothers', or 'sisters'.

NOTES

1 Michel de Certeau, 'L'opération historique', in J. Le Goff and P. Nora (eds) *Faire de l'histoire*, Paris, Gallimard, 1974, vol. I, p. 3.

2 'I do not want to "resuscitate" the female character, because to do this I would have to show that it died, one day, and I do not believe that at all': A. Farge, 'L'histoire ébruitée', in *L'histoire sans qualités*, Paris, Galilée, 1979, p. 19.

3 'It is not my death, but my mortality that I ascertain in the light of the death of others. Here a sort of splitting in time occurs; present death is reflected in the future under the form of inevitable happening': E. Minkowski, *Il tempo vissuto*, Turin, Einaudi, 1977, p. 149; see also p. 150 ff.

4 'Every memory, it seems, contains in itself a *knowledge*. To recognize someone is equivalent to *knowing* that you have seen them before, just as to remember an event is equivalent to *knowing* that that event has happened in the past': ibid., p. 154.

5 See A. Leroi-Gourhan, *Il gesto e la parola*, Turin, Einaudi, 1977, especially vol. II, *La memoria e i ritmi*.

6 Besides general works on the French Revolution, see, on this problem, J. Baskiewicz, 'La Revolution française aux yeux des révolutionnaires', *Acta Poloniae historica*, 1978, vol. 37, especially pp. 89–90; M. Krol, 'La conscience et la pouvoir révolutionnaire: le cas des Jacobins (1793–1794)', in ibid., 1973, vol. 27, especially pp. 70–1.

7 See M. Bloch, *Apologia della storia o mestiere di storico*, Turin, Einaudi, 1969.

8 'History – according to M. Bloch – can engage in the bid to penetrate the future; elle n'est pas, je crois, incapable d'y parvenir. . . . Examining how yesterday was different from the day before, and why, it finds in this comparison, the possibility to foresee in what sense tomorrow will oppose yesterday': M. Bloch, *L'étrange défaite. Témoignage écrit en 1940*, Paris, Seuil, 1957, pp. 155–7.

9 Jacques Le Goff, 'Memoria', in the *Enciclopedia Einaudi*, Turin, Einaudi, 1979, vol. 8, p. 1104.

10 P. Bourdieu, *Un art moyen. Essai sur les usages sociaux de la photographie*, Paris, Minuit, 1965.

11 Le Goff, op. cit., p. 1097.

12 Despite the wish to expand even to non-specialists the historiographic 'practice', a wish present in our movement and in others, I think that apart from some isolated attempts, we are not yet at the point that we 'all' make history. On this point cf. J. Chesneaux, *Che cos'è la storia. Cancelliamo il passato?*, Milan, Mazzotta, 1977.

13 de Certeau, op. cit., p. 4.

14 Farge, op. cit., p. 5.

15 See in particular Carroll Smith-Rosenberg, 'The hysterical woman. Sex roles and role conflict in nineteenth-century America', reprinted in E. Katz and A. Rapone, *Women's Experience in America, An Historical Anthology*, New York, Transaction Books, 1980, pp. 315–37, and S. Schlossmann and S. Wallach, 'The crime of precocious sexuality: female juvenile delinquency in the progressive era', *Harvard Educational Review*, February 1978, vol. 48, pp. 65–94.

16 I am not going into the question of how much the methods of oral history do or do not permit the regaining of a direct memory of

women: a problem which I still think is little investigated. For a stimulating restatement of the questions in this sphere of research, see the paper given by L. Passerini at the 'International Oral History Conference', Amsterdam, 24–6 October 1980.

17 Taking part in a debate among women historians, Carroll Smith-Rosenberg remarked that, after more than ten years of research on the ideology and forms of oppression utilized by men against women, she had become aware that 'this exclusive emphasis on male oppression of women had transformed me into an historian of men'; 'Politics and Culture in Women's History: A Symposium', in *Feminist Studies*, Spring 1980, vol. 6, no. 1, p. 61.

18 de Certeau, op. cit., p. 4.

19 Le Goff, op. cit., p. 1097.

20 This question could be quite fruitful if cleared of mystic apologia on the relationship between woman and nature: menstruation, pregnancy, childbirth, sexuality, although based in natural events, in fact go quite beyond physiology for the meanings that culturally have been connected to them, and that change depending on the era and the geographical area. For this reason I speak of a 'memory' of 'gender' rather than of 'sex', as 'gender' indicates more precisely those historical constructions of a complex of ideas and behaviours built on 'sex' as a physiological fact. The question I asked could introduce the problem of the relationship of women with the social structure, with change and thus with the future. In short the problem comes back to me of the definition of the relationship that the mass of women have had with time and with its scanning, and so with history. However, from this point of view the 'fragments' risk breaking up further until they become babble. I have written on this theme in 'Il tempo ritrovato. Riflessioni sul mestiere di storica', *DonnaWomanFemme*, October–December 1975, Vol. I, no. 1, pp. 37–47.

21 Farge, op. cit., p. 19.

22 Gerda Lerner, 'Placing women in history. Definitions and challenges', *Feminist Studies*, Fall 1975, vol. 3, nos 1/2, p. 5–14.

23 Cf. among others Estelle B. Freedman, 'Separatism as strategy: female institution building and American feminism, 1870–1930', *Feminist Studies*, Fall 1979, vol. 5, no. 3, pp. 512–29.

24 Carroll Smith-Rosenberg, 'Un mondo femminile di errore e rituale: rapporti tra donne nell'America del XIX secolo', *Nuova DWF*, January–June 1979, nos 10–11, pp. 146–73; see *Signs*, 1975, vol. I, no. 1.

25 B. Welter, 'The cult of true womanhood: 1820–1860', *American Quarterly*, Spring 1970, vol. 22, pp. 45–66; reprinted in Katz and Rapone, op. cit., pp. 193–218.

26 See, for example, E. Pleck, 'Wife-beating in nineteenth-century America', *Victimology: an international journal*, 1979, vol. I, no. 1, pp. 60–74.

27 Katz and Rapone, op. cit., p. 17.

28 ibid.

29 E. Du Bois in the debate among women historians, 'Politics and

Culture in Women's History: A Symposium'; see *Feminist Studies*, Spring 1980, vol. 6, no. 1, pp. 28–36.

30 Carroll Smith-Rosenberg in the same debate, ibid., pp. 53–64.

31 It is to be remarked that some women historians have, however, established links of cause and effect between 'women's culture' and the birth of emancipationist movements. Among others, see N. F. Cott, *The Bonds of Womanhood, 'Woman's Sphere' in New England, 1780–1835*, New Haven, Conn., Yale University Press, 1977; Barbara Berg, *The Remembered Gate: Origins of American Feminism, the Women and the City, 1800–1860*, New York, Oxford University Press, 1978; and the 'popularization' of these studies in Katz and Rapone, op. cit.

32 P. Werner, Preface, in *L'histoire sans qualités*, Paris, Galilée, 1979, p. 10.

33 Very different, I think, is the attitude expressed by Rina Macrelli, when right in the middle of her discourse, before quoting the data on the relationship between work and prostitution in the last century, she warns: 'Read slowly, women, it is our skins that are being talked about', where there is no nostalgia, or atemporal levelling out, or victimistic satisfaction, but the sense of a participation in the document, which is the strength of feminist historiography, when it succeeds in being the instrument of awareness; cf. Rina Macrelli, *L'indegna schiavitù. Anna Maria Mozzoni e la lotta contro la prostituzione di Stato*, Rome, Editori Riuniti, 1980; the sentence quoted is on p. 17.

34 A. Kraditor, *The Ideas of the Woman Suffrage Movement*, New York, Columbia University Press, 1965.

35 Freedman, op. cit., and 'The new woman: changing views of women in the 1920s', *Journal of American History*, September 1974, no. 61, pp. 372–92.

36 E. Du Bois, 'The radicalism of the woman suffrage movement: notes toward the reconstruction of nineteenth-century feminism', *Feminist Studies*, Fall 1975, vol. 3, nos 1/2, pp. 63–71. See also E. Du Bois, *Feminism and Suffrage: The Emergence of an Independent Women's Movement in America, 1848–1869*, Ithaca, NY, Cornell University Press, 1978.

Part IV

Philosophy

Chapter 11

Towards a theory of sexual difference*

Adriana Cavarero

ON THE MONSTROSITY OF THE SUBJECT

The 'I' of discourse, that same discourse which I am now thinking and writing in the Italian language, is as it happens not concerned about its being of the masculine or feminine sex. When it is substantivized, it becomes of masculine gender but, extraordinarily, a sex is not due to it. 'I am a woman', 'I am male': the 'I' supports and holds sexuation indifferently, while being, in itself, neutral.

Philosophical discourse can thus legitimately affirm the 'I think' and make this neutral subject a universal. And it can also eliminate the 'think' and simply say the 'I', since it is precisely there that the universal makes itself present. And yet that grammatical masculine gender that the 'I' somehow carries within it irritates and fractures this representation of universality.

The 'I', in the enunciations 'I am a woman', 'I am a man', thus holds sexuation indifferently; but in the second enunciation that which is affirmed of the 'I' seems to fit it with greater exactitude, stemming from the masculine gender which both terms of the enunciation have in common. It seems, in short, that in holding masculine sexuation, the 'I' achieves its intimate completion, specifying in the sexuation the masculinity that its category already announced, all the while keeping it as neutrally available to both genders. That announcement was thus already a signal, a sign of the masculine carried by the neutral and by the universal.

The term 'man' is also, in my language, pregnant with signals.

* First published as 'Per una teoria della differenza sessuale', in *Diotima. Il pensiero della differenza sessuale*, Milan, La Tartaruga, 1985. Translated by Giuliana De Novellis.

In the first instance, man/woman, like male/female, appear as ordinary bipolar couples. But in the discourse which says, for example, 'man is mortal', the man in question is also a woman. In fact, it is neither man nor woman, but their universal neutral. (The enunciation 'woman is mortal' would, instead, give rise to the logical conclusion that man must, then, be immortal. And there is some truth in this conclusion.) 'Man' holds good then, first of all as phenomenon sexed in the masculine, but it also holds good, and precisely because of this, as universal neutral of the masculine gender and of the feminine one.

These announcements and these signals thus reveal the authentic subject of discourse: a masculine subject which raises itself to the universal. Man, as phenomenon sexed in the masculine, carries finiteness within itself, yet with an extraordinary logical rise and fall it absolutizes that finiteness: making it rise to universality through an ascendant dynamics so that universality, through a descending dynamics, can also comprise (specify itself) both that masculine finite which generated it, and the other sex. A sex which now appears for the first time, absent from the logical process and nevertheless gathered up by it, incorporated, and assimilated by it. On this path, man travels the rising and falling curve of sameness: he finds himself and recognizes himself as a particular of his own universalization. Woman, instead, finds herself only as a particular, as the finite other included in the neutral-universal man.

Thus woman is the other of man, and man is the other of woman, but of an alterity which is differently grounded: the alterity of the man with regard to the woman is grounded, in fact, in the man himself who, preliminarily erecting himself as universal, then also admits himself to be one of the two sexes in which the universal becomes specific. The alterity of the woman, instead, is grounded negatively: the universal-neutral man particularizing himself as 'man' sexed in the masculine finds himself in front of the man sexed in the feminine and calls it other from himself.

In this logic, woman's confrontation with man is a mere and irreducible *being in front of*. Indeed, in the logical process of the universalization of the masculine-finite, the feminine-finite is absent, and only at the end is it found, outside the process and incorporated into it. As to why an alterity which is irreducible and originary has been thus incorporated, history might be able to provide an answer, but logic is silent. The logic of discourse assumes such alterity as absent, yet precomprised by the universal and thus controlled by it. The woman is, in this way, something which is foreseen by the specifying of the universal man into man and woman.

Discourse thus carries within itself the sign of its subject, the speaking subject who in discourse speaks himself and speaks the world beginning from himself. There is some truth, then, in the immortality of man, which was announced earlier, in parentheses, almost as a joke: by universalizing the finiteness of his sexuation man surpasses it and sets himself up as an essence which necessarily belongs to the 'objectivity' of discourse. The history of philosophy records, in various ways, the finiteness which the thinking being, precisely because it is such, carries within itself, but it is extraordinarily blind with regard to the finiteness of sexual difference. This difference remains, for philosophy, something unthought, a superfluous determining of man into man and woman, as though finding oneself sexed, which every one of us experiences, being other thus and not otherwise, were too banal an event to be worked on by thought, an event which, at best, must be of interest to the biological disciplines.

So, that to which discourse gives evidence, and philosophy obviously confirms, is the fundamental insignificance of sexual difference, which is (nor could it be otherwise) recorded but not thought in its originariness. Indeed, that finite sexed in the masculine which, by making itself absolute, makes itself universal, in the process of self-absolutization, celebrates its sex, but ignores the difference that is rooted in it, the differing in which the sex consists. Sexual difference comes later, as an unproblematic specification of the universal, but in this coming later, its originariness has already been lost. Here, the hypothesis of two possible philosophies is suggested. One things that being a man or being a woman is something originary which requires a dual conceptualization, an absolute duality, a kind of paradox for the logic of the one-many. The other thinks of the universal man as neutral and holds being man or being woman within it as two cases which have no influence on the validity of the neutro-universal concept. Western philosophy has followed the second hypothesis: it transpires from the pores of language and is the real steel cage which sexual difference must break in order to think itself.

This is not to say that language and philosophy do not attribute meaning to being a man or being a woman.[1] In fact, this meaning, in its millenary evolutions, is well known by women as a story of blood and tears; but it is a derived meaning and consequent to the assumption of the universal man as originary. In this fundamental assumption there is something monstrous, since the logic of absolutizing the finite pays for its daring with monstrosity: after all, the neutral (not yet sexed) or the hermaphrodite (already sexed both ways) have been monsters for a long time. But the true monster, revealed in the logical process, is the neutral male, an unrepresentable monster, and yet so familiar to whomever says: 'Man is a rational animal'. 'Man is the child of God', etc.

But for philosophy, being a man or being a woman is, rather, an accident, as full of consequences as it is ignored by theory.[2] Theory speaks the essence of the universal man (he is mortal, thinking, a fragile shoot, etc.), and then it also takes temporal accidents (the so-called historical conditionings) into consideration; among these seems to belong the case of being born a man or a woman, the latter undoubtedly an unfortunate case.

The concrete self-identification of man and woman in the neutral-universal would, in a strict logical sense, involve the addition of sexual difference to the neutral-universal. We could derive two composite concepts from it: man + masculine gender = man, and man + feminine gender = woman. This type of self-identification would stake its possibility all on the addition. Thus in the neutral-universal man, man and woman are not present and so could not recognize themselves; in the addition of sexual difference recognition is possible but it is completely consigned to that addition. In this second case, however, the content of the universal is the essence which then happens to convey itself in sexed individuals and the gender of these individuals is something external which does not concern the essence.

But something extraordinary happens to the neutral universal concept of man, the extraordinary thing being that the aporetic logic described above is true only for woman. Man recognizes himself fully in the neutral universal without the need for any addition, precisely because of that monstrosity which makes a neutral and a male cohabit in the universal man. In the dynamics of the universalization of the finite through the category of the same, the self-identification of the gendered man with the universal-neutral man has its possibility precisely in that finiteness of the masculine gender which is adopted as universal. Thus in this universal (in the subject, in the I of philosophy) man is present in all the concreteness of his whole being, a gendered living being and not a man + masculine gender, and since he is present in it he recognizes himself, he speaks himself, he thinks himself, he represents himself. The monstrosity of that universal which is at the same time neutral and male does not disturb him since it comes from the logical 'generosity' of a finiteness which takes on the burden of holding true for the other sex as well. When speaking himself and thinking himself man speaks his language and thinks his thought, both of which must, however, forget, because of the constitutive dynamics of the universalization of the finite, this *his* which makes them belong to a fininte gender: they are thus simply language and thought.

The consequence for philosophy is that sexual difference is not thought through, since one of the two sexes is assumed as universal, without ever becoming the theme of an investigation around the true, the originary differing in sex which everyone carries in their flesh like living and dying.

The consequence for woman is that she cannot recognize herself in the thought system and the language of a neutral subject which does not contain her – and indeed excludes her – without accounting for that exclusion. The universal, presuming to hold true for the excluded sex as well, erases the logical space of originary differing, and transfers it to a lower level of consequent differing. Thus woman is the universal man with 'a plus' of feminine gender. We well know how this addition does not empower the universal, but rather disempowers it: in fact the 'plus' is more coherently a 'minus', that is, the neutral-universal man minus the masculine gender which is precisely the real content and the true genesis of this universalization.

The task of thinking sexual difference is, thus, an arduous one since it lies in the erasure on which western thought has been founded and has grown. To think sexual difference beginning from the universal man means to think it as already thought, that is, to think it through the categories of a thought system which stands on the non-thinking of difference itself.

As a something 'more' woman is already, at a logical level, a something 'less'. Western philosophy has recently flirted with the positive value which this 'less' might symbolize at the moment in which the universal neutral, or, more precisely, the subject, is in a state of crisis. For man, who for millennia has set himself up, and recognized himself, as a strong subject, recuperating that weakness generously left in the custody of the 'more or less' of the woman is the flirtation of a subject who is not shaking the foundations of his own representation (and why should he?), but who is freely replaying the same categories of his logic.

However fascinating these flirtations of philosophy might, at times, appear, the road of weak thought is not the road along which woman might arrive at speaking herself, at thinking herself and at representing herself; either for strictly logical reasons, or because it is truly pathetic to wish to speak oneself in the form of a weak subject when woman is lacking a language which would, at the very least, speak her as a subject.[3]

A subject can speak itself as such beginning from itself and not beginning from a neutral which is the universalization which the other makes of itself, setting itself up, however, not as already the other, but as the all.

And here lies the crux of the problem: I, like every woman, am now writing and thinking in the language of the other, which is simply the language, nor could I do otherwise. This language, since I happen to be a woman, denies me as a subject, it stands on categories which compromise my self-identification. How, then, can I speak myself through that which, structurally, does not speak me? How can I think sexual difference through, and in, a system of thought which is founded on not thinking it?

THE QUESTION ABOUT ESSENCE

Woman is not the subject of her language. Her language is not *hers*, therefore she speaks and represents herself in a language which is not hers, that is, through the categories of the language of the other. She thinks herself in as much as she is thought by the other.

Indeed, the subject of this language has, since the very beginning, defined itself as identical to language itself: 'Man is a rational animal' has been handed down to us by a tradition which has erroneously (and in this error there is a profound truth) translated the Greek 'Man is a living being which has language'. That is, language like *logos*, which is both thought and language. Man is thus he who speaks the objects and the world and speaks himself as the speaker. He thinks the all and thinks himself as the thinker. Thought which is identical to being is, apart from thought, nothing. Actually it is not nothing. In Parmenides' affirmation a destiny comes to the word: multiplicity, alterity and difference are declared inexistent and unthinkable. Only the one and compact totality of the identical which does not admit the other *is*; a paralysing totality which runs the risk of blocking itself eternally in this autoaffirmation.

But philosophy soon recognizes this risk and overcomes it: difference continues to be unthought as originary, but it finds space at a lower level, as determined difference. The one diversifies itself beginning from itself, admits the multiple and controls its differentiations, classifying them and dominating them. *Logos* is thus correctly translatable as reason, if reason is thought which orders, rendering difference homogeneous and controllable. Man is he who speaks the world as determined and ordered. Sexual difference which the thinker carries in his/her flesh becomes thus comprised and spoken within the bounds of ordered differing, a difference among others, and much less important than the others, for the theory of that which in principle is.

At a first logical approach it would seem that the two sexes are here in the same difficulty: if the thought of originary identity poses sexual difference as secondary and inessential, both woman and man find their gender as already spoken and controlled in a secondary sphere with regard to the definition of their essence. Their essence is to be rational living beings, and then it is also said that these living beings are divided into male and female. Nevertheless, man (who not by chance appears as the subject in the definition of the essence) is the concrete and historical speaker who produces both the concealment of originary difference and its transposition into secondary difference. Thus man, without apparent difficulty, can speak himself as a rational living being sexed in the masculine, where sexed in the masculine is a superfluous addition, since the subject, in that it is monstrously neutral and masculine, already contains the indication of its sex. And so, calling himself a rational living being is enough for him.

It is well known how history, outside pure logic, is concerned with confirming this theoretical mechanism. Woman represents the irrational, the passional, etc. Sexual difference as secondary difference controlled by the essence, becomes, in effect, something 'less' with regard to essence itself. If this essence corresponds to a neutral-masculine, the feminine, rather than an addition, is a subtraction, a kind of incompleteness as regards the universal essence.

Thus the answer to the question 'What is woman?' can only open tragical aporias. The question asks about the essence of woman, but the reply is already compromised by the coming forward of that universal essence which man has modelled on himself. The most obvious answer would be 'A rational living being gendered in the feminine', but as the rational living being is a universal in which the masculine sex can represent itself, the meaning of the answer is wholly consigned to that addition (sexed in the feminine) which, said like this, is nothing other than an empirical observation, above all, already comprised in the question which specifically asks for the essence of woman. Evidently, the crucial sense of the question comes to light when it is a woman who asks herself it. Indeed, philosophy and culture have already answered this question (the mother, the abyss of voluptuousness, woman is fickle, etc.) but from within a logic structured on masculine categories, which after all, is simply the logic of western language.

In other words, the cruciality of the question resides in the possibility of the woman to speak herself, think herself and represent herself as a subject in the proper sense of the word, that is, as a subject which thinks itself beginning from itself and can therefore recognize itself. Thus the problem of the question about essence cannot be translated into a recourse to a metaphysical establishment which is, now, obsolete, but answers to the need for recognition. The question 'What is woman?' resonates in the daily experience of each and every one of us: 'What am I?' We cannot, evidently, answer it if we *fail* to consider the fact that we are *first and foremost* women.

It is useful to pause briefly on this 'first and foremost'. It indicates, precisely, the essential. Language puts many neutral categories at our disposal to answer the 'What am I?', leaving the feminine gender of this I who questions itself out of consideration. For example: a philosophical scholar, a civil servant, etc., or even an extrovert, an obstinate person, etc. It is easy to sense how the neutrality of these categories covers over the essential, so that the unspeakable, the non-representable is precisely the being a woman. A lived experience, from the very beginning to the very last hour, not spoken, or, rather, spoken in *his* language by one who, from the very beginning to the very last hour, is not a woman but a man.

This destiny of 'unspeakableness' is clear in the most ancient definition, the Greek one, which defines man as the living being which has language. If we wanted to answer the crucial question basing ourselves on this, we could say that woman is the living being gendered in the feminine which has language.

But this would be a resounding lie if that *having* means the profound belonging to the subject which 'has'. Woman does not have a language of her own, but rather uses the language of the other. She does not represent herself *in* language, but rather accepts with language the representations of her produced by the man. And so woman speaks and thinks, speaks herself and thinks herself, but not beginning from herself.

The mother tongue in which we have learned to speak and to think is, in effect, the father tongue. There is no mother tongue, since there is no language of woman. Our language is a foreign language which we have not learned by translation from our own tongue. And yet, it is not ours, it is foreign, suspended in a faraway place that rests upon the missing language. That which we perceive in this foreign tongue, which yet we are and cannot but be, is thus the distance which separates us from it; the tongue in which we speak ourselves but do not recognize ourselves. In this distance is preserved, as a possibility, the missing language, a need for translation which lies in the foreign tongue like a desire to return to the language which has been translated, and is nevertheless missing, present only in the translation like an original which is not lost, but rather has never been granted.

This experience of language's distance gives rise to ways of flight which are well known to us: silence, unspoken residue, body rather than thought. The history which concerns us has always been a history of silences, of reticences, of mute bodies taken to market! The only possible and real way is the one rooted, of necessity, in daily life: being a thought which one is not, and yet inexorably being in this thought, saying and speaking oneself in a foreign language.

Actually, the flight from language is as impossible as it is a living symbol of a purportedly unbearable alienation. If I am the language of the other, I decide to deny this alienation by denying myself; rather than speaking myself in a foreign language, then silence. An impotent symbol, because in silence I speak and think myself even better within that conceptual web containing sounds not uttered by me. In silence, sound is silent not the word.

Certainly the tragedy of knowing oneself alienated in the word belongs above all to philosophy. Poetic or narrative discourse has more yielding and refined instruments to evoke, through the foreign tongue, the possible meanings of the missing language. There exists, in fact, a women's literature which speaks to women; in it, the foreign tongue is transfigured and reaches new and unusual meanings which are yet unfamiliar to us. Philosophy takes a harder road, it must undertake the toil of the concept, beginning from the present conceptual web and from the logical history which it preserves and manifests. This history's most powerful bulwark is the alleged neutrality of thought: an objective universal thought, which, as such, would not exclude anyone, and would, in fact, include the ones and the others indifferently in its truth. To unveil the false neutrality of thought and to show how it is tantamount to woman's alienation, is then the first necessary step towards a system of thought which would contemplate woman as subject, and as a subject which thinks itself.

If it is impossible for woman, as it is for any other speaking being, to get out of language by an act of will, it is possible for her to speak through language her alienation from language. In this speaking her own alienation from language, woman reproduces, in action, alienation itself: the language with which she speaks her alienation is the same, she is thus the place of that alienation which, in understanding itself, reproduces itself.

To recognize as the only possibility of self-representation the speaking of oneself as alienated, in this very speaking confirming and perpetuating her own alienation, seems quite a paltry gain. We might ask ourselves then if the system of thought which tries to think sexual difference might be blocked from the very beginning by the untranscendable structure of thought, that is, of a thought which foresees difference as unthought and confirms it as unthinkable. But we might also ask ourselves whether this self-alienating thought of alienation might be only a logical figure contemplated by western philosophy (and assuredly it is, otherwise I would not be able to speak it), or whether it might also be the conceptual expression of an experience rooted in being a woman.

To the question 'What is woman?' we can thus, for the time being, reply: 'Woman is a living being which has language in the form of self-alienation.'

ESSENCE AS EXPERIENCE OF SEPARATENESS

But this reply is only provisional. It must be verified in experience and not only brought close to experience by analogy.

The problem, as we have said, deals with the essence of woman. As a matter of fact, philosophy has answered in an essential way the question 'What is man?': it recites 'Man is the living being which has language' and not 'Man is a living being which is bipedal, featherless and hornless'. This latter definition lists the characteristic qualities, but not the essential ones, characteristics which can be useful for an external and superficial representation. By using it, man could say what he is like, but not what he is. By speaking himself as a living being which has language, man produces his essence while recognizing himself in this act of producing: he thinks himself a thinker. Thus, for man, having language is the same as being language.

Since woman participates in this essence through being subsumed into the neutral–universal man, she too is language. She is the language of the other. Woman's being consists, then, in an alienation. Not only does she think herself as already thought but precisely in her *thinking herself* she is, from time immemorial, already thought, enclosed and constricted in foreign concepts.

In this thinking herself she produces in action an alienation which differentiates her essentially from the other sex. Even though this essential difference might seem a pittance, since consisting in alienation is traditionally considered to be negative, nevertheless it is a remarkable thing that philosophy makes no mention of it – almost as though it were showing a 'pitying' concern for the misfortune of whomever is born a woman. Instead of reflecting on this essential difference, which is essential in that it is rooted in the definition of man, philosophy is silent, not because of pity so much as because of a logic which foresees sexual difference as unthinkable. In as much as she participates in the neutral-universal essence of man, woman is 'human' and that should be enough for her.

Even if theoretical philosophy, which perhaps more than any other knowledge hovers in the pure space of the neutral object, does not have these preoccupations, cultural tradition has often busied itself around the representations of the feminine. These usually concern woman's body and the 'functions' connected with it. It would seem that sexual difference manifests itself here, and in an overbearing manner: the woman is she who generates, the mother. But the same organs are also a source of pleasure: and then the woman is a whore, the abyss of the senses, etc. Here the universal neutral essence of the language-being is forgotten. The representation of the mother acknowledges trepidation, pain, devotion, death. Thinking is not connaturalized to her unless it be in the form of remembering, of story-telling, of reciting nursery rhymes. The mother has a (sweet) voice but not speech. The representation of the erotic body acknowledges many variations, but it is the opposite of thought (the respite from thought): the voice is no longer even story-telling or reciting nursery rhymes but moans and cries. Sexual difference is then something originary (one speaks of the 'nature' of woman), which is extraordinarily incompatible with that universal essence of rationality which defines the human *par excellence*. Indeed, the interception of woman's nature and human essence disempowers, as we have said, the latter.

However painfully unbearable it might be for many women to think themselves beginning from motherhood, after centuries of exclusion from power because our 'nature' links us to babies, to nurturing, to food and to the home, by means of sentimentalisms played out on images of blood and death which are too indecent even to mention, the act of thinking sexual difference cannot release itself from this thing. It would, however, address it within the precincts of a conceptualization in which it is woman who thinks motherhood and who elaborates around it a symbolic of self-recognition.

In the economy of the present argument it is nevertheless useful, for the time being, to pause again at this contradiction between 'nature' and rational human essence. The contradiction is one among many. The woman mother and the woman whore are also incompatible, as are the woman manager and the queen of the home. The examples are as numerous as the representations of woman which cultural development has produced over the centuries. The recent acceleration of this production (within the general over-production of models in which even the subject has got lost among so many incompatible masks) now renders the alienation, which logic has decreed from the beginning, more evident. Woman's essence thus consists in being loaded with many inessential representations: they are not essential if they are incompatible.

For this reason when woman thinks herself, in answer to the question 'What is woman?', she finds herself laden with a multiplicity of representations of the feminine among which she divides herself in a sometimes extraordinary balancing act. But being obliged to deny a few, or almost all of them through a desire for simplicity, she is frequently the victim of a feeling of incompleteness. This feeling of incompleteness, far from being a superficial and unthought feeling, is instead the real mark of an essential experience.

In the first place, since each of the definitions of herself that woman finds in language comes to her from a language which is not hers, woman is constrained to think herself in a logical movement of interiorization of the external-alien. In other words, when answering what woman is, woman finds answers which have already been spoken (representations already given) by a language which does not contemplate her, and even denies her as a subject, a language which, however, is also her language, while being not *hers*. Thus woman thinking herself is already thought. When she defines herself she finds herself holding a definition of herself already spoken by the other. Yet it is she herself, nor could she do otherwise, who activates this interiorization of the external-alien. There is thus an internal, which is a concrete existent, a gendered speaking living being, who thinks itself as an external, and in thinking itself, reproduces the separateness, between thinker and thought. Separateness which consists entirely in this subject's act of thinking itself. So that what constitutively belongs to woman, what she experiences as a *subject* in the language which is external to her, in spite of or rather in force of its being an external language which does not contemplate her, is separateness itself.

We are, perhaps, coming closer to a more precise definition: woman is a living being which has language in the form of separateness. And *having* has here a completed sense.

It is not surprising, then, that she notices a certain incompleteness when she chooses one or more of the definitions which tradition has provided for her; what woman notices is not the lack of a few definitions, but that logical space of scission which belongs to her as her very essence.

There is in woman's daily life a sense of incompleteness accompanied by the compelling necessity of 'filling' empty spaces to arrive at a completeness, at an identity which would coincide with having thoroughly interpreted all the roles which had to be interpreted, until she corresponded to the totality of the representations of the feminine present in language. Obviously, such representations are frequently incompatible and almost always 'fulltime', but this is not the point. The point is that the completeness which seems to consist in the sum of all the roles, i.e. in managing to be a woman according to all the meanings that language attributes to being a woman, far from being a completeness is a way of deepening that essential experience of separateness.

Thus, the scission which woman carries in herself and renews in thinking herself on the one hand triggers a desire of 'suturation' which addresses the external and attempts to sew together all the representations received in language in an impossible unity. On the other hand, in this very operation the split only confirms and deepens itself: sewing together the external does not fill the split which separates it from the internal. It is the intimate consisting-as-separate of the internal and the external which always manifests itself and asks to be filled. An internal and an external which do not exist each in-itself, in autonomous spheres, to then come together in determined circumstances, but which indissolubly exist each within the other in being a woman. In the experience of thinking herself already thought, the two terms coincide in a constitutive separateness.

It might seem that the search for woman's essence rooted in the category of sexual difference ought to give 'higher' results with regard to what we have achieved, that is, a sort of verification of what woman is at present. And saying 'at present' is saying a lot, since it means referring back to the long history of oppression which has produced this present feminine; a history which emerges in all its negative value in the definition of woman's essence as the experience of an intimate and constitutive separateness of the self from the self.

This difficulty (or disappointment), however, comes from a misunderstanding of the meaning of what we have called essence. If essence is a static content outside time, a truth kept in the mind of God, a being who has always been thus and will be thus for ever, then we really have not found it since it was not what we were looking for. The desire for this type of essence sometimes spurs some historical or anthropological types of research: it is the desire to discover the tracks of an 'original' femininity which history has defeated and concealed, so that woman might reappropriate after the concealment, and in spite of the concealment, that which had *rightly* belonged to her at the beginning. These investigations are obviously legitimate and, furthermore, have the usefulness of utopic representations for the construction of a new image, yet they risk swelling our need for a theory of self-recognition and projecting it into the distance of a painful nostalgia. If an archaeology which calls up and reinterprets the eruption into history of a destiny which has by now been fulfilled is legitimate, it cannot, however, forget that being a woman is now this same destiny, and is necessarily experienced and thought within this destiny. To think ourselves in that essence which has been erased, apart from simply being impossible in that our very thinking ourselves is structured on the categories of erasure, also means a voluntary erasing of our being, *here and now*, as sexual difference which thinks itself. In the representation of a lost essence we can mourn ourselves, but not find ourselves.

Thinking sexual difference can only be the thinking of itself, here and now, of a femininely gendered living being rooted in history. The definition of woman's essence is real only if I, a woman, can recognize my expressing myself in it as I am, and not as I might have been in some improbable era whose sun has set. If this self-recognition does not happen, then yet again the separateness between interior and exterior is reproduced, and, in reproducing itself, again separateness itself is manifest as the essential expressing of myself.

The essence which we are looking for, then, is the historical essence of a real subject who wants to understand itself beginning from itself. There is in this effort at self-understanding an active aspect, which is linked to woman's decision to produce the representation of her own being as a subject. There is also a kind of passive aspect, which consists in the faith of listening to herself, seeking her own value not among the representations which 'have value' in a language which is foreign to her, but in trying to *understand* herself as she is, heavy with a destiny which is not yet a happy one. Even if it might seem dripping with mystery, the essence which is found in this way, through woman's self-interrogation on this 'What am I' of hers, is a thousand times better than aping the enlightened adventures of the masculine subject, which for centuries have relegated her to darkness, while nourishing themselves on this darkness.

The essence found in thinking oneself is thus the experience of separateness. And, here, desire immediately shows itself: this separateness must be filled. It is an overwhelming desire, but perhaps in its very overbearingness blind to gain already made: the experience of separateness which is no longer mute, but has come to the word, and is thus conceptualized, represented, is not separated from the subject which thinks it when thinking itself, which conceptualizes and represents it. In this kind of thought, the woman who is thinking recognizes herself. She is the action of her thought of herself.

THE OTHER/OTHER (WOMAN)*

What has happened then to those masculine categories which structured thinking and impeded unthought sexual difference from thinking itself? How has a speaking woman managed to speak herself beginning from the specifics of her sex, in a language which is founded on the neutralization of the sense of this specificity? Well, she has managed to speak herself not by a miracle, or through having discovered a still intact area of language, but by having recognized as specifically hers the erasure of her specificity.

Language has in fact universalized the specificity of the masculine speaking being and, in so doing, it has set him up as a neutral which also contains the other sex, but the other sex, in the same way that it has not entered the logical process of this universalization, has also remained in it and has preserved itself as alien. In the dynamics of the same through the same, the masculine sex has thought the other as the specifying of itself in the feminine of that neutral universal which he himself is.

But the other has remained the Other.

Language can conceptually erase sexual difference, but it cannot eliminate the presence of its simply being there. In point of fact, feminine sexual difference is not the specifying of itself of a monstrous neutral-masculine. Theory often says: so much the

* Both the Other and the other are feminine, unless indicated as masculine by [m]. [Translator's note]

worse for facts! and, in effect that is what happens. Nor do we want to appeal here to biology, even if we could expect discourses on sexual difference from biology.

Here we have come to touch on an extremely sensitive point for feminine thought, a point which is generally called 'residue'. In discourses among women this term frequently announces the eruption of a breathless, and at the same time, happy linguistic production, the opening up of an imaginary which urges and momentarily appeases the desire for self-representation. I would like, here, to attempt an analysis which would account for the extraordinary effects of the word 'residue' and would at the same time manage to conceptualize it within the confines of a theory of sexual difference.

We were saying then that the other of discourse could not prevent the Other from existing, every time and in every woman, as a presence, even if unthought. This Other is, then, at the very least, a body which is sexed in this way and not in another, and a thinking body: the existent which finds itself sexed in the feminine and thinking, is, in fact, an entirety, an individual living being. We do not need archaeological research to track down this Other here mentioned: every one of us is a living being, thinking, and sexed in the feminine; except that when we think ourselves, the entire and living being which we are, splits: our thought is structured on categories which render sexual difference unthought in its originariness (in its existing from the beginning, in this way and not otherwise in the entire and living being, woman) and reduce it to a secondary difference (the other) beginning from, and at the interior of, a representation of ourselves as entire which, very problematically, should more or less correspond to: 'neutral man + (−) feminine gender'.

Nevertheless woman carries a double alterity. She is the other assimilated in language (I, universal speaking subject which is specified in male and female, each of which is the other of the other both included − foreseen! − by the I). And she is also the Other, an existent to the entirety of which sexual difference constitutively belongs, which the process of universalization of the male has not contemplated as such, but which has still, however, 'materially' survived putting herself forward again as a presence which offers itself to an attribution of meaning from thought. Even if this request has, for centuries, been renewed as evidence of the persistent blindness of thought in its regard.

Indeed, in the process of its universalization the Other [m] (that male living being in the entirety of which difference equally inheres) finds himself in the other [m] as the same, he coincides with it, finding his bearings so well and feeling so at home that he can no longer question himself on his being the Other [m]. Thus masculine sexual difference, in the act of celebrating itself as universal, is lost: it remains an uninvestigated assumption, which gratifies itself in the glories of its absolutization.

In this same process of universalization, the Other, on the contrary, cannot recognize herself and find her bearings in it because she has never been in it, and thus she only finds herself as the other. She finds herself, yet she does not recognize herself. She is the Other who thinks herself as the other, and in this thinking herself she experiences that separateness of the other from the Other, which is precisely the alienation of thought itself from the Other. Alienation which, in a thinking woman, who is in herself the Other-other, manifests itself as separateness, in the self, of the self, from the self.

The miracle of forcing language to speak she whom it does not speak, is thus rather the naming of the alienation that language itself produces, forcing the Other to speak herself as the other.

Unrepresented and unrepresentable in the foreign language, the Other has thought herself as the other, preserving herself as a presence which offers itself to a blind thought, as a mute presence, mute not because she did not have speech, but because speech transformed her into that other, separating her from herself and focing her to consist in this separateness. So perhaps it is here that the extraordinary fascination which the word 'residue' provokes in us is hidden: residue is not so much an uncontaminated nook of our being which has escaped, through stubbornness or divine fate, from masculine language, but the ineradicable presence of an entirety which is forced to self-represent itself in its mutilation.

In speaking herself as the experience of separateness, now the Other shows herself at the window of a representation which comprises her. Separateness actually names the Other as one of the two terms which together consist separately. There does not exist in theory, since there does not exist in sexual difference's current experience, a representation which, in a pure and free contemplation of itself, could give the Other back to herself without her having to pass through the other. It is the Other which experiences herself as the Other-other, the one which represents herself here. Her representation, if it really wants to be *hers*, can only reflect back to her that which she is. But in this reflecting back through which woman represents herself as separate in herself, woman herself coincides with her representation.

The originariness of sexual difference here comes to clarify its meaning: it is not an abstract originariness, which can be understood outside history, as though I could, here and now, decide I were, and think myself as, the Other without taking into consideration my untranscendable being *a here and a now*. The Other which yet I am, appears to me in my current experience of separateness. Naming this experience I speak the originariness of my being the Other as that which has been preserved, in spite of the erasure, and thus as that which can find self-representation only in the form of its having been preserved till now.

OUR BEING ALIKE

It is now necessary to effect a methodological clarification. We have just said that a pure and free representation of the Other which would give her back to herself without passing through the other, with which she consists in separateness, is not possible. To take up a figure explained above, that would be equivalent to being able to speak immediately and without problems in the missing language, overlooking the fact of its existing as always and already translated, in the foreign language. Or more simply: overlooking the fact that the language is missing precisely because it is not there.

Up until now we have privileged a 'realistic' mode of enquiry, that is, an undoubtedly laborious road without triumphal arches, along which woman can arrive at an understanding of what she is and why she is like she is, not what she wishes she were. A road of consciousness and not of pure intention. This, on the one hand, to avoid forward leaps into the void where we risk hurtling against a fullness of masculine representations, which we have simply imagined but not concretely left behind; and on the other hand, to understand better the key of logic which foresees sexual difference as unthought, a logic with which sexual difference must therefore square its accounts if it wants to 'find a way out of it'.

The problem is precisely in the way out: one does not get out of a system of thought simply by thinking of getting out of it, at least not while that thought of a way out is structured on the same categories of thought from which it wants to escape. There is, then, a need for a space of transition, to confront the toil of disassembling and restructuring those categories to find, through them and beginning from them rather than a magic way out, a narrow fissure. Only a beginning, still hindered by mortifyingly difficult obstacles.

But nevertheless a beginning. On this beginning it is perhaps less risky (and frustrating) to gather here and there, with the logical cautions which the case may require, the formulation of a project, the means with which to construct a will to be. Here, the archaeological enquiries which we have mentioned can come into play: from the point at which we have arrived now, the 'truth' of their findings is not so much measured by documental accuracy (did matriarchy exist *historically*?) as by their ability to function as images for a project, where what is lost is what we want to find. And not only the archaeological enquiries in a strict sense, but also all those which are able to provide woman with a symbolic of strong representational value: images in which sexual difference is rendered visible to the Other who watches herself in them.

Of all these disciplines, philosophy is perhaps the slowest, because it measures itself with logical categories which narrow the walls of the fissure of the way out. To the disciplines which are able to create images, it can, however, usefully provide an investigation around the status of the image, which is not severed from the phenomenology of its presenting itself in the context of western thought.

In this perspective the investigation which concerns us now is that of likeness founded in the image.

The being alike of all human beings, that similarity on which the ethics of compassion is based, is established in the book of Genesis on the likeness of the human being to God. We read: 'And God said: let us make man in our image in our likeness. . . . So God created man / in his own image / in the image of God / he created him; / male and female / created he them' (1: 26–27). And nevertheless observe how this passage, which suggests the contemporary creation of man and woman both alike in image to God, is, a little later, contradicted by the affirmation that man was alone: 'It is not good for the man to be alone. I will make a helper suitable for him [like him]'* (2: 18). For this purpose God creates, to tell the truth for the second time, the animals, 'But for Adam no suitable helper was found [no helper was found who was like him]. So the Lord God caused the man to fall into a deep sleep; and while he was sleeping, he took one of the man's ribs and closed up the place with flesh. Then the Lord God made a woman from the rib he had taken out of the man, and he brought her to the man. The man said: 'This is now bone of my bones / and flesh of my flesh: / she shall be called "woman" / for she was taken out of man' (2: 20–3).[4]

This contradiction is extremely important. In the first hypothesis we have the creation of the two sexes in a difference which enables the possibility of two levels of likeness. Both man and woman are in God's likeness and in his image, and that is why, in the reflection of the image back to that of which it is an image, that is, to God, they are also each alike to the other while being different. This is the first level of likeness founded in a transcendent which 'contains' both the sexes, since each of the two is in God's image. The second level of likeness is the one founded on the originary of the two sexed creatures: through it women are alike in Eve, and men in Adam. This level of likeness is secondary because it depends on the former, being in the former already contained: the difference, which allows a being alike in it of differently sexed creatures, is already present in God as it corresponds in image to God. According to this passage of Genesis sexual difference is founded originarily in the transcendent, it is a dual originary where each one of the two sexes resembles God, which is why neither of the two assimilates the other by beginning from itself, grounding the likeness of the other in itself in this assimilation.

The second passage of Genesis has a completely different meaning; not only is woman like man in that she is taken from his flesh and thus derived in a secondary degree from that likeness in God that man preserves, but man also names her, as he had already named the animals, demonstrating in this naming the excellence of his likeness to God, that is, the possession of the naming word as the image of the creating Word. Woman, taken

* The Holy Bible, New International Version, Hodder & Stoughton. The English translation 'suitable for him' is rendered by the Italian 'like him' (see note 4). Direct translations of the Italian Bible will be given in square brackets. [Translator's note]

out of man, will also have the word, not a naming word, but one that repeats the names imposed by man: 'now the Lord God had formed out of the ground all the beasts of the field and all the birds of the air. He brought them to the man to see what he would name them; and whatever the man called each living creature, that was its name' (2: 19).

In the Christian tradition the most frequently quoted version is the second. The first appears in Matthew (19: 4), while the second appears in Paul (I Corinthians 11: 8–12) who emphasizes that woman was created from man and thus for man, and in Augustine (*De Civitas Dei*, XII, 21) for whom the fact that man was created '*unum ac singulum*' unlike the animals is fundamental.[5]

The larger use of the Old Testament passage which foresees woman without an image in the transcendent is confirmed in the New Testament's representation of the incarnation of the divine: Jesus Christ is a man. God becomes incarnate in the masculine body as the Son. That such a becoming flesh should redeem not only men but also women is confirmation of a principle which already showed itself in the creation of woman as in man's likeness. If man is that medium through which woman's likeness to God is transmitted, the incarnation of the divine in the man will be able to transmit its value of salvation also to woman who has been created in his likeness.

In other words: both the second passage of Genesis and the mystery of the incarnation contemplate a correspondence in image between man and God. Since it would be foolish to think that God had wanted to become incarnate in a male body rather than a female body by random choice or by whim, it is better, instead, to question oneself on the meaning of this choice. This choice has, for those human beings who decide to question themselves about it, coherent reasons which can be traced in the second passage of Genesis. It is man '*unum ac singulum*', as Augustine says, who is the highest of the creatures made by God in 'his own image' and likeness, and since God created woman like man (and named by man) that likeness founded, through man, in the divine is extended to woman too, as the image of the image. The direct referent of woman, for her being alike to the other members of the human race, is man, not God. Man as the medium from God and towards God. The incarnation of God in man redeems thus man immediately and woman mediately. Woman, who is sexed differently from that body that bleeds on the Cross, is yet like it, beginning from it, since God has wanted to create her thus.[6]

Here also, as we have already pointed out with regard to philosophical thought, the universal value of the masculine figure pays its price. In the dual originary of the first passage of Genesis, sexual difference appears in the two images equally alike to God, actually being the logical nucleus of duality, and it is therefore visible in that it is conceptually significant. On the contrary, in the second passage, sexual difference does not appear at the beginning, it is conceptually inexistent, and appears only at a successive moment; not referring back to God in being like God, but referring back to man who needs a creature like him. And in this secondary appearing, it is rendered conceptually insignificant in relation to the transcendent, as well as 'tendentially' invisible.

As a matter of fact, in the second passage, when man is *alone*, there is no other sex from which the male can differ. And since it is not there, it is of necessity unthinkable, invisible. Sexual difference becomes visible when God fashions a creature like man but differently sexed; the sexual difference in the second phase is, however, insignificant to the economy of the image of the divine, or, rather, significant in that it reveals that that image, i.e. man, which did not appear as sexed, was sexed in the masculine.

To the originary (masculine) image of the divine something extraordinary happens: it is both not the bearer of sexual difference, and the bearer of masculine sexual difference; but the very extraordinariness can be further logically unravelled as the masculine gender's capacity to be invisible in the image of the divine and visible in relation to the feminine gender. This, after all, reinforces its capacity to stand for the universal. Even if we are dealing yet again with an ambiguous and fundamentally monstrous universal: a being already sexed (but as yet invisible) which shows itself as such only after the event, in its comparability, by difference from the other creature 'derived' from him.

The effects of this invisibility are encouraged again in the mystery of the incarnation: Jesus Christ is a man, and thus he is obviously sexed in the masculine. This simple concentration of our thought on the sex of Christ is, however, in our culture an obscene act: the sex of the Son on the Cross is, in fact, invisible in this culture, it escapes from sight not so much because of a natural modesty, but rather because of the fact that it is conceptually unrepresented. The body of Christ is the body of a man, but on the Cross it is the symbol of a conceptually neutral incarnation in that it is universal in its effect of redemption for men and women.

The value of this symbol for the purpose of a self-recognition of God's human creatures is, naturally, different for men and for women. For the male Christian this self-recognition is immediate, in that he who is suffering on the Cross is like him, alike to God and God himself who is the living image of this likeness. For the Christian woman, however, the self-recognition passes through the mediation of the suffering of the passion. In feminine mystical experiences there is in fact a vivid identification of the woman with the suffering body of this man who is different from other men, a defenceless man, the object of physical violence and, because of this, exalted, raised on the Cross. The physical sufferings of the crucifixion are thus present in all the female mystics great and small, down to Virginia of Leyva, the nun of Monza, and to the poor village women who wind through the streets in the ceremony of kissing the cross. If, however, from a logical point of view, woman's identification with the body of the man who suffers on the Cross seems to require, on her part, a denial of the specificity of her own body, nevertheless the suffering of that tortured body triggers an identification between that suffering and her own suffering, so that this denial of the specificity of her body is really brought into play in the Christian woman, but in as much as it is strongly suffered and only suffered, this passion binds the woman to the passion of the crucifixion.

Obviously, for the Christian woman this identification in passion is all the more easy if she does not think herself in sexual difference, and surrenders herself to that denial of the specificity of her own body to which she has historically been constrained by a culture which foresees sexual difference as unthinkable. Should the Christian woman, however, think sexual difference, self-identification is replaced by the problem of an incomplete redemption, which is the consequence of an incarnation of the divine brought about in the partialness and finiteness of the masculine-sexed body, a problem which is central to the Guglielmite heresy?[7]

From this brief analysis conducted in the field of theology we can affirm, that is, confirm, that the image of woman's essence, the one which for woman would represent her as being first and foremost thus and not otherwise, cannot find its foundation in the discourse of transcendence; or rather, it finds an excellent foundation in that concept of the dual originary of man and woman, equally in God's likeness in their sexual difference, which, not by accident, tradition has neglected.

It is now necessary for us, on the one hand (and this is the task of theological women scholars), to rethink that biblical passage about the dual originary in its unexpressed possibilities, and on the other hand (and in any case) to think an image where our speaking of ourselves as alike to one another finds its foundation in ourselves and not in the other.

OUR BEING DIFFERENT

As a matter of fact, our calling ourselves alike to one another finds a representation only in the negative.

Each human creature's likeness to every other human creature has a double significance in relation to a distinct referent: the human creature's being alike with reference to the human species is different from its being alike to the human creatures marked by the same sexual difference.

The first type of likeness, according to the most frequently used biblical version and, in the final analysis, according to western culture in general, is founded on man's likeness to God which is transmitted to woman through her likeness to man. There is, in short, a concept of humanity represented by the figure man-image-of-God which is extended to woman in that she is created in the likeness of that figure. If we shift from the theological to the philosophical sphere, the schema repeats itself: it is 'the living being which has language', that is, man, who creates the concept of the human, and since woman uses this language, she too is human, a fellow creature within the human species.

The second type of likeness, the one among creatures sexed in the same difference, poses greater problems, at least for women. While for man saying that he is like every other man is a way of speaking which leans on the same biblical or philosophical representation quoted above, the lack of a 'positive' foundation of feminine sexual difference creates, for women, a difficulty in tracing the parameters of this calling themselves alike to one another. There is, in fact, a parameter founded in the 'negative' of feminine sexual difference. Women found their likeness each to the other in the first woman's likeness to the first man, but it is a parameter which only *appears* useful. In fact, the first woman's likeness to the first man is dependent totally on the first man, that is, on the creature which is sexed in the opposite way from those who are constrained to have recourse to it for their being alike.

The argument would seem to be easily resolved by the simple decision to introduce an empirical fact: sexuation is an empirical fact, and all women can call themselves alike simply by virtue of being the same sex. But facts, as mere facts, tell philosophy very little, and in general, they do not say anything if they do not rise to the symbolic level.

In fact I can speak easily of myself as being like my mother, a friend, all women, in that I am sexed like them, but this saying that I am like them seems to rest more on observation than on contents of thought. I can, it is true, raise myself from the level of mere observation by saying that I share a common *destiny* with them which is tied to our sex, but the contents thus found are rather transformed into a problem. Does this same destiny not lean upon the absent thinking of that sexual difference which is tied to it? We are all really alike then in carrying as unthought that sexual difference in which our likeness to each other is grounded. In other words, once again, the sexual difference which we 'carry' is empirically an immediacy which has not risen to the symbolic, it is a presence which presents itself on the threshold of the word.

The experience of separateness which we have defined as the essence of feminine sexual difference, is thus a first step towards the construction of a symbolic which would be able to give a representation to the foundation of our being alike. But it is a first step only; the sign of a progression which would not be a wandering. An opening word of a discourse which would con-template woman as a subject: the first step over the threshold of *her* word. This discourse, the house of woman's language, has no compulsory directions, or, at least, it has directions which as yet cannot perfectly be traced from here, from this poor begin-ning, though we can already foresee that it must, sooner or later, take on the question of motherhood, regardless of our frequent wish for reticence.

It is, however, useful for the moment to examine thoroughly the possibilities which the discourse which we have conducted until now is about to open up. Among these it is fundamental to stress that our being able to say we are alike equally establishes the possibility of correctly naming our mutual differing.

In fact the thinking of sexual difference can perniciously be translated into the theory of an absolute divide which confines the spread of the opaque swamp of sameness*: there would be, in the sexual difference which marks our being as a differing from men, no longer any difference, and of any kind, among us. We would all be the same, all equal. In this way sexual difference would make us not so much alike, but rather undifferentiated. Instead, it specifies the logic of a different differing.

The lack of a thinking of sexual difference actually unfolds the possibility of only one kind of differing: in as much as I am like the rest of the human species, it is with regard to its totality that I must measure my being different. I would thus be more intelligent than Phillip and less creative than Catherine, and my being different from Phillip and Catherine would not be of a different kind. According to the way of thinking of sexual difference I nevertheless differ from Phillip essentially and, just as essentially, I am the same as Catherine. The same in *essence* as Catherine, but not the same in intelligence, character, personal experience, etc. These differences mark my differing from Catherine which is completely different from my essential differing from Phillip.

Thanks to this essential differing, which is at the same time my essential being the same as every other woman, even my differing in individual characteristics, which at first seemed indistinguishable whether compared to one or the other sex, can now be revised. It is by definition inessential, but it assumes a different meaning according to the sex against which it is examined. Between a man and a woman it is an inessential differing within an essential differing, as a result of which it means very little, since the essential differing between a man and a woman makes the meaning of every other differing superfluous. Between a woman and a woman it is an inessential differing within an essential sameness, so that it takes on the significance of an unfolding of determined differences which rest upon a common essence which makes the two women alike.

It is thus necessary to understand the conceptual meaning which

* In Italian, *uguaglianza* means both equality and sameness. [Translator's note]

distinguishes being alike from being the same. Being the same in essence refers to our common being women, that is, it answers that crucial question 'What am I?', which showed itself to be necessarily rooted in the *'first and foremost a woman'*. In this question the I is not a neutral, but neither is it an abstract. The I which questions herself about her own essence is in fact an individual charged with her insuppressible uniqueness, which cannot simply correspond to this essence, but which wants to understand her uniqueness beginning from this essence which acts as its foundation. This foundation defining the being a woman of every woman, is the same for every woman, but since every woman is this unique woman, the same foundation is revealed to be always and necessarily incarnated in the infinite unique existents who are alike in it, but who do not correspond to it like monotonous replicas of a mould which allows no variations. Being alike marks a tension between a same and a different, and if it is completely resolved in one or the other, it dissolves. Being alike is thus structurally the medium which holds together the same and the differing and gives to each of them a meaning which is such only in this relationship. Outside this concrete relationship, the same is an abstract and the differing is an indeterminacy.

The 'myth' of sameness/equality between women is thus revealed to be a making absolute of the foundation of their being alike and it triggers the possibility of many risks. The major risk becomes evident on the political level where the terms 'equality' (sameness)★ and 'difference' when referring to the problem of power take on a meaning which is immediately loaded with consequences: the particular gifts of some are humbled or repressed, not only by group dynamics, but also by self-censure. Another risk is that the sexual difference which should make us perfectly equal, would become a wall behind which the inessential differences survive, inessential, but the only ones which it is not necessary to deny, so that the determined differing proper to every individual woman ends up measuring itself, and thus meaning something, only in relation to the other sex. The third risk, and perhaps philosophically the most pernicious, is the one rooted in the concept of abstract sameness: the same which allows no differences leaves no space to mediation. Only the 'being alike'

★ See translator's note on p. 215.

as tension between the same and nevertheless different, makes possible the self-recognition of the one which is a passing through the other to understand itself as different in a common essence, so that the two sides of the differing and the being the same may be safeguarded, but not absolutized, in the mediatory category of the being alike.

The thinking of sexual difference is then revealed to be fundamental not only to the representation of an essence which logically establishes our being alike, but also to show us the direction of a theory which would not substitute a new cage for the old cages. In other words, the symbolic which we are seeking is not a beautiful image in whose fixedness each one of us must correspond as an individual reflection, but an image which restores to the individual her essence, while reflecting back the richness of her individuality. So that in the image, each woman, in recognizing herself, would know herself.

ALMOST A CONCLUSION

Here, where our intention to think sexual difference has been able to find an uneasy beginning, there is no theoretical space for a conclusion. However, there is, perhaps, the possibility of glimpsing the feasible paths of a future development of this mode of thinking which is now only at the initial stage. The provisional conclusion is thus rather a patient gathering together of theoretical threads which have been unravelled from the initial discourse.

Among these, is the necessity of the dual.

Philosophy questions itself on the originary, but precisely because it questions itself about it, it does not form it but rather finds it, and tries to discover its meaning. This originary is as such an *already there*, a presence which presents itself to an attribution of meaning by thought, so that thought could say what this 'already there' is. Thus the task of thought is an almost subservient one, and yet so powerful in its ability to decide the essence of that which presents itself to it in its simple presence and consigns its whole destiny to the defenceless act of this presenting itself. Already present is thus the world, in the infinite multiplicity and variety of its presenting itself, and in the world, a world itself, the thinking being, a presence which is presupposed to its thinking itself, presenting itself to the power of its thought: it is that which thought decides that it is. But it is above all, from always and for ever, this simple *already there*. A factual originary, in its minimum significance, an originary presenting itself to its own meaning in its maximum significance.

This 'already there' of the human creature contains precise connotations, and it is in the totality of these that it presents itself to its own meaning: it is living, mortal, sexed, thinking. Thought actually decides, for example, on the most painful of these connotations, death; it says what it is, and even manages to transform its presence in the concept of the immortality of the soul, but always beginning from this presence, from the human creature's being already, and from always, mortal, from its being thus and not otherwise. An unthought death would remain a simple presence, a sudden unexpected dying, each time singularly experienced in stupefied silence. But that is not possible! Of course, it is an absurdity.

Why? Because death is visible. It is a presence which continuously presents itself to the eyes and thus consigns itself to an investigation on is own meaning. The same is true of life and of language. The Greeks said: 'Man is a living being which has language', and in the term 'living being' dying was also comprised, less painfully; that dying which as a protagonist resonated in their most ancient name for human beings, 'mortals'.

Why not sexual difference then? Does it not belong to the presence of the human creature which presents itself, the being already from all time sexed in difference thus and not otherwise?

Perhaps because thought is truly powerful, to such an extent that it denies visibility to that presence which presents itself to it constitutively without defence and thus allows that among the possible meanings which could be attributable to it, would be included that of its own erasure.

Thus it has happened that no meaning has been attributed by thought to the self-presenting presence of sexual difference; blindness has produced its invisiblity. Human creatures were, and still are, there: the originary presence which renews itself in every single new appearance, which describes itself as living, mortal, sexed, thinking, a presence which as a whole entity presents itself to be defined by 'What is it?', and every time it reverberates in this definition as a mutilated whole, or rather as a monstrous neutral sexed in the masculine.

The presence presents itself in sexual difference, it tirelessly repeats its *already there*: 'I am two: either the one or the other.'

But, at the very best, thought replies: 'You are a gender, and I define you as a neutral gender, then I also allow you to become specified in the one and then in the other.' Thus the originary presence in the whole of its sexuation has no meaning for its own being, as a whole being, sexed in difference, either the one or the other. It is one in its *essence*, an essence which does not contemplate the two, even if it agrees (observes) that it takes form itself, through a cunning reproductive mechanism, in the one or in the other according to chance.

The dual originary of the human creature is not a less than new find, engendered by the imagination, a kind of game (we have tried with the one, now let us try with the two) but the attempt to give meaning to a presence which has never tired of presenting itself to thought.

The thinking of sexual difference, recognizing the dual originary as an unsurpassable presupposition, excludes a logic of the assimilation of the Other. For the *feminine way of thinking* difference, the Other is theoretically a not yet investigated entity, and probably one which could only be investigated in the ways allowed by a logic of the dual which at the moment is only advanced as right and necessary, but not yet developed. This logic nevertheless presents itself to us as of now conflictual with regard to that logic of the one which has suffocated its historical possibility. It is a conflict which is not carried out with cudgel blows (or maybe it is, I do not know), but rather requires the suspension of trust, being suspicious of thought, with regard to the entire conceptual castle of the logic of the one. We women are at present inside, not outside, this castle: it is thus also necessary to refine our weapon of self-diffidence. This means that we should not paralyse ourselves with self-censure, neither, for goodness' sake, should we paralyse other women with cries of 'sexist' or similar labels. It means, instead, to be suspicious of the purported neutrality of language, of its scientific objectivity, and also of its beauty. So that in this beauty being a woman would no longer be the enchantment of a creature who is mute in front of the word.

NOTES

1 A very precise investigation of this meaning, conducted through the analysis of the texts of the major philosophers (Plato, Aristotle,

Descartes, Hegel, Freud, etc.) can be found in the work of Luce Irigaray, a thinker to whom my research, and any philosophical research on the theme of sexual difference, owes a lot.

2 We can find an exception to theory's ignorance in Hegel and Freud, and, to a certain degree, in Plato's *Republic* (453 b and *passim*). On the meaning and limits of this exception see Cristiane Fischer, Elvia Franco, Giannina Longobardi, Veronica Mariaux, Luisa Muraro, Anita Sanvitto, Betty Zamarchi, Chiara Zamboni, Gloria Zanardo, 'La differenza sessuale: da scoprire e da produrre', in Adriana Cavarero *et al.*, *Diotima: Il pensiero della differenza sessuale*, Milan, La Tartaruga, 1985.

3 See Rosi Braidotti, 'Modelli di dissonanza: donne e/in filosofia', in Patrizia Magli (ed.) *Le donne e i segni*, Ancona, Il Lavoro Editoriale, 1985, pp. 24–37.

4 In the Greek text of Genesis 1: 26–7, we find the term *homoiosis* for 'being alike'; this is repeated in the second passage (Genesis 2: 21) where 'alike' is *homolus*. In Genesis 2: 18, however, which the Italian tradition translates as 'I want to make him a helpmate who would be like him', we have in Greek the expression *kat'auton* which indicates rather the concept of relationship and of correspondence. This is confirmed by the Hebrew text where we find in Genesis 1: 26–7 the term *dmwt*, and in Genesis 2: 18, the term *neged*, which indicates in its more ancient use the concept of counterpart and also of correspondence. It seems thus that a confirmation can be found on a lexical level of these two different meanings of likeness, where the second one is a likeness of woman to man through a derived correspondence.

5 I use a note and the materials thereof, from Hannah Arendt's *Vita activa*, Milan, Bompiani, 1964, p. 354 (see her *The Life of the Mind*, vol. 2, *Willing*, London, Secker & Warburg, 1978); she adds, however, with reference to the two biblical passages, that their 'difference indicates a lot more than a different evaluation of the importance of the woman': this 'a lot more' refers to the faith-action and faith-salvation connection. This notation is in keeping with the neutral investigative style present in the volume: for example, the problem of the despotic power of the master of the household over women and slaves is considered worthy of consideration with reference to the slaves, but not to the women. The logic of neutral thought which is thus in evidence throughout the book is all the more significant when it is seen at work in a thinker whose quality is, for those adepts of her work, unanimously recognized as truly excellent.

6 See Luisa Muraro, *Guglielma e Maifreda. Storia di un'eresia femminista*, Milan, La Tartaruga, 1985, p. 138 and *passim*.

7 I once again call to your attention the excellent work of Luisa Muraro in ibid. It demonstrates how the Guglielmite heresy, in its principal or *Ursache* Guglielma, is born from the notion that the incarnation of God in the man Jesus Christ was an incarnation in sexual difference, a truly human incarnation in its sexed partialness, which demands that the incarnation be thought in the feminine sex, according to Guglielma (probably) achieved in every woman, according to her followers in her personally. The monstrosity of a neutral man (Jesus Christ who

incarnated all humanity, while being only a man) was born of the masculine mind. In the Guglielmite way of thinking, God knows sexual difference and does not create monsters; his incarnation belongs in sexual difference and only in this form will humanity be saved. The Guglielmites affirmed that non-Christians will be saved thanks to Guglielma: the non-recognized partialness of the divine incarnation in Jesus Christ was thus the reason why many of them stayed outside the Church

Chapter 12

Jumping*

Angela Putino

Thinking for oneself. Responsibility: to think the event, to question the event. One might believe that the highest level of responsibility is found in a superior organization, an ideal, an idea, a game plan. But sometimes in these circumstances individual responsibility is evaded when faced with the event, and singularity becomes a contingent aspect, if not a conspiracy regarding what constitutes the *we*. Here, the singular seems forced to find its identity in a *we*, a *we* resulting from what is authorized in the discourse. And in the discursive authorizations, the past and its foundation appear.

I think that responsibility is thinking for oneself, based on oneself. But this leads to another line of questioning: where is the self? Does it really split or distance a *we*? I am not talking about a social *we* and the fake and mutilating individual–society dialectic, but about that *we* so often pronounced among women. That *we* which becomes a desire for a subject identity or an intrasubjectivity, or at other times merges into the indistinct. It is not always a homogeneous *we* which is articulated, but a *we* tied to several discursive levels and therefore changeable; each of these levels embodies the dangers of a *we* which burdens the shoulders, and I would say that every woman is familiar with the perspectives and dangers regarding only the *we* with which she is concerned and confronted.

One sometimes complains of not being able to say 'We were, we are', and to show the rich country and the temples and the castles. The anguish goes parallel to a fragmented, separate *we*, which cannot say *we* and which looks for security in an identity

---

* First published as 'Saltare', in *DWF*, 1988, no. 5–6. Translated by Laura Benedetti.

or at least an apparently sound biological realism. Sometimes, the world is eclipsed and, without a *we*, trees and fields and living beings do not succeed in naming themselves and the word of things does not become a word for a woman. In this case one tries to find a solution in a sound referent and defines reality according to economic laws: what is real is real because it is ratified by consent. But can one not say that sharp splinters, if not a large country, appear? That even if a tree is not so named, the voice nevertheless travels across a soft leaf?

And can one not say that, if the universal subject is declining, so perhaps is the subject? That the world itself, in representation, is a foreign grid? That neither foundation nor unity nor consent can move our questioning?

Hinted at by presenting, it is an unrepresentable *we*, a *we* one can get close to and savour as annual flowers savour spring. It cannot avoid showing us its terrible condition of being on the edge, far away and alienated. Even when it is close it winks in a balanced calm.

Hinting at the unrepresentable by presenting. Nostalgia wraps a presentation which is insufficient and which does not clearly indicate 'this was before you and after you', but which accompanies us while letting us go.

The *we* of the presenting of the *we* is immemorial because we can never associate it with our history although it seems to be going in that direction. Nevertheless it produces a growth, a joyful impulse, an imagination which exceeds and calls itself 'a-human'. An imagination which jumps on the male imagination with which it believed itself to be assimilated.

What can this *we*, unrepresentable and yet always yearning to be present, be? A conquered word, an acquired gesture, a form of behaviour unusual if compared to common behaviour and yet not eccentric because it closely follows the everyday aspects of our life. To receive energy from a woman and to return it to her, without transferring it to the world or to others as usually happens in the human condition. Something taken and then something returned to the same woman or another woman, not to society in general, nor to culture or philosophy. Only in this way can we obtain a useful and usable knowledge. Only along this path, as light as a gesture, between two or more women, comes a *we*. This perhaps leads to the liveliness of some moments. A dense dialogue, which never stops for other models, which yearns to talk without rejecting any method, neither the sweet nor the cruel one. The pacified gestures of some figures of women close to each other, one head brushing up against another as if they were both part of a new time and tension. The letters written from one woman to another, to explore, to express. Some ceremony, a little carpet of kindness laid out for another woman. Clues which hint at a we. Only here does the bravery of thinking for oneself stand out, without withdrawing into arrogance. *We* is a horizon open to thinking for oneself, not a verification or a confusion on a level of equality.

What does a woman's thinking for oneself think? Often: 'Run away, run away, don't let them catch you, if you're there you won't be here any more.' Not wanting to be tamed, this is thinking for oneself. A flickering, a revolt which combines the joy of being in the world and the desire to be strangers. An adolescent game which invents not another street, but another space. The intensity of the untamed in my thinking makes me turn to another woman, a concrete other, with a name, or to other women with names. Maybe here, without pronouncing we, I say we. We is a challenge, it is not familiar territory. It is a race dissociated from the word which expresses not a designation of the human species but a map of connections, glances, remedies, writings: a map of the untamed, a worn threshold of invincibility. The word 'race' conveys the dream, the challenge; separate from its value as having human significance, separate from its sad history, it is marked by our individuality. It wants to be like a desert, an expanse of clouds, a penetrable space where the limiting configuration of a landscape, either foreign or familiar, does not appear. Without being tamed by the landscape, here I move and another woman moves. If I am able to look at her in this space she is clearly visible, not far from me but separate. If I have this space I know her difference and mine, my fear and hers, but also her courage and my fear; here I can be joyfully surprised by her bravery, more daring than mine, and perceive her, watch her route, and listen. But without imitating her, without identification, because in this space, which is impossible to manipulate according to external limits and signs, we are at the same time a tribe and individuals, and each woman fights her own war.

Holding one's own. I have often thought that the real point of the battle of courage is 'holding one's own'. A deep passage of fear opens up whenever one finds oneself in this position or sees another woman who does not give up. Of course fear does not exist when everything legitimizes an opposition or makes it convenient, when the context itself calls for a skirmish, when the matter arouses quarrelling and boasting. I am talking about another way of holding one's own which does not depend on the effectiveness of one's weapons, a way in which words do not move like a parade pleasing the speaker and the listener. Here words stop, distancing the proper order of the discourse, the cunning values of a certain competence; here words are nothing but barriers. The other woman or we who pronounce these words do so as if sewn to them. The adhesive force that pushes them against us like a dress which one cannot stop wearing is knowing that there is a resistance.

I remember the pull of fear when I heard a woman say: 'And yet I know it is like that.' She was forcing me to take a position, but I would have liked it to have been clarified by one of the many discursive arguments we use to give value to what we say. But it was not. She was excluding herself from this territory and affirming that something was visible precisely because of her exclusion; she was forcing the other woman to make the same jump, because only from that place would another understand what she was saying. The affirmation needs no justification, it rarely emerges and its rarity cannot be predicted. This is where discursivity is interrupted. This is scary: we are forced to accept responsibility for this affirmation without justifying it. It has an authority which cannot be confused with despotism. I do not think one feels a moral obligation here, but rather a slight feeling of timorous courage upon which, from one moment to the other, either the fear of ridicule or the conventional blanket of interpretation may fall.

Often, the event which does not experience tameness is destined to disappear. It fades, it is covered by a fog of insignificance or of reduction.

I want to prevent another woman from disappearing, erased by the approximations; I want the thread of the argument which defines her, which makes her understandable, not to disappear, even if it is a thread which does not yet have a precise outline. I do not want it to become as weak as a voice, the inflection of which is impossible to recall because of an imperfect memory.

Because my only perception of that 'I know it is like that', of that *holding one's own*, was in the fleeting moment of our encounter.

This is unexpected knowledge of myself and the other, but it is so unpredictable that it easily disappears. One asks the other to make herself known, to bring back the same face forcing one to have the same glance, to find a remedy for what may disappear if we catch a glimpse of it. Recalling is not for her, but for us. It is also true that we cannot tolerate the injustice of erasing, like a supplementary or anticipated death. And yet I call her so that what has appeared between the two of us, almost a threshold, will not move far away.

I cannot alone recall even what I had already seen in myself. Without having been myself I would not have been able to see her. As a person I am a vantage point, a tall mast of a ship boarded by a castaway. My Self and her Self rise up between the *I* and the *she* to say a *we* which does not have anything to do with our lives. When *we* say *we*, we are in a realm of consciousness without knowledge, we jump at the beginning. When we are above our heads, we make something of that *holding one's own*, of that invincibility which is now between us like the *we*.

It is a strange bridge, the one laid by the *we*. This is exactly where I want to 'hold my own' in the face of the other woman. Between us the *we* is now used to create distance: to circumscribe spaces, to define their perimeters, to maintain a position, so as not to lose ground. I want to define my route, not lose what makes me say *I*. I do no want to lose the things I have loved, for which I have suffered, and thanks to which I will never be able to forget having been an inhabitant of the earth.

At the same time there is another desire: that the other woman not forget all this and therefore not imitate me, not identify herself with me, nor agree with me before feeling happy about herself. The truth is that I do not want to meet somebody who resembles me, I want an otherness, but one which does not rub against me.

The other she represents cannot come from the acceptance of what is tamed in her; she cannot accept it in order to disagree with me. Shamelessness towards the world is the true characteristic of disagreement with another woman.

I think that a woman never wants a man to talk on her behalf; my wish is that a woman not talk on my behalf either. I want to meet, but meeting does not imply substitutions. In a different context of desire, Murasaki says that women of great renown and high social status do not show false pride: they take what is worth taking and do not measure themselves against the world. Maybe a famous woman does not want a substitution, but she dares to become light: she knows how to make herself attracted.

Tragic, maybe, but also comic. Have laws anything to do with responsibility?

To disobey means above all to elude two concepts: guilt and expiation; to undo the link between the two, to displace it, to bypass it. Every time a structure moves while maintaining the strict order of these two terms, the centre is a model based on a majority, which is part of the male culture. We start another movement which is intended to disrupt the realm of laws and weaken them. Therefore, we cannot respect the consequentiality of this order. The link between punishment, guilt and pain can be loosened. We jump over, we cut the bond between them. We can transform pain into a gratuitous feeling: we cannot eliminate it from our life, but we can loosen or unfasten its tie with guilt and expiation.

To sever the ties which determine the ordered consequentiality means to limit the capacity of the system of laws: the system's structure, and therefore order, can impose itself in fact only because of its solidity. Ours is an operation of circumventing, deceiving, approaching differently; this means always wanting something else to be accepted, always being able to propose another initiative. In this way the importance of disobedience lies not in what has been denied, but in what one has tried to say. If suffering ever follows, it will not be as an atonement for the violation of the laws, but as going down in a war, falling in a battle. Falling does not mean giving up your memory, your thoughts, your rules. No woman atones for her sins or pays the price of guilt, but rather she crashes, collides, resists, feels pain, dies. We no longer give alms to morality.

We do not pay because we contract no debts, we do not pay because we do not believe, because we smile, we express irony. After all, we never really took seriously these laws and their claim to be the only ones. We never really believed – and here, to believe means to think that one's freedom is in step with the laws.

Far away, we do not disobey or betray or give up. These laws have often constrained us, at other times they have bound us, they have always besieged us, but we paid nothing but what was owed the victor. Above all, we do not atone for our sins because we have not interiorized the guilt. Sometimes we put guilt between us like a written page beyond which we could not see ourselves; but we always tried to write other signs on the other side of the page. We mark the other face and nobody can tell whether or not it is close to the transcription of the laws. We only know that it is time to turn the page.

Our pain, our suffering, very often seemed useless and gratuitous to us: we want them to remain useless because we do not want them to be construed as atonement. Pain is not a loss, it is the heroism of war. I think it is fair that men do not have heroes any more: these heroes are only useful for marching in columns in the armies, like ghosts perpetuating a power structure. For us it is different. Pain for us is a great narration because it is one of the events of disunion; it is a duel which separates us from the general community in the human race. What is painful, what is cruel, is taken and transformed, becoming a myth and a rite and a plot in our memory. Guilt does not cause movement; it turns dark and internal, it becomes neither wind nor sand nor a call.

Of course not. We interiorized a law, but in a perverted way. Since it did not include us, or concern us, or give us our due, we felt excluded, like strangers. This alienation worried us. It made us strangers among ourselves, incapable of justice and of having rules. A reciprocal squint. To which we want to react with a displacement. We were suspicious, squirming nervously even when we seemed to respect completely the formalities of certain obligations. An abyss opened up in our lives between us and the laws before we could even ask: 'Which laws? Is this a law?' We tried to go unnoticed. We played like children, born again, like adolescents, hiding without recognizing the commands but listening to them only in order not to capitulate under the first inquisitions. All one has to do is begin, then everything follows.

Laws were like Captain Hook to us, we sent a crocodile with an alarm clock after them. We fled, making others flee, with imperceptible shrewdness. Using a little, hidden audacity we tried to control the insurmountable aspects of the laws. We experience a comic tension, an innocence which can remain as such since it does not recognize a correspondence between disobedience and punishment, since it does not bond them together with guilt.

Some women think that women's space should be a homogeneous and neutral country, a cautious country of equals. I do not wish to talk to women who consider this true, desirable and tolerable.

Chapter 13

On the female word and its 'spirit'*

Gabriella Bonacchi

Completely at home in the modern world yet perfectly unsure of herself, completely at the centre of dominant narratives yet perfectly marginal; she who becomes a woman today concentrates in herself the spirit of our time.

However, women are not simply a component among others of the sociopolitical scene. They evoke a primary, anthropological, emotional dimension, both linked to history and in conflict with it, which for the sake of convenience is often called sexuality. Women evoke an unrelievable tension between the sayable and the unsayable – not what is still unsaid, but what resists being said. This again, for the sake of convenience, has sometimes been called the relationship between nature and culture; meaning, it would seem, the relationship between the known and the unknown, between *heimlich* and *fremd*, which creates the *unheimlich*, the 'Uncanny' within the very sphere of domesticity, of day-to-day experience.

For what could be more domestic – literally – than women? Yet women's words – some women's words – have sounded uncanny, disturbing.

The reason for this, I believe, is that alongside the reassuringly familiar (and complicit) voice of the *Nebenmensch*, men have heard in women's words undertones of the *Fremde*, of the alien, the trace of an otherness which would unveil itself in sudden flashes in the features of their mothers, sisters, daughters, or companions.

Within the domestic walls, in bedrooms, kitchens, bathrooms, woman's word has revealed itself as *other*, upsetting the symmetry which has been obsessively pursued by our culture.

* First published as 'Della parola femminile e del suo "spirito" . . .', in *Reti*, 1989, no. 2. Translated by Maureen Lister.

What has been so disquieting and frightening in woman's word is not so much its difference, as its *asymmetry*. For asymmetry is wild and multiform, whereas difference can be made to fit a certain context. Asymmetry occupies a privileged position in the construction of sense, whereas difference can be moved down to a lower level of consensus.

I shall return to the more general relationship between '*Zeitgeist*' and the asymmetry of woman's word. First of all, I want to draw attention to the genealogy of this speaking-as-woman on which are founded both our most recent experience, and the possibility of communicating it: to ourselves – to the women we have become – as well as to other women.

Let it not be forgotten, the truth we have created originated in a *promise*: the event of a promise which is fulfilled at the very moment women affirm each other's presence, addressing to one another unheard-of words. This is how I would describe what the Libreria delle Donne (Milan) named the 'thread of happiness' circulating among women. Women's being-together has created a new language, whose founding act was originally prelinguistic, but which can only be expressed in language.

This founding act was the loving, 'thoughtful' addressing of a word, for the first time destined by woman to woman. I believe that this reciprocal address precedes all other more sociable (that is, expressible in sociological categories) forms of entrustment. Reciprocal address has transformed being female from a fact into an *event* which established relationships among women. This relationship is the originary event of our movement's history and politics; from this relationship – in momentary detachment from the current moral modes – the new ethic implicit in speaking ourselves was born.

In the Middle Ages *homines* gained their identity as such through belonging to a community. Whether they were nobles or plebs, men were men because they were acknowledged as such by their place of origin – lineage or corporation.

Being-man was not a discovery, but an invention. In the same way, being-woman today means inventing ourselves, venturing out towards the secrets held by that originary mutual acknowledgement, which each of us created and possesses. Everything has a market price: but being-woman is still considered imperfect goods, because we have rejected the logic of emancipation. For though it is no longer founded on the gift economy of ancient anthropological realities, it still resists being entirely governed by the rules which structure the game of supply and demand.

THE SITE OF FEMALE REFLECTION

Women are undoubtedly affected by the heteronomy of patriarchal time and reality, a reality which has not been defined by us. But in being-woman, there is – there can be – the *moral feature of provocation*, a challenge towards the doings of that part of the world over which we have no control. In order to do this, however, we must keep the memory of the way in which we have created, through our practice of reciprocal address, a world of women.

So the various stages of this process should be reconstructed, beginning with *autocoscienza*. The peculiar richness of Italian feminism lies in the special attention it has dedicated to the issue of relationships. This also explains its relative weakness in achieving social 'progress', compared to the feminist movement in other countries. The practice of *autocoscienza* marked the transition from the traditional 'realistic' form of relationships between women to a metacognitive exploration. Belonging to the female gender was no longer an immediate fact of consciousness directly linked to biological reality, and was transformed into a sort of 'alchemist's secret', which must be learned in the being-together with other women.

This rite of passage – impure and characterized by the fusion of emotion and cognition that marks the initial stage of all knowledge – is the true matrix for critical detachment from the dominant culture. But how did this 'knowledge of knowledge' evolve, consciously guarded as it was, by a secret which we do not seem willing to reveal even now? One hypothesis is that it came about by means of self-representation. In the groups of the 1970s, each woman was first of all a mirror, where the other woman could recognize her own 'body'. This recognition has created culture, weaving the web of interpersonal relationships which we have been taught, in the west, to call 'soul'. Sometimes, the groups succeeded in the delicate cognitive process of constructing a bodily image as *object* (whole), at the same time considering this image as *subject*, that is, as an active source of self-representation. This, as far as I can see, provides the basis for the tranformation of women into rationally, morally conscious, responsible individuals who are capable of *owning* their actions introspectively, recognizing them and representing them as their own: all actions, including the intentions and emotions of an interior world objectified and rendered subjective at one and the same time.

The groups were, sometimes, the site of female *reflection* where the body was extended into a soul which became its virtual 'internal' dimension.

The intimacy, the 'Dionysian' element of women's being-together, led to an inevitable rupture of the usual connection between the public and the private. In order to discover the relationship between intimate reality and its authentic expression, the normal channels of communication between the self-elaboration of a political subject and its entry into the public sphere had to be severed. The resulting 'separatism' and 'secrecy' make today's task of reconstructing the groups' work almost hopelessly difficult, even without taking into account the amnesias which normally affect all participants in historic events.

Another effect of 'separatism' and 'secrecy' has been a one-sided focusing on certain aspects, selected according to criteria of obedience to differing – but equally exploitative – political liturgies. The 'thread of happiness' is claiming victory for the irreversible maturity of a female symbolic which is even capable of swaying opinion in male strongholds. The intention of the 'Women's Charter'[1] was to restructure the citadels of male power using female passion and votes: from the new Italian Communist Party* all the way into Parliament.

What has been violated in both cases is just what I would be tempted to call the *Dionysian intimacy* of an experience which needs to remember is originary destination in order to speak itself.

It is this 'immaterial' foundation which has made feminism a child of our era but also, as we shall see, the interpreter of a temporality which partly oversteps the limits of the present postmodern curve.

THE SPIRIT OF OUR TIME

Our epoch is marked by the end of community, including the 'residual' spiritual community of modernity. Atheism, the *atheon* of values in the official symbolic order, has been substituted for

* The Italian Communist Party has now changed its name to 'Democratic Left-Wing Party' (Partito Democratico della Sinistra). [Translator's note]

the 'polytheism of values' typical of modernity. This has led to a crisis in all the substantialist movements, beginning with the working-class movement, whose point of reference is a foundation, or a metaphysics. Today we have entered the era of the 'unmentionable community' (Blanchot), or the 'negative community: the community of those who have no community' (Bataille).

Women's political presence is a hybrid. It testifies on the one hand to this movement of history towards the 'unmentionable community', a community without foundation; on the other hand to the anxiety about the lack of foundation – or lack of symmetry, which amounts to the same thing – and to the search for a new, solid foundation which can fill the void left by the traditional one. So our political presence has on the one hand witnessed the impossibility of proposing the traditional basis for political action, which was rooted in class or social structures (a reference to the 'transversality' of our political presence). On the other hand, recent developments reveal how difficult it is to bear this experience of a presence without a foundation, and how difficult it is to react to the inertial forces of our historical inheritance. For I interpret women's search for a new foundation as a rootedness in a past which our presence originally intended to deny, and effectively did so.

THY FEARFUL SYMMETRY

In an article in *La Stampa* (8 March 1989), Guido Ceronetti wrote that today the entire French Revolution could be completely reinterpreted 'in the light of its hunger for symmetry'. Commenting on the image of the 'fearful symmetry' of Blake's tiger metaphor and the 'Dionysian intimacy' of the industrial revolution (which was much more violent than the French one, just as Albion's ironworks were much more bloody and pitiless than the all 'too human' virulence of Marat, Charlotte Corday's *monstre égorgée*), Ceronetti writes that 'the western mind is manacled to symmetry and even imagines Nature and the Creator as forgers of symmetry'. Our epoch is full of 'mind-forg'd manacles', forged more by the industrial revolution than by the events in France, where the Dionysian element did emerge momentarily.

Our epoch has caught only glimpses of the difficult *freedom of the assymetrical*, and has never fully accepted it. According to

Ceronetti, all that remains of the asymmetrical today are acts which fill the empty space of symmetry and of which one is ashamed. If all symmetry is *fearful*, the revolution, being symmetrical, is 'horrifying'.

The working-class movement is a child of the symmetry of the French Revolution and has, as we have said, sharper claws and teeth than the French Revolution, which still bore too many traces of the premodern. Modernity owes more to the industrial revolution than to the storming of the Bastille, and the working-class movement is more modern than the people of the Parisian barricades.

We are left to contemplate the great ruins, our prophecies being rendered weaker and weaker by our infinite discouragement. What conclusion can we draw from the ruined symmetry of the working-class movement? That 'intellectual thing' that is a tear? Or the courage to continue. But in which direction?

What Ceronetti, following Blake, calls manacles, Heidegger calls the western metaphysical tradition, with its nihilist destiny, leading to total destruction. Some believe, with Irigaray, that to name this *destiny* and unmask the gendered nature of its claim to neutral universality means defeating metaphysics. The mask is torn away in the name of the face: I know what you are playing at, some are saying to metaphysics, your disguised features hold no more secrets for me. Your features are the ones I have always known, those of the father. But the face is, in turn, another foundation, which is stronger because it is truer, *natural*, and not artificial like that of the mask.

The substantial mechanism of metaphysics is rootedness in a foundation; for, according to Heidegger, the search for a foundation is the theo-teleological inheritance which ensnared the 'guardians of universality' during the century-long sway held by the eldest discipline, philosophy. And this passage in Heidegger constitutes a point of no return for all contemporary thought.

Does not rootedness in nature – biological gender – the foundation of a symbolic order which is *other* – mean succumbing to a new metaphysical expedient?

Women's most recent ideas are haunted by a ghost: a horror of asymmetry, which may also present itself as a metaphysics of symmetry, rootedness in a natural foundation of new manacles. But these manacles could simply serve as a tempting replacement for the old, decaying symmetry: which would be a strategy to avoid the *horror vacui* of the relationship with the Other as a free choice, with no foundation outside of its same existence.

Many competitors crowd the postmodern market-place of values: the search for a solid foundation may be an attempt to avoid the risks of competition, presenting itself as the competitor with the best qualifications for the refoundation of an alternative culture. But what cultural alliance can be formed on the basis of the cancellation of true asymmetry, the asymmetry of a relationship between two subjects which has no other foundation than its own ephemeral presence, when it constructs and realizes itself each time?

WITNESSES OF 'GREAT RUINS'

History has taught the lesson of death more often than that of life. And we should not be afraid to face the inexorable fact of the losses which it helps us to identify. It is useless to deny that the contemporary thinker's sole role in western culture seems to be that of contemplating the great ruins. This, as Benjamin's angel pointed out, is history's precious lesson. The culture of the western working-class movement has also shared this destiny of annihilation of the foundation. But as a ruin and no longer as an object of immediate historical identification, it might lead us to some untimely and therefore more productive reflections.

But how can the history of the working-class movement as a 'great ruin' be any use to us?

I would say that the culture of the working-class movement represents a courageous effort to evade the competition dominating modernity. In the middle of the twentieth century the theory and practice of the worker's organizations claim a strong subjectivity, the first-born's right credited with maximum objectivity. The very capitalistic mechanism that had caused the oppression of labour was supposed to lead to its liberation: liberation of the self and of the other. Here we see dialectic at work – the culmination, according to Heidegger, of western metaphysics – in the form of an 'astute' mechanism according to which the greatest oppression entails the greatest potential for liberation.

At the heart of the working-class movement, and its culture, we find the cross – not the cross of myth, as in premodern movements, but the cross of western metaphysics: the dialectics of liberation.

As I am familiar with historical procedures, I shall attempt to organize my account along the classical historiographic line of division into periods. I shall try to trace the differences between the characteristics of modernity, whence the working-class movement was born, and the features of contemporaneity, whose daughter is women's political presence.

As I have already stated, my thesis is that the contemporary radicalizes the features of modernity and that our political presence has been a hybrid. On the one hand we have constituted a *novum* profoundly rooted in the contemporary radicalization of modernity. On the other hand, almost frightened by this *novum*, we have tried to present ourselves as descendants of more or less illustrious dynasties, claiming the substantialist inheritance which still assails the protagonists of modernity, not least the working-class movement.

A word of explanation. When I was trying to order my ideas, intellectual modesty made me shrink at the idea of naming the time in which we are living in order to distinguish it from the past (in so far as such operations are possible or useful). I wondered if the term 'postmodern' still has any validity. Can it still be used without evoking, as its sole identifying definition, that mixture of libido and economics, electronics and cynicism, computers and cheap seduction, esotericism and pretence which some of Lacan's and Derrida's trivial popularizations have led us to become suspicious of?

During my search for a respectable family father with acceptable credentials, I came across the name of Max Weber, a forbidding and rather obsolete personality. His definition of the modern world as a world dominated by 'polytheism of values' kept echoing in my mind (I consciously refrain from mentioning the greatest of all indecent thinkers, Nietzsche and his gay science; I would rather refer to the more sober corrosiveness of Pascal and his elaboration of the three orders – the order of the flesh, the order of the spirit and the order of values – whose principles are not reciprocally transposable).

Another name crossed my mind, a person who is equally underestimated in fashionable genealogies: Paul Valéry, the Valéry who wrote *La politique de l'esprit* and *La crise de l'esprit*. These two texts, to a certain extent, take us beyond Weber, as they state that these different orientations, this 'polytheism of values', not only swarms the macrospace of society, but also the individual micro-universe. According to Valéry, this pluralism, which is a characteristic of 'all cultivated heads', constitutes the essence of modernity.

PLURALISM AND PLURALITY

Let us pause to consider the consequences of the hyperpluralism which characterizes our lives today.

Theoretical 'polytheism' interacts with the very definition of the areas under discussion. Let us take, for example, the relationship to nature: where does this begin? With the exploitation of raw materials, as the economists say, or the transfer of energy, as the ecologists say? Or with the relationship to internal nature, as the followers of critical theory hold?

Each of these approaches corresponds to a profoundly different attitude towards life: life as individual survival, life as service to the species, life as pleasure, life as 'getting on at all costs', life as 'waiting for the fatal moment'.

With Nietzsche, philosophy bids farewell to Hegel's obsession with the unity of reason. The labour of Sisyphus undertaken by Hegel, in taking up Kant's unified decree after years of work around the separate spheres of different types of reason, is interrupted. Twentieth-century philosophy has accepted the more theoretically relevant challenges of Einstein's relativity, as well as those contained in Heisenberg's indeterminacy theory and Gödel's theory of incompleteness, shifting from strategies of unity to strategies of multiplicity. This is the direction of the exchanges between contemporary philosophers and Prigogine's theory of dissipative structure, Thom's catastrophe theory and Kuhn's thesis of paradigm transformation.

In this perspective, postmodern thought constitutes a radicalization of the basic tendency of modernity and of its essence, which was already formulated, as we have seen, by Weber and Valéry. Postmodernism is the final separation from any desire for unity and its oppressive aspects. We could indeed consider postmodernism – in as far as it is useful to employ this label – as a radicalization of the pluralism of modernity, in the sense of its transformation into a 'radical plurality'.

The main difference between pluralism and 'radical plurality' is that the former relies on a sort of two-stage model, the first stage being the hard core of certainties which form the basis of consensus: that is to say, the old basis which permits the coquetry and capriciousness of the second stage, which is tolerated exactly because it is considered part of the so-called superstructure. This two-stage model has undergone a final crisis in the contemporary era, where dissent has taken hold at the roots, giving rise to vertically different versions of the world. This could also explain, for example, the radicality of the new fundamentalisms with which our world abounds and the violence of their reciprocal antagonism: the ecological, religious and even feminist neo-fundamentalisms. Today, differences are no longer conceived as variations on the same theme, but as irreconcilable conflicts.

We are facing a radical crisis in the metahistorical narratives which have shored up the ideologies of modernity: the emancipation of humanity in the Enlightenment, the full realization of the spirit in idealism, the hermeneutics of meaning in historicism, the liberation of humanity in Marxism.

It is the working-class movement's ideology that has set most store by the hope of realizing in history the recomposition of humankind into a totality of good. But we know that coercion and terror are the other face of that totality – the worker's state, the socialist monoculture.

But if women are not to base their word on a foundation, not even that of the gendered character of the human genoma, where can the charismatic force of women's word come from?

We thus return to our initial ideas on the 'immaterial' foundation of feminist political subjectivity.

Being-together, which engendered the expression 'addressed from woman to woman', has constituted – and here I will spell out what I only hinted at earlier – the ultimate community, in fact the community of those without a community, a community of the dispossessed in our century.

Let us now recall some aspects of what has been a truly different, asymmetrical presence (in Ceronetti's sense) of women in recent years.

FROM RUINS TO THE COMMUNITY OF WOMEN

I think back with affection to the 'poverty' of women's earliest texts, in comparison with the richness and boldness of the texts which are being written today. I am thinking of the leaflets, the small anthologies full of platitudes about our misery; the usual texts of the few 'unhappy' women who were our points of reference: Virginia Woolf, Sylvia Plath and Emily Dickinson. Then came the rich and authoritative words of Irigaray, who spoke of philosophy and psychoanalysis, re-creating a new common sense, a new museum of wisdom, where new female divinities could be erected: the sea lover, Nietzsche's unsaid, Descartes' silences, Plato's unsaid, everything that western thought had silenced was investigated, scrutinized, stolen back and spoken aloud. Never had closer attention been paid to the shadowy areas around the margins, to the turns and folds of thought, to its difficulties and failures. In order to be rich, negation must be applied to brilliant, rich materials, it must demolish the great works. It cannot deal with experience that has not been articulated, and proclaimed.

The fascination of a style, or, rather, a *manner*, resists unchanged the transformation of its field of application and immediately infects the critique which wants to upturn it. A great positive often produces only a great negative which is more affectedly stentorian than the original it claims to be criticizing.

The risk of *manner* can never be overemphasized: whatever it is and however it is represented, manner cannot but be manneristic, cannot but oppose the most secret and intimate *experimental songs* – I am still referring to Blake's *Songs of Experience* – which the harshness of experience feeds upon.

In the face of the monumentality of certain types of women's writing today, one almost misses the poorly written, hesitant, almost illiterate work of the 1970s, which often bore witness, in its clumsy uncertainty, to that pure presence of women on the threshold of expressing their own self-experience, their *own* in so far as they were subjects living in the fire of that experience.

THE DIFFICULTY OF REPRESENTING PURE ESSENCE

The women's movement of the 1970s demonstrated that, without a project, a plan, or a conspiracy, *explosive communication* was able to affirm itself, in unexpectedly happy, party-like meetings which upset social forms. The possibility opened up for each woman, irrespective of age, class, or culture, to approach any woman who chanced to come as someone already loved, because the other woman always represented the familiar-unknown. The collectives had no other project than themselves and the women who caused them to exist. There was just one single item on the agenda: the desire to be together without any utilitarian interest. This being-together restored every woman's right to equality in sisterhood, by virtue of the freedom of speech which exalted everyone. Every woman had something to say, or something to write. It didn't matter what.

Communication was uninhibited, it was nothing other than transparent, immanent communication with oneself, in spite of the conflicts, discussions and disagreements that arose from almost pure effervescence rather than from calculating intelligence.

There was no serious attempt at reform but an *innocent* presence which appeared to men – and women – in power as a sort of masquerade, or a carnivalesque replica of their own discomfiture.

Innocent or 'common presence' (René Char), which ignored its own limits but which was political in its awareness of universal immediacy, whose only challenge was impossiblity, but which had no well-defined political will and was therefore at the mercy of any sudden turn of the institutions.

A presence which consists of a spontaneously realized utopia has always been ambiguous: without future and without present, it is a presence which is not historical but anthropological, like the presence of those shamanic figures that have peopled all tribal cultures. The community of women was not made up of women from any particular social or political area; it was the refusal to assume any form of power, or, above all, to delegate any form of power. It was important to be present, not as individuals or subjects but as demonstrators in a sisterly, anonymous and impersonal movement. In order not to limit its potency, the community of women accepted non-action: the refusal to be part of any duration.

With the intervention of duration, history, the attempt to stabilize the persistence of vision and the community of women, the presence of the women's community was no longer there: because it was at one and the same time the dissolution of the social pact and the reluctant insistence on re-creating it in a sovereignty which could not be circumscribed by law, though it still founded a law.

All this happened because women's being together was at that time an example of what Maurice Blanchot calls 'unmentionable community'. The working-class movement was community and then became history; and the same thing happened to the political presence of women when it was transformed into the women's movement: when the charismatic presence of the community of women took the direction of exodus. In its place the empty husks of duration, project and structure have remained. In place of unfounded presence – founded only by itself – the foundation, a rootedness, has remained which this time was the gendered nature of the genoma instead of the mechanisms of capital accumulation.

In a mercantile society commerce certainly exists, but never community, never any knowledge which is more than an exchange of 'good manners'.

When women decided to enter the world of social intercourse, they learned how to deal with institutions but became to all effects powerless. More and less powerful at the same time, powerful only in terms of their measurable force. This, it is worthwhile emphasizing, is a precious possession.

But let us not try to get back what we have lost by investing in our demands for proportional representation, or for the legislative regulation of assaults on our reproductive system, a charisma which they cannot and must not have. As secular women, we must live our mourning in a secular manner, without asking the rape law to stop at the threshold of our intimacy.

The Dionysian intimacy of the movement and the secret of its presence were inaccessible as long as they existed: now they are inviolable because they no longer exist. We are left with business to be dealt with because we no longer house poetry. I mean that poetry no longer lives in women being-together, and no gendering of the genoma will ever be able to restore to the female word its originary potency.

We now live in times of industriousness, works, doing, careers and decisions: this is all very well but we cannot expect this time to preserve the flavour of poetry, or, as Bataille said, of 'inactivity'. We have to choose, if we are active, we must inevitably take our leave from the suspension of historical time suggested by 'inactivity'.

Otherwise we are making fools of ourselves.

ETHICS WITHOUT A FOUNDATION

What ethics can we found on something that had a foundation just when it had no foundation, when it had no other foundation than an unfounded and unfoundable presence, founded because it was unfoundable?

If the community of women, the presence which constituted the foundation of all laws denying all present laws, no longer exists, and we know that it existed because it no longer exists, because it can manifest itself only in its absence, in never having been – feminism never was – where do we speak from when we talk about a female moral subject?

Perhaps from the ruins of the community of women . . .

For, as Blanchot says of his 'unmentionable community', farewell from the community cannot neglect the awareness of the 'always uncertain end' which is inscribed in its destiny. One of the characteristics of the community is in fact to give the impression, when it dissolves, of never having been able to exist, although it actually did. How then, in what words, Blanchot wonders, can one speak of a reality whose past could never be experienced, and of which one can retrace only what caused it to exist by default?

The reply is that this 'unmentionable community' still has a binding political meaning which will not permit us to lose interest in the present time. Opening unknown spaces of freedom, Blanchot says, this makes us responsible for new relationships, ever threatened, ever hoped for, between what we call action and inaction.

By inaction what I think might be meant is the word-still-to-come in the dominant temporality; because it has *always already* existed in the *other* time of the originary promise whose memory we must keep, in order to maintain the capacity to address words to other women, which 'thoughtfully' preserve not only difference but also asymmetry as their highest value.

What 'legal' corpus can be derived from asymmetry?

Let us try to whisper some principles.

If the other, as Levinas states, is always a little closer to God, and it is upon this that I found my true need of, and my availability for, the other, it is not enough to claim the right of difference to exist and express its vision of the world. If anything, what must be claimed is the right for the relationship between differences to express itself in truly different ways, truly in contrast with the laws of symmetry, the fierce tiger of the industrial revolution which attacked the very roots of the living world, multiplying but casting doubt upon its symbolic universes. I would like our voices to become fainter – though certainly not when we are speaking to Donat Cattin;[2] fainter when speaking to each other – in order to allow that which is only different to become asymmetrical.

But this implies that the ethics be transformed into aesthetics, in the sense of the Greek word *aisthesis*, which means, in fact, *perception*.

NOTES

This paper was first presented at a seminar on the birth of the female moral subject, organized by the Centro di studi e Ricerche delle Donne of the Istituto Gramsci, Rome, 11 March 1989.

1 The influence of feminism was seen in the Charter of Women Communists, published in Italy in November 1986; for extracts from it see Paola Bono and Sandra Kemp (eds), *Italian Feminist Thought: A Reader*, Oxford, Blackwell, 1991, pp. 340–8.
2 Donat Cattin, the ex-Minister of Health, well known for his reactionary politics.

Index